A LONG TIME COMING

A Long Time Coming

THE STRUGGLE TO UNIONIZE AMERICA'S FARM WORKERS

Dick Meister and Anne Loftis

MACMILLAN PUBLISHING CO., INC.
New York

COLLIER MACMILLAN PUBLISHERS
London

Macmillan Publishing Co., Inc.
866 Third Avenue, New York, N.Y. 10022
Collier Macmillan Canada, Ltd.

Library of Congress Cataloging in Publication Data
Meister, Dick.
A long time coming.
Bibliography: p.
Includes index.
1. Trade-unions—Agricultural laborers—United States
—History. I. Loftis, Anne, joint author. II. Title.
HD6515.A29M44   331.88′13′0973   76-54510
ISBN 0-02-583920-9

First Printing 1977

Printed in the United States of America

To Mary R. Nevins, Fred Ross and the farm workers of America.

CONTENTS

PREFACE

"The Impossible Victory"

They began arriving early that morning of July 29, 1970, swiftly filling a bright new hiring hall on the edge of a sleepy little San Joaquin Valley town named Delano, in the heart of California's grape industry, 140 miles northeast of Los Angeles. They waved brilliant red banners as they waited. They sang. *"Nosotros venceremos, nosotros venceremos . . . we shall overcome, we shall overcome. . . ."* They chanted. *"Viva la huelga! Viva la Virgen de Guadalupe! Viva Cesar Chavez! Viva!"* They were brown-skinned Mexican-Americans, most of them; poor, judging from their well-worn work clothes, and fiercely proud, in the manner of Emiliano Zapata and other heroes of the Mexican poor whose portraits looked out sternly on the joyous, anxious crowd, flanked by images of religious saints and newer, gentler heroes, Robert Kennedy, Mohandas Gandhi and Martin Luther King.

At precisely 11 o'clock, as a blistering morning sun beat down on a dusty field outside, Cesar Chavez stepped before this group of some 200 of the men and women who had followed him through five years of struggle. Chavez wore an elaborate white wedding shirt by way of celebration, his impassive Indian face made even darker by contrast. He spoke softly, almost shyly, and he did not smile. But he, at last, had the word: "Victory." Delano had fallen. The country's largest grape growers would sign union contracts; the growers of other crops would follow soon. Farm workers would have their own effective union, that hope which had been held up to them for more than three-quarters of a century as the way out of economic and social deprivation.

"Viva! Viva!" Chavez lowered his head as the farm workers cheered. Beside him at a long table studded with microphones sat his fellow officers of the United Farm Workers Organizing Committee, now to become a true union with enforceable contracts. Beside them were men from the AFL-CIO, promising the continued and full support of the world's most powerful labor movement, and men high in the

Roman Catholic hierarchy and in the Protestant Church, also firm in support. The grape growers were there, too, plain, blunt-spoken men in open-neck shirts. Their relentless opposition to unionization had been no less intense than that of growers elsewhere, but they had made the ultimate concession by coming to the UFWOC hiring hall to sign union contracts in front of reporters and cameramen from all over the world.

UFWOC had forced the growers to the table with a worldwide grape boycott. It was part of a remarkable campaign that had fashioned a movement—*La Causa*—from what had been another seemingly hopeless strike by still another powerless group of farm workers when it began in September of 1965 in the isolated vineyards around Delano. The boycott helped forge a potent coalition of clergymen, industrial unionists, young activists and civil rights advocates, liberal Democratic politicians, socially conscious shoppers and others. They also waved crimson banners, sang the songs of the vineyard strikers, chanted the slogans and espoused nonviolence, on city streets, outside supermarkets, in meeting halls. They were united in a determination to halt the sale of grapes everywhere, and ultimately they forced the growers to grant recognition to the strikers' union and sign the contracts.

Boycott pressures were threatening to "destroy a number of farmers," declared John Giumarra Jr., the young lawyer who spoke for the growers. The growers once had called Chavez and his followers "Communists," "outside agitators" and worse. But now they smiled, albeit uncomfortably, in response to cheers from workers who once had booed very loudly, and called *them* names. But Giumarra didn't dwell on the past. He smiled broadly, dismissing the bitter exchanges of the previous five years as the natural exaggerations of warring parties. He supposed that "we're starting a new relationship here, a relationship that's going to be a very important one. . . . The world will be focused on Delano to determine if this has really been a revolution in labor relations and if social justice will prevail. If this works here, it will work well throughout the rest of the world."

Chavez also looked to the future: "Today's really, truly, the beginning of a new day. We give hope to millions and millions of farm workers . . . and we will not disappoint them. We thank God for all these things, and we thank you, too. . . ." Whatever Chavez might have said next was lost when a photographer shouted for him to shake hands with young Giumarra. He did, Giumarra held up two fingers in a victory sign and the audience broke into noisy, joyous applause. It was then that Cesar Chavez smiled.

It was "the impossible victory," declared John Henning, director of the AFL-CIO in California—a victory won against astounding odds.

Most U.S. workers in private employment are guaranteed the right to organize by the National Labor Relations Act. They merely need demand union recognition, prove they want it by a vote, and employers are obligated to bargain with them on pay and working conditions. But grower allies in Congress excluded farm workers from the law when it was passed in 1935, and have kept them excluded. The growers' political allies have made certain as well that the few laws that are designed to protect farm workers are enforced generally by grower-oriented government agencies.

Growers also have won subsidies to maintain or increase the price of certain crops, irrigation water at far below the actual cost of delivery, and other state and federal benefits that have strengthened them even more vis-à-vis farm workers.

Much of the government aid was originally intended to help small independent farmers, but the main beneficiaries have been large corporations, which have used it to enhance the preeminent position they have held in agriculture throughout the twentieth century. The corporations, long the principal employers of agricultural workers in this country, treat farming as an investment and seek to extract the maximum possible profit from the labor of the workers.

Farm workers had struggled against these employers for decades. But the workers, most of them impoverished immigrants or the equally poor residents of rural slums, were so preoccupied with eking out a living they had little choice but to accept the primitive labor relations system, poverty-level pay and generally miserable working conditions imposed by the growers. The workers and their children had to work whenever they could in order to survive—whatever the conditions. They did not have the time and energy, or the education, experience and leadership, to develop the political and economic strength necessary to overcome their employers' power to dictate the terms of employment.

The workers obviously needed organization, and others had tried to bring it to them from the very beginning of corporate control in agriculture. First came the Industrial Workers of the World, storming across western fields at the turn of the century, then Communist Party organizers, socialists, industrial unionists. Their struggles drew fierce, often violent, opposition from growers and government alike. But without them there would have been no victory in Delano, no hope for "millions and millions of farm workers."

We can't afford to lose our jobs, so we keep quiet and don't complain and the farmers think we are happy. You whistle in the fields and you go out and get drunk on Saturday night because you can't face the truth—that you are so damned poor, that the kids are sick and that your life is depressing. In the fields the bosses shout at us in front of our wives and families. They insult our womenfolk and bully our children, and because we are so poor, we cannot afford to lose the job. We take it. This destroys the family and it destroys the men as individuals. . . . When we tried to fight back in the past, we found the grower was too strong, too rich, and we had to give up.

—Ernesto Loredo, a California farm worker, November, 1968

A LONG TIME COMING

1

Outcasts

It was sung on street corners usually, by rough men in dirty work clothes—a bit off-key, God knows, but with wondrous zeal: ". . . Come, be a man, join the union grand; come organize with us in harvest land. Down in harvest land, united we will stand . . . to make old Farmer John come through. . . ."

A union of farm workers? Only these zealots would seriously consider such a thing, these men in that utopian band called the Industrial Workers of the World. They were barely into the twentieth century, in the midst of a clamorously capitalistic society where labor's duty was not to sing songs of rebellion but to dance to the tunes of dull obedience played by employers. True, some men in the cities had banded together in unions, but they had skills to offer employers, something beyond mere raw manpower. What chance had farm workers for unionization, as they drifted from harvest to harvest, certain to be replaced from the full and endless stream of three and a half million other penniless, unskilled migrants if they as much as whispered the word "union"?

Few outside the fields even knew of the farm workers' miserable conditions. But *they* knew, these men of the IWW—Wobblies, they were called—and their dogmatic insistence on trying to improve the farm workers' lot against overwhelming odds would focus public and union attention on the forgotten workers.

The Wobblies began their agricultural organizing in California, shortly after the IWW was founded in 1905 in Chicago by a group of socialists and dissident union organizers as an alternative to the nineteen-year-old American Federation of Labor. The Wobblies' message was worker solidarity above all else, and they saw the AFL as dividing workers by ignoring the racially and ethnically mixed mass of unskilled workers in favor of the far fewer skilled and semiskilled white craftsmen who were organized into separate AFL unions ac-

3

cording to their crafts. Thus the AFL was denounced as a major obstacle to the IWW's goal of creating a classless society through organizing the unskilled—an elitist, racist handmaiden of the capitalist class which controlled the country's wealth and means of production, keeping most workers at or below the sustenance level. The IWW would organize all workers into *One Big Union* regardless of race, nationality, craft or work skills, call a mammoth general strike and wrest control from the capitalists.

The revolutionary message was presented in the simple language of the workplace, in street corner oratory, in satirical songs set to familiar melodies and in a tremendous outpouring of publications, including a dozen foreign-language newspapers which were distributed among the many unskilled immigrants from European nations where unions advocated similar goals. Workers were told again and again that they all had the same problems, the same needs, and faced the same enemy. It was they who did the work, while others got the profit; they were members, all of them, of the working class. To aspire to middle-class status, as the AFL advocated, would mean competing against their fellow workers and chaining themselves to a system that enslaved them. Organized religion was also a tool of enslavement, to keep the worker's eye on "pie in the sky when you die" while he was being exploited in this world. Patriotism was a ruse to set the workers of one nation against those of another for the profit of capitalist manipulators.

IWW organizers carried the message to factories, mines, mills and lumber camps throughout the country, and to farms in the Midwest and California, whose agricultural industry was an ideal target for the Wobblies. Its large-scale operations attracted masses of poor workers with no attachments save to each other; they shifted constantly from employer to employer and community to community, living together in hobo jungles, camps and dilapidated rooming houses, sharing what little they had to survive. They had been abandoned, furthermore, by the AFL. The labor federation had organized a few small groups of farm workers early in the century and had set up several locals for California fruit pickers in the area south of San Francisco, but these had disappeared after a few years because of the AFL's general lack of interest in unskilled migrant workers.

The bulk of California's farm workers, in any case, were Chinese and Japanese immigrants who had long been treated as enemies by orthodox unions. Isolated by legally sanctioned discrimination, deprived of basic civil rights, the Asians were pitted against white workers, who demanded better pay and working conditions than the Chinese and Japanese were forced to accept. The battle raged for decades, with the unions and their white members denouncing the Asians for being "cheap labor" and employers promoting their continued immigration for that very reason.

California growers began hiring the Asians in the 1870s, but they had always relied on cheap labor. The first to be used were native Indians, who harvested the small wheat and barley crop that was grown in the period of Spanish and Mexican rule before California was ceded to the United States. Most of the occupied land was used for cattle grazing, however, and this meant individual land holdings were huge, running to hundreds of thousands of acres, and parceled out by government grants to only a few hundred people.

The pattern of large holdings continued after California became a U.S. possession in 1848, through a provision in the cession treaty that honored the old land grants. Other parcels were grabbed up by speculators who secured new Mexican grants, some of them fraudulent, on the eve of U.S. occupation. The federal government later granted other huge tracts of land to the Central (later Southern) Pacific Railroad in the form of sections along the rights-of-way of the transcontinental and intrastate lines it began building in 1863. By then, most of the state's 128 million acres of arable land belonged to only a few thousand people, even though California's population had increased twentyfold since the discovery of gold in 1848. The railroad alone owned 20 million acres. Few of the owners farmed the land themselves, however. They rented their holdings to individuals and corporations or had them taken over by squatters.

The growers moved to large-scale cultivation in the 1860s, primarily in response to a heavy foreign demand for wheat. They greatly increased their wheat plantings, in speculative ventures that required relatively few risks, since land could be rented and then abandoned if the market dropped or the fertility of the soil declined. Costs were minimal, since wheat required little irrigation in years of normal rainfall. Too, the use of harvesting machines meant that only a relatively few workers were needed, and they could be found among Indians, down-on-their-luck miners and newly arrived Europeans who would do the work for lack of other opportunities.

A general economic depression in the 1870s provided growers with even more recruits, but it also cut their profits. They were hit as well by a drought, which forced them to borrow heavily from banks to finance irrigation projects, by competition from new wheat-growing regions in Russia and the Mississippi Valley, by wide fluctuations in world prices and by constant increases in the freight rates charged by

Southern Pacific after the transcontinental railroad was completed in 1869.

Completion of the railroad proved to be a blessing for the growers, however, because it enabled them to shift into much more profitable fruit and vegetable crops. Southern Pacific provided freight cars that would carry the highly perishable produce east without spoilage and, in laying off most of the 10,000 Chinese laborers who had helped build the western half of the transcontinental line, made available the workers necessary to begin the shift in crops.

There were no machines available for fruit and vegetable harvesting; it took lots of hand labor and, if a large profit was to be realized, men who would do it cheaply and move up and down the state constantly to work for a number of growers whose aim was to harvest their crops as quickly as possible. It was a system that would come to dominate California agriculture, and the Chinese fitted it perfectly.

More than 50,000 Chinese, beset with floods, famine and local insurrections in China, had streamed into California with the other fortune hunters. They were heavily in debt to merchants in China and California who financed their passage, found them jobs, arranged for their wages to be sent to the families they left behind and generally controlled their lives in this country. The Chinese worked in gangs, not only on railroad construction, but also in the mines and in light manufacturing in several cities, principally San Francisco, the booming gateway to the gold fields. But when the high wages and plentiful jobs of the early Gold Rush period declined and settlers from other states flooded California via the newly completed railroad, anxious white workers began driving the Chinese out of the mines and cities, aided by laws that prohibited the Asians from taking legal action against citizens who did them harm. As a result, thousands of other Chinese joined the former railroad workers in the rapidly expanding orchards and vegetable fields. By the 1880s, the Chinese made up at least half of California's farm labor force.

Most of the Chinese had been tenant farmers in their home country and were highly skilled. They taught their employers the intricacies of fruit and vegetable growing, and did much of the work of building levees, reclaiming marshlands and developing irrigation systems that opened large new areas of the state to farming. A group of Chinese workers called the first recorded strike in the history of U.S. agriculture, a brief walkout in the Kern County hop fields in 1884, and another group briefly operated as a union; but generally the Chinese were undemanding, and, after the harvests, returned quietly to San Francisco and rural towns, where they lived together in overcrowded ghettos, lonely single men cut off from the rest of the community. Growers were so pleased with their labor that they imported thousands more workers directly from China, with the help of merchants and others who also profited from the immigration.

But though fruit and vegetable growers were highly satisfied, smaller growers who continued cultivating wheat were no happier about the competition of cheap labor than were white unionists and small manufacturers. The wheat growers, manufacturers and unionists formed an alliance through a Workingmen's Party organized in San Francisco by union leaders and joined with others to win enactment of a federal law to prohibit immigration of Chinese laborers after 1882, when the number of Chinese in California had grown to 100,000. A further law, passed during an economic depression in 1894, was intended to force growers to deport many of the Chinese already in California; when growers ignored the law, bands of unemployed white workers invaded camps where Chinese were housed and forced workers to flee to the cities, where they took jobs that would keep them from competing directly with the hostile white workers. The Chinese worked as domestic servants, laundrymen and in restaurants and other establishments in Chinese settlements.

Growers retained the upper hand, however. The general scarcity of jobs enabled them to hire desperate white workers for as little as 75 cents a day, compared with the $1.40 that had been the most recent rate paid the Chinese. The white workers tramped from farm to farm, quickly harvesting the crop and moving on, a haystack or an open field often their only resting place. Some tried to settle down; but the pattern of large land holdings had already been set and few small homesteads were granted by the government to settlers. They did farm small plots of land as squatters, but the owners often appeared and seized the land, improvements and all.

Growers, however, overextended themselves; fruit production became so great they couldn't profitably market the output. Then the state was hit by a drought. Many orchards were abandoned and a depression settled on California agriculture. Growers needed a new intensive crop to maintain their large holdings and make a quick profit to recoup their losses. They found it in sugar beets.

A new high tariff on imported sugar guaranteed growers a profitable market, but they needed a large supply of cheap labor to exploit it. This they found in the thousands of Japanese they recruited to work in California beginning in 1890, when the Japanese government relaxed a ban on emigration. Some came directly from tenant farms in Japan; others arrived after working as contract laborers on the sugar plantations of Hawaii. By 1900, there were nearly 25,000 Japanese farm workers in California, making up the bulk of the work force in sugar beets and other labor-intensive crops, which accounted for half of the state's agricultural output.

The Japanese were as highly skilled in farm work as the Chinese they replaced and willing, at first, to work for even lower pay. But they were independent, since they were not in debt to moneylenders; many were young and single, ambitious and aggressive, and they were organized into crews headed by bilingual contractors. Once growers began hiring Japanese crews extensively, the crews began making demands; they might sign on at low wages, but then stage slowdowns or threaten to walk off if pay wasn't raised. In some cases, crews demanded a share of the crop.

Crews struck in the fruit orchards in 1902, and in 1903, crews in the sugar beet fields joined in a strike with Mexican workers, formed a union with more than 1000 members and asked the AFL for a charter. The union collapsed, however, because AFL President Samuel Gompers said it could not be chartered unless it excluded the Japanese members, and the union, its Mexican secretary declared, would not accept any charter "except one which will wipe out race prejudice and recognize our fellow workers as being as good as ourselves." The AFL's Labor Council in Los Angeles backed this stand, in a resolution declaring that "the most effective method of protecting the American workingman and his standard of living is by universal organization of wage workers regardless of race and nationality." Nevertheless, most union leaders and their members shared Gompers' view that the Japanese, no less than the Chinese, were unfair competitors who seriously undermined the pay and conditions of U.S. workers and should therefore be kept out of the country.

The Japanese were not generally interested in union organization anyway. There was an abortive attempt by members of a radical Japanese political group to organize pickers into a union in 1908, but the organized activity usually was limited to spontaneous efforts aimed at winning concessions from particular growers in particular harvests.

The principal impediment to lasting organization—and the reason the Japanese ultimately would be subjected to even stronger discrimination than the Chinese—was that many of the Japanese worked for others only until they could manage to become independent growers themselves. By 1910, one-fifth of the Japanese in California were farming their own land, as owners, lessees or sharecroppers. Many southern European immigrants followed the same pattern, but though the dominant Anglo-Saxon growers grudgingly tolerated this white competition, they bitterly resented the Asian incursion.

The Japanese holdings included large sections of land they had reclaimed, and their farming methods were more productive than those of many white growers. Hence the growers soon joined white workers in regarding the Japanese as unfair competitors; Japanese holdings were infringing on the growers' large holdings and the heavy output of produce by the Japanese was infringing on the growers' profits.

The growers, and unions and patriotic societies, formed organizations dedicated to combating what they called the "Yellow Peril," and in 1913 helped win state enactment of the first of two alien land laws that were designed to keep Japanese from owning or leasing land. Although the laws were circumvented to some extent, the Japanese found it difficult to retain land and to buy or lease other property. Eleven years after passage of the first alien land law, a federal act virtually halted all immigration from Asia.

Growers continued to employ many of those Asians who were already in California, however, including the Japanese, several thousand East Indians and some Koreans, along with a few Middle Easterners and a growing number of Mexicans. They were assigned the roughest "stoop labor" in areas where growers declared it "was not white men's work worth a white man's wage," although the native white drifters and southern European immigrants who made up the rest of the farm labor force actually were paid very little more.

The foreign groups were separated from each other and from the larger society by language and culture. For the many workers who could not speak English, the only contact with the outside world was through bilingual labor contractors who found them jobs, food and lodging, often at great personal profit, and who were in effect their bosses. This system blocked the workers from dealing directly with growers; the growers dealt solely with the contractors, deciding whom to hire, at what pay and under what conditions without giving the workers an effective voice in the matter.

The groups were kept apart from each other on the job, too, since California's farm laborers commonly worked in crews consisting only of their fellow nationals, were paid differing rates according to nationality and were generally encouraged to treat those of other nationalities as competitors. When mixed crews were used, it was often for the purpose of destroying the sense of solidarity that naturally developed within homogeneous crews.

It was a system quite purposely designed to keep wages low and workers disorganized, and bringing the disparate, mutually suspicious groups of workers together seemed to be an impossible task. The AFL, of course, would not even attempt it. That was left to the Industrial Workers of the World, for the very purpose of the IWW was to unite such workers.

The Wobblies' boldest attempt to organize the farm workers was launched in the summer of 1913 at a hop ranch outside a nondescript northern California town called Wheatland. The ranch, owned by the Durst brothers, was the state's largest single employer of agricultural labor and, like other large growers, the Dursts recruited far more workers than they actually needed for any particular harvest. It was a way to keep pay as low as possible, and since pay was on a piece-rate basis, a way to get the crop picked swiftly without adding a cent to overall labor costs.

The Dursts needed 1500 workers at the most for their three- to four-week harvest in that summer of 1913; but there were masses of unemployed workers in the West, and more than 2800 of them swarmed into Wheatland in response to newspaper ads that promised steady employment for 2700 workers at the locally prevailing rate of $1 for every 100 pounds of hops picked. Half the recruits were aliens, of twenty-seven nationalities; the others were local workers and native white drifters. Among them were some 1400 women and children from nearby towns and perhaps 100 members of the IWW, including two experienced organizers, Richard (Blackie) Ford and Herman Suhr.

Ford and Suhr were among the IWW "job delegates" who roamed the West organizing spontaneous strikes aimed at improving working conditions. During the previous eight years, they had helped lead strikes in the fields and lumber camps, had hopped freights with migrant workers as they made their way along the Pacific Coast and had taken part in highly publicized "free speech fights." The "fights" sent hundreds of Wobblies and Wobbly sympathizers to jail and subjected them to beatings and other abuse from police and vigilante groups that waged a veritable reign of terror to try to silence the IWW's revolutionary message of working class solidarity.

The Wobblies' refusal to back down until they finally won a measure of tolerance for their right to freely hold public meetings, on street corners or anywhere else, to distribute their literature and to maintain headquarters in the dozens of towns from which they had been chased gave the IWW a status greatly out of proportion to its numerical strength. In 1913, the IWW had only 5000 members in California, less than 10 percent of the work force. Yet many employers, political leaders and others in the established community perceived the IWW as a serious threat to the very existence of capitalism. It was true, at any rate, that the IWW was a serious threat to the one-sided system of labor-management relations preferred by many of the established groups. For though workers might have only imperfectly understood the IWW's purpose, they were singing Wobbly songs all over the state, applauding the Wobbly message and generally treating the IWW as a champion of their rights.

The IWW's job delegates had no difficulty reaching the hop pickers who had flocked to the Durst Ranch for the harvest. Conditions were so appalling, even by the low standards of California agriculture, that many workers were in fact demanding action on their own, quite apart from suggestions by Ford, Suhr or any of the other Wobblies.

The workers were crowded together in a treeless, sun-baked camp about a mile from the hop fields. They slept on piles of dirty straw, pallets or hard canvas squares, many without blankets—in the open or in ragged tents rented to them for 75 cents a week. There were only nine shallow, doorless privies to serve as toilets for the thousands of workers and their families, many of them suffering from dysentery; garbage was tossed into nearby irrigation ditches to rot; wells that supplied drinking water were contaminated and some soon dried up altogether. The stench was nauseating; flies and disease were every-where.

Workers, women and children included, went off at 4 a.m. to the fields where temperatures soared to more than 100 degrees by noon and heat prostration was common. There were no toilets in the fields; and there was no drinking water—only a sour concoction of acetic acid and water that was sold by a member of the Durst family for five cents a glass. There were so many workers that even the Durst hop fields, the world's largest, sometimes could not contain them all. On some days, as many as 1000 stayed behind in camp while the others swarmed through the hop vines, then stood in long lines at stations where supervisors carefully examined their pick to see that it was "extra clean" of excess leaves, dumped it on a scale and gave them pay chits based on the weight. The rate varied according to the num-ber of workers in the fields, but none ever made more than $1.90 for the twelve-hour work day. And 10 cents of every $1 was held back as a "bonus," to be paid only if the worker lasted the entire harvest season—or was allowed to by the Dursts. Much of what little money the workers did make was spent on groceries sold at inflated prices in a camp store owned in part by the Dursts. Workers had no choice but to buy there, since local stores were prohibited from bringing delivery wagons onto ranch property.

Groups of angry workers gathered regularly in the squalid camp to voice their mutual complaints. Encouraged by Ford and Suhr, and by indications that the Dursts might heed them, workers called a mass meeting four days after the harvest began to draw up a list of demands. They wanted fresh drinking water brought to the fields twice a day; the assignment of "high polemen" to pull vines down to the level of the women and children working in the fields; one privy for every 100 people, with separate facilities for men and women; and a firm pay rate of $1.25 per 100 pounds of hops picked, with no "bonus" withheld. The workers formed a committee, headed by Ford, to present their demands to Ralph Durst, the ranch manager.

Durst told the committee he would provide fresh water in the fields and more toilets in the camp. But he flatly rejected the other demands and angrily fired Ford and the other committee members; they were dangerous IWW "agitators," as far as Durst was concerned. Ford warned Durst he was inviting a strike; furious, Durst struck him across the face with a heavy glove and demanded that a local constable run Ford off the ranch. When the constable was unable to produce a proper arrest warrant, Durst rushed off to the nearby city of Marysville for help.

A sheriff's posse of eleven armed men was hastily assembled and quickly set off for the ranch in two autos, led by District Attorney Edward Manwell, who also happened to be Ralph Durst's personal attorney. As they sped toward the ranch, bent on arresting Ford, some 2000 workers were gathering under his chairmanship to debate on whether to strike. The workers closed tightly around a makeshift platform as Ford and others addressed them excitedly in several languages. Reaching down from the platform, Ford took a sick infant from a mother's arms and held the child up to the crowd. "It's not so much for ourselves we are fighting," he shouted, "as that this little baby may never see the conditions which now exist on this ranch!"

The crowd began singing a Wobbly song about "Mr. Block," a worker whose faith in capitalism was attributed to a head "made of lumber and solid as a rock." The last chorus was dying away as the deputies jumped from their cars and started toward the platform, attempting to disperse the tightly packed crowd and seize Ford. A deputy grabbed at Ford, a platform railing collapsed and the crowd surged forward. On the edge of the crowd, a deputy fired a shotgun blast into the air—"to sober the mob," he later asserted. Suddenly, there were more gunshots—"a hideous racket," as one eyewitness described it, "that sounded as if someone had thrown a box of cartridges into the fire." As panic-stricken workers and deputies flayed about in confusion, a young Puerto Rican worker dashed from a tent, clubbed several deputies, seized a gun and began firing. Deputies returned the fire. The shooting lasted thirty seconds, perhaps a minute. When it stopped, four people were dead—the young Puerto Rican, District Attorney Manwell, a deputy sheriff and a boy who had been passing by the edge of the crowd, carrying a bucket of water. More than a dozen others were wounded or injured. Deputies and workers alike ran quickly from the scene of what would be known thereafter as the Wheatland Riot of Sunday, August 3, 1913, and quiet descended on the Durst Ranch.

The governor sent four companies of state guardsmen onto the ranch the next day; they found only a few hundred workers, huddled together, as a contemporary newspaper account noted, in "hovels and gunny sack tents." Many of the stragglers were arrested on riot charges, and Durst and other growers, insisting in near-hysterical terms that they were facing revolution, hired the Burns Detective Agency to scour the West for Wobblies. Although there had been no rioting until that "sobering" shot was fired by a deputy, authorities placed full blame on the IWW.

More than 100 Burns operatives ranged through California and Arizona, arresting several hundred Wobblies with the aid of local authorities, who held them in jail incommunicado for weeks at a time while Burns men tried to extract "confessions." Even IWW lawyers couldn't find the prisoners, who were deliberately moved from one jail to another. Conditions were so bad at the Yuba County Jail in Marysville that one Wobbly prisoner went insane and another committed suicide.

The special targets were Ford and Suhr. Ford had been unarmed during the riot and had in fact counseled nonviolence, but a Marysville coroner's jury demanded his arrest on grounds that the district attorney's death had come from a "gunshot wound inflicted by a gun in the hands of rioters incited to murderous anger by IWW leaders and agitators." Suhr had not even been in Wheatland when the outbreak occurred, but he was sought because he had sent telegrams to IWW locals throughout California, asking them to rush to the aid of the workers in Wheatland on that day.

Suhr, a quiet, slow-witted man, was captured in Prescott, Arizona, by Burns detectives, and according to a Wobbly account,

confined like a beast in the refrigerator of a box fruit car . . . poked with clubs and bars to keep awake . . . taken to Los Angeles and tortured in that jail . . . to Fresno for further torture. Thence to San Francisco, thence to Oakland. Here for four days three shifts of Burns men tortured him by keeping him awake. In order that no marks should show on his person, they rolled long spills of paper and thrust the sharp points into his eyes and ears and nose every time his head dropped. He was placed in a three-foot latticed cell so that these animals could easily torture him without danger from his fists. He went crazy, signed a "confession," and the judges of Yuba and Sutter counties and the district attorneys thereof have tried to make it impossible for him to swear out a warrant for his torturers.

Ford and Suhr were brought to Marysville and tried there for murder in January of 1914, despite pleas by their attorney that they could not get a fair trial in that city. They were tried along with two young workers who were present at the riot, but who had very little connection with the rioting. Authorities acknowledged they chose the two at random from among the hundreds of workers who had been arrested, and admitted as well that Ford and Suhr had not taken any part in the violence. But the prosecutor, assisted by the dead district attorney's son, argued they were guilty through being members of an organization that had sent men to Wheatland to provoke workers into dangerous and, ultimately, fatal action. The IWW searched the state for witnesses who testified that the defendants had not incited anyone to riot, and Suhr retracted his pretrial confession. The young workers were acquitted, but the jury convicted Ford and Suhr of second-degree murder. Nine months after the riot, they were sentenced to life imprisonment.

The trial was highly publicized throughout the country, as were attempts afterward to free Ford and Suhr. They quickly became labor martyrs, even to conservative AFL leaders and others whom the IWW denounced as class enemies. The "respectable citizens" denounced the IWW in turn, but they formed committees all over the state to work for release of the two Wobblies; they argued that, while the IWW was indeed a dangerous organization, Ford and Suhr had been unjustly convicted of something they had not done.

The riot and its aftermath drew the public's attention to issues far broader than the treatment of Ford and Suhr, however. For the first time, the plight of farm workers was exposed to general view, through newspaper stories and government reports which elicited a strong response. The popular press continued to attack the IWW, but now also attacked Durst and other growers for what the Sacramento *Bee* called their "oppressions and inhumanities" and "absolute disregard of the rights of others." The public outcry brought action from the Progressive administration of Governor Hiram Johnson of California, who had been elected with heavy AFL support, along with a large body of reform-minded legislators. This coalition had enacted more than three dozen laws to improve the conditions of working people, including one creating a Commission on Immigration and Housing, which was now assigned to clean up the conditions exposed by the Wheatland Riot.

The commission investigated farms statewide, finding conditions generally not much better than those on the Durst Ranch, and began enforcing a state Labor Camp Code that set standards for sanitation and living accommodations.

But the reforms were only temporary. Further, they were linked to a campaign to suppress the IWW and thus keep workers from taking collective action to successfully demand improved conditions on their own. It was a pattern that would hold for the next half-century; farm workers would get some minimal and fleeting gains through strikes, but, almost without exception, they would be denied the opportunity to form effective unions to win meaningful advances. The most they could expect would be mild reforms forced on employers by paternalistic liberals, or initiated by growers themselves to block unionization. Pay might be increased, working and living conditions improved, but the basic need for lasting self-organization would not be met.

The pattern emerged after the Wheatland Riot, when Carleton Parker, a young University of California economist who served as executive secretary of the Commission on Immigration and Housing, issued his report on conditions at the Durst Ranch. Parker, whose report was extremely critical of the Dursts, said the IWW had "volunteered the beginning of a cure; it is to clean up the housing and wage problem of the seasonal worker." He assured Governor Johnson that the commission

now has the funds, the men, and the organization to clean up this abuse this coming summer, insure a decent standard of comfort to the seasonal worker and take away the argument and talking weapon of the agitator. The most important labor problem in California is that of the seasonal agricultural laborer, on whom the IWW plan to concentrate this summer. I am convinced that our opportunity here is real and vital and our service will be as imperative and essential to the farmer and employer as to the farm laborer.

Conditions were improved on farms throughout the state under the commission's prodding. The Durst brothers, for instance, installed bath houses at their camp, water hydrants, enough enclosed toilets so there would be one for every ten residents and set up a garbage disposal system.

The IWW, well aware that the improvements could undermine its organizational efforts, attacked them as illusory and sought as well to combat the commission's warning to workers that strikes and other organized activity would not improve their conditions. A Wobbly poster told workers:

The Politicians and the Kept Press are working overtime to make you believe the Hop Fields will be Heaven this year. You Know Better. . . . Unless FORD and SUHR are free by August, let Carleton Parker and his Commissioners pick the hops.

The IWW invited attempts to undermine the organization by refusing to deemphasize the goals and methods that had been largely responsible for the conviction of Ford and Suhr. Wobblies adamantly refused to adopt the AFL concept of collective bargaining in which job conditions were determined bilaterally by workers and employers. There was no place in the IWW doctrine for such compromise; Wobblies would replace unilateral control by employers with unilateral control by workers. They continued "to teach," as one IWW advocate explained, "that the worker on the job shall tell the boss when and where he shall work, how long, for what wages and under what conditions . . . that gradually the worker will get more and more power until finally he will take over the industries." The IWW proclaimed these views louder than ever, now that Wobblies had the platform they had sought to broadcast their message widely and increase their influence on migrant workers, however much their revolutionary position might undermine other support for Ford and Suhr.

Wobblies warned there would be a general strike if the prisoners were not released, and threatened sabotage. They affixed signs to fruit trees with copper nails, advising workers that "as long as Ford and Suhr are in jail, don't stick copper nails in fruit trees; it kills them," and spoke openly of burning haystacks and barns. In IWW parlance, "sabotage" generally meant slowdowns on the job and other "conscientious withdrawal of efficiency," and the Wobblies' bark was always far worse than their bite. But growers, government officials and newspapers seized on the IWW's purposely inflammatory rhetoric to wage a massive scare campaign against the organization.

Growers formed a "Farmers Protective League" and spent hundreds of thousands of dollars to hire private guards and detectives to keep Wobbly "agitators" off their property and to lobby the state and federal governments for suppression of the IWW. Some actually feared Wobbly violence, but the growers' real concern was the IWW's growing success in winning adherents among the farm workers. By 1914, just a year after the riot, the IWW had forty locals in California, and hop growers were losing millions of dollars because of the IWW campaign to force release of Ford and Suhr. The campaign, endorsed by the AFL, called for workers to either stay out of the hop fields or, if they did take jobs, to strike and engage in slowdowns.

By 1915, agents of the Commission on Immigration and Housing who had been assigned to oversee the improvement of conditions at farm camps were acting as spies to uncover IWW activities. The chief spy was an AFL representative who had been hired over Carleton Parker's objection at the insistence of the state AFL's secretary-treasurer, Paul Scharrenberg, a commission member. The AFL spy posed as a Wobbly, infiltrated IWW strategy sessions and reported regularly to the commission as he traveled the state with Wobbly organizers. The reports frequently were imaginative accounts which translated IWW threats into deeds; but they helped convince Governor Johnson, who had supported Wobblies in their earlier "free speech fights," that the IWW had become a serious menace.

Parker was replaced as the commission's executive secretary by his assistant, George Bell, who directed a campaign to suppress the IWW; the commission joined growers in seeking federal action against the organization, and Johnson, who had shown sympathy for Ford and Suhr, now took a hard line against them. The governor conceded that justice might have been less than perfect in their case, but said he couldn't consider granting clemency to individuals who belonged to an organization that advocated sabotage and class warfare. The state AFL had filed a seventy-eight-page plea for release of the prisoners, but Johnson convinced the federation to abandon the case, even though some AFL affiliates continued to back the campaign for clemency. The Building Trades Council in Alameda County, for example, denounced the governor's stand:

You admit that Ford and Suhr could not have had any part in the alleged campaign of violence, and yet they are to be punished as long as "threats of injury and sabotage continue." . . . The real murderer was the man responsible for the original crime. . . . Durst ought to be on trial for the murder of the District Attorney.

Despite the pressures, the IWW's influence grew rapidly, to the point that it established the country's first broadly based farm workers union, the Agricultural Workers Organization, at a conference in Kansas City in the spring of 1915. The AWO became the IWW's primary concern under a new general secretary, Bill Haywood, and others who shifted the IWW's basic approach. They did not stress the dissemination of propaganda for revolutionary goals; rather, they concentrated on organizing around workers' immediate needs, as the first essential step toward revolution. Wobblies abandoned street corner speechmaking to devote full attention to the activities of the job delegates who were bringing together workers at farms and lumber camps to demand higher pay, shorter working hours and better food and lodging; most workers wanted those things far more than they wanted the revolutionary "Cooperative Commonwealth of Workers," which previous IWW leaders had held up to them as the primary goal.

The AWO was extremely successful in its initial campaigns among the 250,000 men who worked in the grain belt of the Midwest, traveling by freight trains from Oklahoma to Kansas, to Nebraska, to the Dakotas, to Montana, to southern Canada and back again, working at a farm for a week, maybe two weeks, and then moving on. They were at the mercy of holdup men, cardsharps and bootleggers; brakemen and railroad police beat them, shot at them or demanded payoffs to let them ride unmolested. To escape detection, they often lay on boards placed between metal rods under the speeding boxcars, just ten inches from the track, or squeezed inside accordion-pleated couplings between boxcars.

A depression had forced thousands of urban workers into the migrant stream, and their main concern was simply to find a job, whatever the conditions. They worked from dawn to dusk in stifling heat. The fortunate ones slept in barns; others slept in the open, and the food was no better than the lodgings. "What the farmers raise they sell," as one Wobbly explained it. "What they can't sell they feed to the cattle. What the cattle won't eat they feed to the hogs. What the hogs won't eat they eat themselves, and what they can't eat they feed to the hired hands."

IWW delegates rode the freights with the migrants, organizing them to forcefully resist those who preyed on them. The IWW's red membership card became a means of protection against the holdup men and railroad bullies, who came to fear Wobbly retaliation; in some cases, the red card was the equivalent of a train ticket. Job delegates gathered migrants in camps on the outskirts of the small towns along the grain belt or in storefront offices and clubrooms in town and formed committees to seek work. This gave workers the companionship and sense of belonging they were denied elsewhere in the farm communities, a feeling of solidarity, and loyalty to the IWW.

The workers' unity helped them win better pay and conditions, but in part because grain growers, flooded with heavy orders from warring European nations after the start of World War I in 1914, were willing to meet the purposely moderate demands the IWW's new leadership was making rather than risk disruption of their very lucrative harvests. There were strikes and slowdowns, but the mere threat of such action often was enough to win the demands of the Agricultural Workers Organization for basic pay raises, overtime pay after ten hours, adequate food and lodging and a pledge of nondiscrimination against members. In the 1915 wheat harvest, the AWO got basic pay raised 50 cents a day to $3.50, and by the end of that year had 18,000 members contributing more than $50,000 in dues and initiation fees, and 100 job delegates in the fields signing up at least 100 new members a week. By 1917, the AWO had 70,000 members, thousands of other adherents, and had proved to the satisfaction of IWW leaders that similarly successful organizations could now be set up in industries outside agriculture.

By 1917, however, the United States had entered World War I, and the repression that had begun against the IWW in California after the Wheatland Riot spread throughout the nation. The IWW had aroused widespread opposition by holding antiwar and antidraft rallies and otherwise vigorously opposing U.S. entry into the war. "This war is a businessman's war," one IWW leader declared, "and we don't see why we should go out and get shot to save the lovely state of affairs which we now enjoy." The war was being waged for the profit of capitalists, said Bill Haywood, and "it is better to be a traitor to your country than to your class."

Once the United States entered the conflict officially, the IWW was careful not to openly oppose U.S. participation; but neither would it adopt the mandatory wartime attitude of "my country, right or wrong." Wobblies continued espousing a revolutionary philosophy considered alien and thus subversive during a period when superpatriotism, unquestioned loyalty and extreme nationalism were demanded of all citizens. Worse, the IWW would not abandon its commitment to strikes and other organizational activity, even after the federal government banned strikes in industries "vital to national defense," including the industries—agriculture, lumber and mining—in which the IWW was most active.

Industrial strife, whatever the reason for it, was considered a hindrance of the war effort, and Wobblies were equated with such wartime enemies as spies and draft evaders. Growers and AFL leaders seized on the opportunity to picture their IWW foes as traitors, and the press regularly carried imaginative articles about crops being destroyed by treacherous Wobblies—some, it was reported, in the pay of enemy agents from Germany. "While this country is at war," said the Cleveland News, "the only room it can afford for IWWs is behind the walls of penitentiaries." The San Francisco Chronicle insisted that

Wobblies "are worse than the Germans" and should be "imprisoned or put out of existence."

Growers formed vigilante groups to chase IWW organizers from farm states, with the support of law enforcement officers and the popular press; there were beatings and at least one lynching. Soon, workers who dared demand more than the "going wage" offered by growers were branded as Wobblies and driven off, to be replaced from a supply of compliant workers whom growers recruited through a new National Farm Labor Exchange organized in the name of patriotism. The new workers included Boy Scouts, YMCA groups, children from detention homes who had to give 40 percent of their meager earnings to the homes, and a women's corps, whose members worked for $2.50 a day and provided their own board and lodging. That wage, typical of what growers were offering, was of course much less than the prevailing rate the IWW had helped set for farm workers. But though workers' pay declined, grower income and profits continued to rise steadily because of wartime sales.

The wartime pressures finally moved the federal government to take the direct action against Wobblies that George Bell had been advocating since soon after he took over as secretary of California's Commission on Immigration and Housing. Bell, backed by Governor Johnson and the governors of seven other western states, had first laid his request for a federal investigation of the IWW before President Woodrow Wilson in 1915. In July, 1917, he proposed a plan of action designed to immobilize the IWW. Wilson had at first refused to act because of findings by a presidential investigator that the IWW's membership was too small and too disadvantaged to be dangerous; but in the political climate of 1917, the government could not resist the insistent nationwide demands for action.

On September 5, raiding parties from the Justice Department burst into the IWW's national headquarters in Chicago, into the homes of Wobbly leaders and into regional IWW offices in more than twenty cities around the country, seeking information on an alleged plot to disrupt the war effort. The offices were torn apart, tons of books and papers carted off, funds seized, and more than 500 people arrested, including the IWW's chief national and regional officers. They were charged with violating the Federal Espionage Act, in part by striking employers who held government contracts, urging people not to work for certain employers and discouraging others from serving in the armed forces. Its leaders jailed, its records and funds impounded, the IWW all but ceased to function as a labor union; it became a legal defense organization. The IWW was hampered in that, too, since the evidence seized by the raiders was denied to Wobbly attorneys, the Post Office Department barred IWW literature from the mails, and raids were conducted regularly on the offices of IWW defense committees.

The IWW got no help from the AFL, but did get strong support from civil libertarians such as Roger Baldwin, who founded the National Civil Liberties Bureau (later the American Civil Liberties Union), mainly in response to the campaign against the IWW. Baldwin and others argued that the raids and subsequent government actions were blatantly unconstitutional and urged President Wilson not to prosecute those arrested. But their pleas were in vain, and Baldwin concluded bitterly that "by prolonged and deliberate misrepresentation in the press the IWW has come to be so outlawed by American public opinion that almost any injustice toward them can be perpetrated without protest."

It was public opinion, surely, that led to the conviction of more than 150 of those who had been arrested. Government prosecutors presented no evidence showing that any of the individual defendants had engaged in any specific criminal acts. Nor was there any evidence that the IWW officially advocated striking or otherwise withholding labor for any purpose except to improve working conditions, or that it advocated draft evasion or any of the other acts of subversion that had been alleged. Federal attorneys merely cited letters and other documents that had been seized in the raids as evidence that Wobblies generally were involved in a conspiracy to commit sabotage. The material talked boldly of sabotaging recalcitrant employers and angrily attacked the war and the government that waged it. It was enough that Wobblies spoke of such things, and that newspapers and the prosecutors *claimed* Wobblies had carried out the threats; whether they actually *did* anything criminal seemed beside the point to juries caught up in war hysteria.

The initial trial was held in Chicago. After four months of testimony, a jury deliberated less than an hour before finding all 100 defendants guilty of conspiring to commit every one of some 10,000 criminal acts charged to the IWW by the federal prosecutors. Kenesaw Mountain Landis, as unyielding a judge as ever sat on the bench, levied fines totaling $2.3 million and imposed sentences ranging from five years' imprisonment to the legal maximum of twenty years on most of the defendants, including IWW General Secretary Bill Haywood, who was among those sentenced to the maximum term.

Another major trial was held in Sacramento, California, in December of 1918. Half of the forty-six defendants who finally came to trial had been held in jail more than a year while government prosecutors awaited completion of the proceedings in Chicago. They had been arrested in a raid on the office of the IWW's Agricultural Workers Organization in Fresno; the others were arrested after Governor-elect William Stephens received a bomb in the mail, even though federal agents had been unable to link any Wobblies to the alleged assassination attempt. At one point, fifty prisoners were confined for sixty-four days in a cell twenty-one feet square with only a single cotton blanket each, and had to take turns sleeping and standing. Five of the prisoners died in the influenza epidemic of that year. The IWW's defense committee offices were raided periodically while the defendants were in jail; records were seized and committee members arrested. In the meantime, public hysteria mounted, to the point that California newspapers were suggesting that the prisoners in Sacramento be lynched.

The IWW had gone into the Chicago trial almost eagerly, naively anticipating acquittals that would finally free Wobblies from government harassment; but the IWW carried no such illusions into the courtroom in Sacramento. All but three of the California defendants decided to offer no defense at all; it was the only way, said one of them, "to preserve the self-respect of ourselves as members of organized labor." The forty-three defendants issued a declaration that "the labor movement of America will judge us. We will not put a single witness on the stand. The prosecution has harassed our defense in its efforts to organize and prepare a legitimate case. The blame rests on them. We are ready for your farce." After that, they lapsed into silence.

Government attorneys produced two former Wobblies who agreed to testify as paid witnesses in exchange for the dropping of charges against them. The witnesses claimed they had set fires, poisoned farm animals and committed other acts in an IWW "sabotage campaign." They named none of the defendants as participants in the "campaign"; and the government, while citing a dozen or so fires that had been set on farms three to five years before, did not even prove conclusively that the alleged acts of sabotage had taken place. But prosecutors sought only to prove conspiracy and merely needed to read inflammatory IWW literature to convince the jury that the Wobblies had *inspired* sabotage. It took the jury only about an hour to return guilty verdicts against all the defendants. They were sentenced to from one to ten years' imprisonment each. Then, after six weeks, they broke their silence. They sang "The Internationale," and Fred Esmond, leader of the IWW's defense committee in California, rose to proclaim:

We, the outcasts, have been framed up on, clubbed, beaten, slugged, martyred and murdered. Is it any wonder that I do not consider myself bound by your procedure when this court and its proceedings are a disgrace to the United States? You have done more than any IWW could possibly do to drag your Stars and Stripes through the mire.

The end of World War I in 1918 did not end the persecution of the IWW. Opponents turned to the IWW's open support for the Bolshevik revolutionaries in Russia as new evidence of treachery, using as their main weapons against Wobblies the criminal syndicalism laws which were enacted in twenty-one states between 1917 and 1921, subjecting violators to from one to twenty-five years' imprisonment and fines up to $10,000. Typical was California's law, enacted in 1919 after Governor Stephens declared that Wobblies "must be suppressed with a determined hand." The law forbade "advocating, teaching or aiding and abetting the commission of crime, sabotage . . . or unlawful methods of terrorism as a means of accomplishing a change in industrial ownership or control, or effecting any political change." Typical, too, was Governor Stephens' characterization of Wobblies as "huns of industry . . . terrorists . . . the bitter enemies of all honest workers [who] during the war did all in their power to aid the enemy."

The IWW's postwar strikes and organizing efforts were crushed by mass arrests of strikers and IWW members, who invariably were charged with engaging in "Bolshevik conspiracies." In California, more than 500 Wobblies and IWW sympathizers were jailed during the first five years after enactment of the criminal syndicalism law there. The IWW tried to combat the harassment by calling for a general strike in 1923 and by declaring a boycott against fresh fruits and canned goods from California; but it was virtually the last gasp of a dying organization. By 1924, the IWW was bankrupt, financially and otherwise; the organization had few members, and the leaders who remained were split into warring socialist factions. Most of the tacticians who had guided the IWW's meteoric rise were gone. Many of the foreign-born among them had been deported; the others who had not been imprisoned had died or had left to work with the AFL or the Communist Party. Haywood himself had fled to the Soviet Union, where he soon died, a shattered man still dreaming of the "Cooperative Commonwealth of Workers."

The IWW's Agricultural Workers Organization retained one local in California, but by 1926 it, too, was gone. Government harassment wasn't the only reason for the AWO's decline; the IWW had done little to attract the Mexican immigrants and family groups that had joined the farm labor force in large numbers after World War I. The AWO continued to concentrate on the much smaller group of single men who migrated from farm to farm via freight trains, ignoring the families that worked their way through farm states in automobiles, camping together along the roads rather than living as isolated individuals in hobo jungles. These workers didn't need the fellowship of the IWW or the protections that its red membership card afforded those who rode the freights.

The martyrs of the Wheatland Riot finally were paroled—Blackie Ford in 1925 and Herman Suhr in 1926—but they and their organization were no longer considered menacing. After his release, Ford was tried in Marysville for the murder of the deputy sheriff who had been killed in the riot with the district attorney. This time, however, Ford was acquitted, with assistance from the American Civil Liberties Union. Many of those who had been arrested during the postwar period nevertheless remained in prison, despite efforts of the ACLU and others on their behalf. Some were not released until the 1930s, just as the law that had been used to imprison them was being used to jail a new generation of radical organizers, these from the Communist Party.

Some leaders from the AFL had talked of trying to organize farm workers but they feared the entrenched grower power that had destroyed the AWO. As a result, there was very little organizing in California during the half-dozen years between the AWO's demise and the beginning of efforts in the 1930s by the Communists and others outside the established labor movement. There were almost no strikes during the period and almost no other organized activity—except by growers. They strengthened their already powerful position in labor relations by forming associations through which they recruited masses of poor workers—so many that workers were forced to quietly accept whatever growers chose to offer them or get no work at all. These workers, noted one happy grower, were "free from Bolshevik tendencies."

Farm pay dropped steadily, from an average in California of 30 cents an hour in 1920 to half that ten years later. Working and living conditions worsened as well. The reforms initiated by the state's Commission on Immigration and Housing after the Wheatland Riot all but disappeared through lax or nonexistent enforcement of the laws that had been enacted during the IWW's rise.

It was almost as if the Wobblies had never existed. They had vanished as swiftly as the reforms they had inspired. They had not negotiated union contracts farm workers could use as the basis for further gain; they had left no organizational structure on which the workers could build. The IWW had left only a small band of lonely, frustrated men ineffectually sputtering anticapitalist slogans, subjected to the ultimate insult of being unheeded now by even their enemies.

Yet though the Wobblies lost their battle, they were not failures. No one before them had even attempted to organize farm workers on such a scale. They proved it could be done; and that lesson, even the very tactics they had employed, would one day help guide others to victory. The Wobblies' courage, their songs, their literature, their speechmaking, their organizing efforts, had focused workers on a common body of ideals; and though the workers had not yet the means to act on the knowledge of their own rights and dignity brought to them by the IWW, they would act someday. Even the oppression that crushed the Industrial Workers of the World provided a crucial lesson. Civil libertarians would henceforth be on guard; they would take nothing for granted. They now knew just how undemocratically their democratic government was capable of acting when confronted with a serious threat to society's dominant economic interests.

2

"We Can't Live on That!"

There were 400, maybe 500 strikers milling about the dusty vacant lot, muttering angrily among themselves. There had been a pitched battle between pickets and a posse of growers outside a cotton field a few miles away, and seventeen of the pickets had been taken to a justice court just across the highway from the vacant lot. The strikers had sent a delegation to the sheriff to demand the pickets' release, but that had done no good.

In the center of the angry crowd, a strike leader named Pat Chambers stood on a soapbox—a short, slender man straining mightily to be heard. As the noonday sun warmed his florid face, he spoke of the evils of capitalism, of the worth of the proletariat; Chambers was a Communist Party organizer, and he often spoke of such things, but his purpose now was to divert the strikers from thoughts of storming the courthouse. That, he said, would be "leading a bunch of working people to slaughter." Out beyond the crowd, a line of automobiles had been drawn up to the very edge of the vacant lot. Members of the grower posse stood beside the cars.

Chambers persuaded the strikers they should cross the highway to a dilapidated two-story brick building near the courthouse that served as the local headquarters of their organization, the Cannery and Agricultural Workers Industrial Union. They'd hold a meeting there, beyond the hearing of their grower foes, and *then* decide what to do. They started across the highway. Suddenly, the posse members ducked behind their cars, leveled rifles and fired. Strikers scattered down the highway, running full-tilt, dashed into their headquarters building, or dropped to the ground in panic. Most escaped—but not all. Two men were killed. Seven men and one woman were wounded.

The date was October 10, 1933; the place, Pixley, California; the incident, the most violent and dramatic of a series of violent and dramatic events that once again riveted public attention to the farm workers of California. Gone was the quiet despair that had pervaded the state's fields after destruction of the Industrial Workers of the World nearly a decade earlier. In its stead was the angry desperation of workers driven to the starvation point by the Great Depression of the 1930s. Farm pay spiraled steadily downward, even as crop production continued to rise; urban workers and migrants from other states swarmed into the fields to compete for increasingly scarce jobs; and farm workers were denied even the relief afforded industrial workers by the reforms of President Franklin Roosevelt, which granted the right to unionization, a minimum wage and other protections.

The result was strife never before experienced in U.S. agriculture. There were no less than 140 strikes on California's farms alone between 1930 and 1939, involving more than 125,000 workers, and drawing an even fiercer counterattack than the IWW's activities had provoked. Many of the strikes were spontaneous uprisings; but grower interests nonetheless found a new menace to blame for the unrest and to justify their violent reaction to what they would once again picture, not as efforts to improve pay and working conditions, but as efforts to violently overthrow the government. The posse that had fired on the strikers in Pixley, for instance: Eleven of the riflemen were positively identified by witnesses, eight were brought to trial for murder—and all eight were acquitted by a jury that was told they were patriotically defending their justice courthouse from attack by "Communist agitators."

The new unrest in California's fields first surfaced among the Mexicans whom growers began hiring in large numbers after the Mexican Revolution of 1910 forced thousands of destitute workers to flee across the border. There were only 8000 Mexicans in California in 1910; by 1920, there were more than 120,000. Many were working on farms, including some who had been hired directly from Mexico during World War I as contract laborers. By the late 1920s, there were more than 350,000 Mexicans in the state, providing growers with a ready supply of low-paid laborers to substitute for the Chinese and Japanese who were now denied them by restrictive immigration laws. Mexicans made up at least half the farm labor force and, like the Asians before them, were subjected to blatant discrimination. They were barred from Anglo schools, restaurants, movie theaters and other public facilities in the farm communities where they worked, and treated as necessary evils who were encouraged to harvest the crops quickly and cheaply and return to Mexico until the next harvest season, lest they become public charges.

The Mexicans were forced to draw together in *barrio* settlements where they formed mutual aid societies to provide such things as unemployment benefits and legal help. Eventually, some of the societies took the form of unions and, beginning in 1928, staged a series of strikes in the Imperial Valley near the Mexican border, an extremely fertile region that had been desert until the Colorado River was diverted into the area two decades earlier and Mexicans hired to help develop the land. Growers smashed the Mexicans' strikes by calling in authorities to arrest and deport strike leaders; but the very act of striking, and the strong response of growers to actions that often amounted to no more than protests against pay reductions, instilled a sense of angry solidarity among the Mexicans, the Filipinos who worked beside them in the fields, and the Anglo workers in nearby packing sheds.

The Filipino workers were among 31,000 young single men who had come to California in the 1920s, some after working as contract laborers in Hawaii. They migrated throughout the state in the same manner as the Mexican workers, and were also thrown closely together, isolated from the rest of society, and discriminated against because of their race.

The unrest attracted organizers from a Trade Union Unity League, which the Communist Party established in 1929 to organize the masses of workers who had been left jobless by the Depression, as well as farm workers and others who had been ignored by the craft unionists of the AFL. Like the Wobblies, the Communists sought to form a classless society by bringing unskilled, discontented workers into organizations that cut across racial, ethnic and craft lines and were dedicated to Marxist principles. The Communists saw an ideal opportunity in the Imperial Valley where, in 1930, the Trade Union Unity League joined in strikes started by the Mexican unions. The Communist league took over leadership of some of the strikes and, after several months of activity, called a conference of delegates from every farm and packing shed in hopes of forming a union that would encompass all of the valley's agricultural workers. But just a week before the conference was to be held, sheriff's deputies raided the league's headquarters and the homes of its representatives and supporters. One hundred people were arrested for alleged violation of California's criminal syndicalism law, and eight were eventually convicted and jailed for as long as three years.

Neither the Communists nor the desperate workers would be so quickly suppressed, however. Within a year, the Communist Party had set up the Cannery and Agricultural Workers Industrial Union— a political action group that attempted to assume the leadership of dozens of strikes, often at the invitation of the strikers. In 1932, the CAWIU put a corps of idealistic young volunteers into the fields, headed by Pat Chambers, a thirty-one-year-old construction worker who was recruited by party members in Los Angeles to be the chief organizer, and an executive secretary, Caroline Decker, whose impassioned, eloquent speechmaking belied her youth—she was only twenty—and her look of college girl innocence. Decker had been involved in a bloody coal mine strike in Kentucky and other party activities among workers, but she was not familiar with agriculture. Neither were Chambers and most of the volunteers; but the organizers were convinced they could bring California's farm workers into a single movement by helping bring about effective unified action in the strikes that so many separate groups of workers were calling.

The young CAWIU representatives could scarcely keep up; they were constantly on the move, sometimes helping workers win modest gains, but often losing in a matter of days. They hitchhiked or drove beat-up cars from area to area, relying on supporters for shelter and temporary office space, spending their own meager funds to put out leaflets, gleaning information on commodity prices and other essential matters from sympathetic small growers, and trying to act quickly, before the large growers who were the strike targets could mobilize against them.

The CAWIU's first major strike came in late 1932, among some 400 workers in the fruit orchards around Vacaville in northern California. The strikers held out through several months of extreme harassment. Strikebreakers threatened them with lead pipes and pruning shears, and, at the height of the strike, a masked mob of forty men took six CAWIU leaders from the Vacaville jail, drove them to a lonely road twenty miles away, flogged them, shaved their heads and poured red enamel over them. A Communist Party delegation sent to organize a defense committee for the strikers was chased away by 180 deputized vigilantes.

But though the strike in Vacaville was broken, waves of other CAWIU-led strikes broke out as crops came to maturity elsewhere throughout the spring and summer of 1933. Three thousand pea pickers struck, one thousand cherry pickers, and hundreds of workers in grape vineyards and peach and pear orchards. In most cases, strikers won wage increases, but at least one striker was killed and many others injured by hostile deputies and vigilantes who, as Chambers recalled, often "descended like locusts."

By late summer, the CAWIU had set up a network of locals throughout the state and planned a series of crop-wide strikes, the

first of them in the peach orchards of seven San Joaquin Valley
counties. Chambers organized the strike against the largest of the
peach growers, the 4000-acre Tagus Ranch, by slipping past armed
guards between 2 and 3 o'clock in the morning to meet with pickers
on the ranch property where they lived. The pickers quickly won a pay
increase, and the smaller peach growers who also had been struck
settled within a few days on the same terms as the huge Tagus Ranch,
whose lead they usually followed. The success in the peach orchards
attracted an enthusiastic group of local organizers who helped wage
the other strikes that had been planned by the CAWIU. In all, the
union led two dozen strikes during 1933, winning pay raises in every
one of them but four, for more than 35,000 workers.

The most important of the strikes was the conflict that prompted
the outbreak in Pixley on that October day when two men fell before a
posse's bullets. Pixley stood in the center of a mammoth cotton-
growing region that spread across six San Joaquin Valley counties, a
region 114 miles long, 30 to 40 miles wide, dotted with more than
2000 farms. Up to 20,000 workers swarmed into the area for each
fall's harvest, camping in the open or living in flimsy weathered cabins
in grower-owned farm labor camps. Three-fourths of them were Mexicans, who regularly migrated from Mexico or from the Imperial Valley
after the seasonal harvests there were concluded; but there also was
a substantial number of families from the southwestern United States,
some of them black. They began coming into California's fields in
1910, in response to grower advertisements for experienced "southern
help" to handle the skilled and arduous task of picking cotton. It was a
relatively new crop in California then, and not widely cultivated. But
California growers, faced with declining prices for other commodities,
soon found that their irrigation techniques enabled them to produce
three times more cotton per acre than growers in the South and that
their cotton would fetch a higher price because of its quality. So by
the 1920s, cotton was California's number-one crop.

The Depression cut deeply into the cotton growers' income, however. They were getting $1.46 an acre in 1930, but by 1933, the re-
turn had dropped to 72 cents an acre, and many growers were heavily
in debt to banks that had loaned them money for planting and to the
cotton ginning companies that had also provided loans and processed
their crops. As a result, workers' pay dwindled. Pickers, who had
commonly made $1 for every 100 pounds of cotton they picked, were
paid 40 cents per 100 pounds in 1932. Helped by subsidy payments
from the Roosevelt Administration and hoping to avert action by the
CAWIU, the cotton growers' association set the rate a full 20 cents

higher for the 1933 harvest. But the union, flushed with its victories in other crops, demanded a rate of $1 per 100 pounds and urged cotton pickers to stay off the job until they got it.

The crop matured late that year and so the harvest crews arrived almost two weeks before picking actually started. CAWIU representatives roved continuously through the cotton-growing region to set up locals, pass out leaflets, make speeches and meet with groups of idle workers—listening, persuading, explaining, giving rudimentary lessons in leadership. When the harvest got under way in early October, thousands of workers stayed off the job.

CAWIU leaders had counseled strikers to stay in their labor camps, but growers evicted them when they refused to work and, in doing so, gave the union a powerful organizing tool. The CAWIU gathered the homeless strikers into tent cities, including one, in the Kings County town of Corcoran, that housed more than 3000 people—more than lived in the town itself. Union guards stood outside the enclosed camps, "sanitation patrols" made certain county authorities would have no excuse to shut them down, and residents elected their own racially-mixed committees to conduct camp business and strike affairs. Caravans of trucks and autos moved out of the camps regularly to drive along the edges of cotton fields bearing huge strike signs. A caravan would stop at a field where nonstrikers were working, a bugler would sound a call and strikers would pile out of the vehicles to shout, "Strike! Strike!"

Ultimately, there were more than 15,000 strikers in the cotton-growing region—and lots of furious growers. Some local working people sided with strikers, as did some small growers who felt that they, too, were being exploited by the larger growers who set the pickers' pay rate and otherwise controlled agriculture in the San Joaquin Valley. But banks and other dominant community interests with large financial stakes in farming sided with the growers, and local merchants who wavered were warned they would be boycotted if they did business with strikers.

County authorities, backed by state officials, rejected grower demands to deport Mexican strikers, declare the strikers' camps health hazards and close schools so students could replace strikers. But local courts and law enforcement officers, who allowed grower vigilantes to be armed and deputized, lined up firmly behind the growers. As one undersheriff explained, "We protect our farmers . . . they are our best people. They are always with us. They keep the county going. They put us in here and they can put us out again, so we serve them." The Mexicans who made up the bulk of the strike force, added the undersheriff, "are trash . . . we herd them like pigs." Some law enforcement officers carried their support to the point of arresting strikers merely for the act of picketing. "There's no law on mass picketing," as one sheriff explained. "But I can make law . . . and I can go before any court and win my case."

Local newspapers wrote provocatively about a "Communist conspiracy" to seize the valley and joined growers in warning strikers they were being manipulated by leaders dedicated to "social anarchy and red revolution," as a typical editorial declared. An editorial in the Corcoran *News* informed the Mexican strikers camped in town that they were

visitors to this country, here only through our sufferance. You have been fools, many of you, trying to reach a goal that is not possible for you to reach, the right to dictate to American employers what they shall pay, whether they can pay it or not.

Emboldened by such support, growers formed "protective associations" of armed men who patrolled the cotton fields provoking fights with strikers, broke up strike meetings, joined the squads of deputies and state highway policemen that surrounded the strikers' camps, and urged their fellow citizens to act. One grower group placed a newspaper advertisement that declared:

We, The Farmers Of Your Community, Whom You Depend Upon For Support, Feel That You Have Nursed Too Long The Viper That Is At Our Door. These Communist Agitators MUST Be Driven From Town By You, And Your Harboring Them Further Will Prove To Us Your Non-Cooperation With Us, And Make It Necessary For Us To Give Our Support And Trade To Another Town That Will Support And Cooperate With Us.

The ad appeared in the town of Tulare, where the CAWIU's main field office was located, just one day before the men were killed in Pixley, seventeen miles to the south. On the same day as the Pixley shootings, a striker was killed and several others injured in Arvin, a town farther south, by grower allies, although strikers rather than growers were arrested after that incident.

The deaths focused widespread public attention on the strike. Urban liberals, radicals, students and clergymen joined workers in a procession of 3000 mourners that marched quietly through the streets of Bakersfield, on the edge of the strike area. The outside supporters helped to greatly intensify the strike, joined in protests against the treatment of strikers by local authorities and urged Governor James Rolph of California to dispatch state troopers to the cotton fields to halt vigilantism. Rolph didn't send troops; but under pressure from federal officials and the public, he did order the state's Relief Administration to supply food to the hard-pressed strikers, who had been denied county relief.

Growers had previously rejected attempts by the federal Labor Department and the state Labor Commissioner to mediate a settlement, but were now under heavy pressure to end the strike. The pressure was heightened considerably when Governor Rolph appointed a fact-finding board headed by a University of California economist to hear testimony from worker and grower representatives and recommend a pay settlement. Grower witnesses claimed pickers could live adequately on the pay rate of 60 cents per 100 pounds that had been offered before the strike, and asserted they could not afford to pay more. But CAWIU representatives claimed that rate netted whole families of workers only $3 to $3.50 a day and, as a striker asserted, *"We can't live on that!"*

The fact-finding board recommended a raise to 75 cents per 100 pounds, and it was accepted by both sides—albeit with great reluctance. Growers began paying the rate after a federal lending agency threatened to withdraw guarantees for the loans they needed to plant and process their crops, and strikers began returning to work after state officials warned that their relief aid would be cut off and county officials moved to condemn their camps. So, after three weeks, the great cotton strike of 1933 was over.

That so many thousands of farm workers had stayed out together for so long under such trying conditions was a major accomplishment that would be a source of important instruction and inspiration for farm workers and organizers in the future. But the immediate returns were slight. A 15-cent raise wasn't much to show for three weeks of grueling strike activity in which 3 people had been killed, 42 wounded, 113 arrested, and strike leaders put on a growers' blacklist that would keep them from ever working again for the men they had dared challenge. Nor had the extraordinary efforts brought the farm workers a lasting organization. For when their strike collapsed and CAWIU organizers moved elsewhere, the local organizations they had put together to wage the strike also collapsed.

The strike had not even done a great deal of damage to the growers; they managed to harvest three-fourths of their cotton that season, and most showed a profit. What the strike *had* done was to resolve growers and their allies to crush any further attempts to challenge their unilateral control of farm labor relations. They had been caught off guard by the militancy shown by workers in the 1933 strikes, but they were well prepared when workers in the Imperial Valley struck under CAWIU leadership at the start of the winter lettuce and pea harvests in January of 1934.

A party of deputy sheriffs, deputized growers and American Legionnaires broke into the strikers' initial strategy session and dragged eighty-seven workers and CAWIU leaders to jail for alleged violation of the criminal syndicalism law. Other raiding parties roamed through the valley in a manhunt for CAWIU representatives and supporters, in open defiance of a federal court injunction that had been secured by the American Civil Liberties Union. To underscore their defiance, vigilantes abducted the ACLU's chief attorney from his hotel room, beat him, dumped him in the desert outside El Centro and forced him to make his way back to town barefoot. When the strike continued nevertheless, raiders invaded the strikers' main camp, driving out 2000 workers and their families with tear gas and burning their shacks and tents to the ground. The CAWIU strike was broken, two months after it began.

It had amounted to a flagrant disregard of basic constitutional rights by law enforcement agencies on behalf of growers who were "paying less than a starvation wage," according to a commission of inquiry sent to the Imperial Valley by the Roosevelt Administration. Simon J. Lubin, a prominent commission member, reported that Imperial Valley workers were averaging as little as 56 cents a day and living in "filth, squalor, and entire absence of sanitation," in "totally inadequate tents or crude structures built of boards, weeds and anything else that was at hand." As for local authorities, Lubin reported angrily:

They forbid free speech and assembly. . . . Brutally they break up public meetings conducted in private halls. They interfere with the organization of labor. . . . Indiscriminately they arrest innocent men and women under fake charges . . . fix exorbitant bail . . . threaten to ruin a few residents brave enough to show sympathy with unfortunate workers. They scoff at our Federal courts. They threaten to prevent, by bribery or force, the feeding of starving women and children by Federal agents. Their so-called peace officers do the bidding of their masters with the able assistance of pistols, machineguns, tear gas bombs, hard wood sticks. . . .

The federal commission recommended that the state and federal governments guarantee the workers' civil rights, improve their living conditions and encourage collective bargaining. But government authorities refused to take any meaningful action and grower violence and intimidation continued. Workers and organizers were constantly harassed and mobs of vigilantes beat three of the attorneys who came to the valley to defend strikers who had been arrested.

Much of the violence was waged by a group of Imperial County growers who had formed an organization pledged to help struck growers harvest their crops and to act as "special deputies . . . in the event of disorders arising out of picketing and sabotage." The group's inspiration, and that for similar organizations in twenty-five other agricultural counties, came from a report on "labor trouble" distributed by the state Chamber of Commerce; the report claimed that 90 percent of the strikes that began breaking out in 1933 were instigated and financed by Soviet interests seeking to sabotage U.S. production.

The Chamber, backed by the California Farm Bureau Federation and the state Agriculture Department, brought the county groups into a statewide organization in May of 1934. It was called the Associated Farmers; but the financing, and most of the control, came from outside groups with heavy stakes in keeping growers' labor costs and prices low and their harvests free from disruption. They included northern California's major private utility, Pacific Gas & Electric; the area's major grocery chain, Safeway Stores; and banks, railroads, oil companies, real estate firms, farm implement manufacturers and food packers.

The Associated Farmers joined the Chamber of Commerce in blaming farm labor unrest on "agitators who are more interested in the overthrow of our American system of government than in the welfare of the workers," and announced that the new organization's main purpose was to ferret out the "agitators." In the Associated Farmers' view, farm unionization per se was "un-American," because, the organization claimed, it would destroy agriculture. Hence the Associated Farmers opposed "unionization of farm labor on any basis" and branded all those engaging in union activity as "agitators." As one farm worker noted, "Anyone asking for a nickel raise was a Communist."

The Associated Farmers kept files on these "agitators" and published their names in bulletins that warned growers to avoid hiring them. The organization made a patriotic show of turning the names over to federal agents and the "red squads" operated by local law enforcement agencies, which eagerly assisted in running the troublemakers out of the fields. The cooperation was so close that all of the state's agricultural counties adopted ordinances that virtually outlawed picketing and other farm union activity. A typical ordinance, in Tulare County, prohibited "unauthorized line-ups of automobiles, concentrations in camps for which permits have not been obtained and meetings of more than 25 persons without permits." Most of the counties also adopted ordinances that allowed growers to mobilize for "emergencies and disasters"—including strikes.

The county chapters of the Associated Farmers, some with more than 2000 members, kept well prepared for mobilization. Members were drilled by former Army officers and were issued twenty-inch-long pick handles. They stood guard outside orchards and vegetable fields surrounded by barbed wire, regularly receiving reports from grower supervisors inside who listened carefully for talk of strikes and other "subversive activity."

CAWIU organizers waged nine more strikes after they left the Imperial Valley in March of 1934, but the organizers were no match for the veritable army now massed against them. The last of the CAWIU strikes were called in the fruit orchards across the bay from San Francisco, not only to support better pay and conditions but also to demand removal of state troops who had occupied San Francisco's waterfront after a general strike was called in that city with the active support of the Communist Party. In one of the CAWIU strikes, Contra Costa County authorities, under the guidance of the Associated Farmers, used an antipicketing ordinance to herd 200 strikers into a cattle pen, arrest the leaders and escort the others across the county line.

The general strike in San Francisco, called in July to support the demand of longshoremen for recognition of their union, was cited widely by labor foes as evidence of a conspiracy among unions and the Communist Party to overturn the established order, and used to justify attempts to suppress union and Communist activists throughout the state. Authorities moved on the CAWIU in the same month as the general strike. A raiding party broke into the organization's service center in Sacramento, broke up furniture, seized records and arrested Caroline Decker, Pat Chambers and seventeen others on vagrancy charges, then ordered them held for trial for allegedly violating the criminal syndicalism law. After a four-month wait, fourteen went on trial on charges that they had advocated, taught, aided and abetted "the duty, necessity and propriety of committing crime, sabotage, violent and unlawful terrorism . . . by justifying personal violence to all police officers, militia and all other law enforcement officials. . . ."

The trial became a cause among civil libertarians, for the CAWIU representatives actually were tried on the basis of antigovernment statements in Communist literature that the prosecutor introduced, and because, as the prosecutor complained, CAWIU activities had cost growers "millions of dollars." The defendants boasted of their Communist affiliation; but, Decker told the jury, "If you vote for acquittal you are not voting for communism; you are voting for the right of the American people to say what they please."

Chambers declared that conviction of the Communist organizers would be "the opening gun in an attack on the wages" of farm workers. He urged the jury members:

Go to the agricultural fields and see for yourselves how miserable the conditions of life are there. You will see children with the terrible imprint of hunger on their faces. I swore to fight against all organizations that use their power to browbeat the poor. I swore above all that these children would not go hungry. I have seen so much misery, starvation, brutality, I am glad that I took part to a small extent in the struggle against them. They now want to force wages back. . . .

After four months of testimony, Chambers, Decker and six other key CAWIU leaders were convicted and imprisoned. Some were paroled a year later and the others released two years later by an appellate court, but by then the CAWIU no longer existed. In 1935, shortly after the trial, the Communist Party had dissolved the union and the Trade Union Unity League as part of its shift to a "Popular Front" policy. There would no longer be an independent Communist labor movement; henceforth the party's labor organizers were to work within the AFL.

The death of the CAWIU was inevitable anyway, quite apart from the shift in Communist Party strategy. It's true that CAWIU organizers called for strikes rather than for revolution, for pay raises rather than for worker control of agriculture; but like the IWW organizers before them, they saw the strikes as essential steps toward their Marxist goals. Growers knew this, the government knew this, and so did many unaligned people who otherwise might have supported the union and its activities. It kept many potential backers away, and gave grower interests an excuse to viciously suppress any attempts to better the conditions of farm workers—and, eventually, to destroy the CAWIU.

Relatively few workers supported the CAWIU because of revolutionary beliefs; they desperately wanted better pay and conditions and, in the course of four extraordinary years, the union helped them get what they sought, either directly through nearly fifty strikes or indirectly through the independent actions of growers seeking to head off union activity. It raised the average pay of California's farm workers by fully one-third, greatly diminished their feelings of hopelessness and brought them the sympathy of outsiders who had largely forgotten them after the destruction of the IWW.

But though the farm workers' powerful opponents had been forced to make concessions, they had not been forced to step down from their commanding position. Nor had the CAWIU left workers the means to continue challenging them effectively. In their rush from strike to strike, CAWIU leaders had not left behind grass roots movements that could have been built into a true farm workers' union—a union with goals set by the workers themselves, and led by the workers, rather than by urban intellectuals dedicated to class warfare and the other tenets of Marxism *they* thought the workers should follow. Organizers were instructed in their basic manual to "be extremely careful to bring the rank-and-file into the leadership," and the union did develop temporary rank-and-file leaders during its strikes, but most of them were no more committed to carrying on the CAWIU's program than were the masses of workers who took part in the strikes. The CAWIU had relatively few real members—just followers who heeded the union's Communist organizers as long as the organizers were active and holding out the prospect of improved conditions. The CAWIU had tried to give workers a way to continue on their own, by demanding formal recognition of the union in several of its major strikes. But union recognition, said Pat Chambers, "was a utopian idea in that era."

The disappearance of the CAWIU did not kill the hope the organization had raised for creation of an agricultural union that would include all the industry's workers, from the fields to the processing plants. That kind of union could arm agricultural workers with the united strength that might match that of their employers, who had integrated their operations through marketing cooperatives and other organizations that recruited workers, set pay and prices and generally developed common policies for harvesting, processing and selling produce, as well as for dealing with labor.

The former CAWIU organizers and other radicals who became active in the AFL tried to push the federation into forming an integrated union; it seemed a necessary and logical development to them, since the AFL already was organizing cannery workers, and one of its most aggressive affiliates, the Teamsters, was attempting to organize "everything on wheels"—including the trucking firms that hauled farm produce. Groups of workers held two conferences to discuss the idea and petitioned the AFL to set up a broadly based International Union of Agricultural Workers. But though the plan was backed by one of the most prominent of the AFL's statewide leaders, Harry Bridges of the longshoremen's union, other members of the federation's executive council rejected the idea. They protested that it violated the AFL's basic concept of setting up unions according to craft rather than by industry.

It was clear the AFL still had little interest in organizing field workers under any circumstances. "Only fanatics are willing to live in shacks or tents and get their heads broken in the interests of migratory labor," declared Paul Scharrenberg, the AFL's former secretary-treasurer in California.

The prospects for organizing California's farm workers were dimmed even more by an influx of migrants who began pouring into the state in the mid-1930s—tenant farmers and sharecroppers who had been driven off drought-parched land in Oklahoma, Texas, Arkansas, Missouri and other south-central and midwestern states by a plague of swirling dust storms. More than 300,000 Dust Bowl Refugees, as they were called, made their way to California between 1934 and 1939, many in response to grower advertisements promising a substantial number of jobs at good pay. They were highly skilled, desperate enough to take whatever work they could find, and so numerous that growers no longer felt a need for the Mexicans who had been the mainstay of their labor force. Many of the Mexicans returned home on their own, and more than 50,000 were deported at the behest of local authorities who did not want to carry them on relief rolls crowded with Depression-stricken workers. By 1935, Dust Bowl Refugees had supplanted Mexicans as the major group in California's fields. They made up half the farm labor force, providing growers with an overabundance of cheap skilled labor.

Union organizing seemed out of the question now that the fields were flooded with so many penniless workers competing desperately for jobs at whatever pay and under whatever conditions growers provided, eroding the gains union activity had won just a few years earlier. Growers sometimes found themselves with as many as five to ten times more workers than even they wanted for particular harvests, some of them sleeping in the fields, between rows of vegetables or under fruit trees, to make certain that someone else wouldn't get their jobs come morning.

Battered autos piled high with bedding and household goods rattled over California's rural highways as the Dust Bowl Refugees searched for the work that often could not be found. They camped beside streams and irrigation ditches, in groves of trees, under bridges, in tattered tents or in crude shelters made from cardboard or corrugated paper. Typhoid fever and other diseases were common and hundreds

of infants died. Children rarely attended school; they were needed in
the fields to help their families fight for survival. If the migrants were
lucky they might eat beans, but boiled dandelion greens and potatoes
or perhaps fried cornmeal might be their only food. For even when
a job could be found, a whole family might get no more than $1.25
for an entire day's work.

The work was grueling. In picking prunes, as one worker who followed the fruit crops noted:

All the kids work, even the little ones four or five years old. . . . The
prunes are shaken from the trees by "shakers" who use long poles. . . .
Pickers must crawl on their knees to pick the prunes. . . . When the
prunes get hot they get sticky and your hands are caked with gummy mud.
Your knees hurt like hell from crawling on the ground, and your back
aches like double-be-damned hell.

In berry picking, it is . . . hot as hell. There is no shade. Working hill-
sides you can be standing up straight and your nose will be two feet from
the ground . . . the heat reflects back into your face until you can hardly
breathe.

In picking wine grapes, the hazards are sunstroke, cuts from the [cut-
ting] knife and starvation. Eating wine grapes causes bellyache.

In picking cherries, you get a cent a pound . . . if it don't rain and
split all the cherries. If it does rain you get in debt, or go hungry waiting
for the next job. When you have your bucket filled you get down and dump
them in a box, then turn the bucket over and sit on it for awhile (your back
will be aching plenty from hanging on the ladder). That is, you do if you
haven't a large family of small kids to support. If you have, you take everything but the rest period.

Many of the workers were literally starving, but they got little sympathy from most Californians, who were having serious troubles of
their own in the Depression years and bitterly resented having to ab-
sorb a flood of refugees. The migrants all became "Okies"—a term as
scornful in California as "nigger" was in southern states. They generally were treated as shiftless, dirty parasites who had flocked to
California to steal jobs from hard-pressed local residents who were
finding it extremely difficult to get work themselves, or who had come
to take advantage of the state's relief programs. The programs did provide more than the virtually nonexistent programs in the migrants'
home states, but local authorities invoked residence requirements and
otherwise made certain that migrants were all but denied the slight
aid that California did offer the needy. Most of the aid they did get

came through sympathetic federal officials who supervised relief programs.

Rather than aid the newcomers, community leaders attempted to drive them out, sometimes giving them a tankful of gasoline to make certain they kept moving, at other times using more forceful methods. AFL officials were no different from other community leaders; they joined bankers and businessmen to form an association dedicated to halting the "Okie invasion," for it was undermining the job security of AFL members. The association and other citizens' groups demanded that the government oust the migrants from the state and deny relief payments to anyone who had not lived in California for at least three years. Legislators introduced bills to do just that, as well as to prohibit further migration from other states. The bills didn't pass, but communities made do with ordinances outlawing the migrant camps on their outskirts. Los Angeles city officials even ordered police to erect "bum barricades" on highways leading into the state from the east; they managed to turn back "unemployables" for several weeks in early 1936, until a court ruled that the procedure was unconstitutional.

After state officials took over supervision of relief programs from federal authorities in 1935, migrants and all others on relief—including strikers—were ordered to take work in the fields or lose their payments. "Help the state's harvests," said Governor Frank Merriam sternly, "or get off the dole." State employment offices in urban areas sent relief recipients to farm jobs hundreds of miles from their homes, and the growers who had agreed to hire them warned the workers openly that they would lose their jobs and their eligibility for relief if they raised any complaints about the pay and conditions the growers had set without consulting the state, much less the workers. There were so many of these workers that in 1937 California's entire hop crop was picked by relief recipients, as was most of the cotton crop.

The Associated Farmers considered such a work force ideal, and worked closely with the state in recruiting the workers. For their presence was important in protecting growers from the "labor agitation" which the Associated Farmers continued to oppose vigorously. After helping crush the CAWIU in 1935, the organization sponsored formation of a paramilitary group, the California Cavaliers, which promised to "stamp out all un-American activity among farm labor." That assuredly included union activity for, as one of the Cavaliers' officers explained, "We aren't going to stand for any more of these organizers; from now on, anyone who peeps about higher wages will wish he hadn't!" Members of the Cavaliers joined other vigilantes to burn crosses near labor camps at the start of harvest seasons and to generally terrorize farm workers. The Associated Farmers also cooperated with sheriffs in making "preventative arrests" of workers accused of planning strikes and had state employment officials and sheriffs screen job seekers. They kept out workers who had engaged in strikes and asked those who were hired to report the names of any strikers they had known and to report their own job complaints directly to the sheriff.

Not too surprisingly, there were very few strikes after the death of the CAWIU, despite a continued decline in farm pay and worsening of working conditions. Most of the strikes that did break out were quickly and violently suppressed. There was only one major strike in all of 1935, in northern California apple orchards near Santa Rosa; it was crushed after a group of 250 vigilantes, including city officials, a state legislator, American Legionnaires and leading business and professional men, broke up strikers' mass meetings, tossed tear gas bombs at strikers' houses and drove their leaders out of the area after beating and tarring and feathering them. The San Francisco *Examiner* hailed the action as "a direct American answer to the red strike fomentors."

There were two major field worker strikes in 1936, both waged by one of the Mexican unions that had been formed before the creation of the CAWIU. The strikes, among celery and orange pickers in southern California, lasted almost a month each and resulted in slight pay gains. But several hundred strikers were arrested for vagrancy and jailed for periods that coincided with the length of the harvests, and others were beaten by the armed guards which patrolled the struck fields, or were violently evicted from their labor camps.

The most important agricultural strike of 1936 was not called by field workers, however. It was called by members of an all-white AFL union in the packinghouses of Salinas, in the heart of the Salinas Valley's vast lettuce-growing region. The strike began after the Associated Farmers set out to destroy the union, for fear that the AFL would get a foothold in packinghouses and canneries, which were as important as field operations to the profits of the organization's members. Growers were worried, furthermore, that the radicals now working within the AFL might yet move the federation into the fields, especially if the AFL secured a strong position in the packinghouses and canneries.

Employers launched their campaign against the AFL's packinghouse union by refusing to renew a two-year agreement they had signed with the union in 1934. In response, 3000 packinghouse workers struck, joined by 500 Filipino lettuce pickers who had formed an independent union. Salinas took on the appearance of a city under siege. Packinghouses were rimmed with barbed-wire barricades; anxious guards stood atop the roofs, cradling machine guns, as spotlights played over crowds of pickets below. Buses full of strikebreakers recruited in Los Angeles and San Francisco by the Associated Farmers pushed through the pickets and made their way to long rectangular buildings inside that looked for all the world like military barracks. Some 2500 armed vigilantes prowled the streets, those without guns carrying axe handles made in local high schools and issued to them by the Associated Farmers under authority of the county sheriff. He had allowed this "Citizens Army" to form by ordering the mobilization of every able-bodied man in Salinas between the ages of eighteen and forty-five. The "Army" beat strikers, attacked their camps, bombed the Salinas Labor Council's offices with tear gas, chased a newspaper reporter and photographer from town by threatening to lynch them, and threatened to kill any radical organizer who set foot in Salinas. In a month it was over. The strike was crushed. The union was crushed. And AFL officials hardly raised their voices to protest.

But eventually the vicious, unchecked oppression and the steadily worsening conditions of the workers attracted the attention of civil libertarians, liberal political figures and others who came to the farm workers' support. They were appalled by newspaper accounts of grower excesses and by reports of widespread misery. In July of 1937, for instance, the national field secretary of the Gospel Army reported that 70,000 migrants were starving in the San Joaquin Valley after being lured there by grower ads calling for many thousands more workers than they could possibly use. The workers and their children were getting as little as 15 cents a day for picking cotton.

Public concern intensified in 1938, when there were more than a quarter-million migrants wandering through California. The San Joaquin Valley was hit by a disastrous flood that year and newspapers and national magazines told the country of thousands of homeless and starving families and of local officials and growers who fought to keep federal agents from bringing in food and medical supplies. Thanks in large part to the publicity, the relief came nevertheless, and author John Steinbeck and others continued to chronicle the misery of the workers and the conduct of their employers. Steinbeck reported in *Their Blood Is Strong*:

The workers are herded about like animals. Every possible method is used to make them feel inferior and insecure. At the slightest possible suspicion that the men are organizing they are run from the ranch at the point of guns. The large ranch owners know that if organization is ever effected there will be the expense of toilets, showers, decent living conditions and a raise in wages.

Workers got some help after a liberal Democrat, Culbert Olson, was elected governor of California in 1938. Olson, the first member of his party to hold the office in the twentieth century, was backed strongly by the migrants, who brought their traditional support for the Democratic Party with them from their home states. Olson relaxed the regulation that required the unemployed to take farm jobs or lose relief payments and revived the Commission on Immigration and Housing, under an executive secretary, Carey McWilliams, who was an outspoken critic of corporate agriculture and supporter of the strikes and other activities of farm labor unions. Olson also backed bills to improve the conditions of farm workers, although most were blocked by a Republican legislature and the Associated Farmers' influential lobbyists.

A new union also was active, under the sponsorship of labor leaders who had left the AFL to form the Congress of Industrial Organizations in 1936, with the aim of organizing workers by industry rather than by craft. The CIO union in the farm industry was chartered in 1937 as the United Cannery, Agricultural, Packing and Allied Workers of America. The union, led by Communists and other radicals, intended to do what its name implied—bring cannery, packinghouse and field workers into a single organization, which could be helped by having members of other CIO unions, such as longshoremen and warehousemen, refuse to handle produce until the agricultural workers' demands were met.

Many of the union's members lived in camps the Federal Resettlement Agency and Farm Security Administration set up to try to ease the migrants' plight. The camps provided simple but clean housing, bathing and laundry facilities and other amenities, and served as islands of security where residents could set their own rules. They were not like the camps operated by growers; residents could not be evicted for striking or taking part in any other union activities, and organizers could contact them openly. But since relatively few workers could be accommodated in the government camps, most continued to live in their own makeshift camps or in the grower facilities.

The chances for improving the situation seemed better than they had in several years, however, given the posture of the state and federal governments, the liberal sympathy that had been aroused, and the CIO union's proclamations of militancy. Additionally, growers were in a poor position to argue against demands for improvement, since farm income finally had risen above the pre-Depression level.

But grower interests stiffened their opposition. They denounced the federal camps for being union staging areas and intensified their use of vigilante tactics to meet what they saw as a serious new threat.

The CIO union helped workers win some minor concessions in nine strikes during 1937 and 1938; and, in 1939, the state's Commission on Immigration and Housing intervened after vigilante action had broken a cotton pickers' strike and forced growers to raise pay nearly as much as strikers had demanded. But strong Republican opposition to Governor Olson kept the state administration from moving more forcefully. Nor could the union establish the base necessary for a successful assault on grower power.

The union was not a grass roots organization that drew strong commitment and leadership from within its own ranks; that came from the union's president, a New York intellectual, Donald Henderson, and its other officers. They found it very difficult to convince the politically orthodox migrants to accept their left-wing views and take the collective action that, in the political climate of the time, was considered radical, if not revolutionary.

The Dust Bowl Refugees who made up the core of the union's membership were poor union material in any case. Although hardship and persecution and the encouragement of sympathetic outsiders moved them to take part in union activities to try to improve their working conditions, their hope generally was not to become part of an organization of workers. Most considered themselves farmers rather than farm workers, and their real hope was to reestablish themselves on small farms of their own. Sometimes, in fact, these workers sided with struck growers, many of whom were also transplanted southerners.

The CIO union's campaign also was hindered by the AFL, which continued organizing cannery workers and produce truck drivers, who were protected by federal labor laws guaranteeing them the right of collective bargaining and thus were easier to organize than the unprotected field workers.

Finally, in 1940, the CIO abandoned the organizing of field workers and its hope of forming an integrated agricultural workers' union; it concentrated on what had developed into a bitter jurisdictional dispute with the AFL over organizing cannery and packinghouse workers. The CIO dissolved its farm industry union and put another radical-led union, the Food, Tobacco and Agricultural Workers, into the fight. The new union had some success in organizing packinghouse workers, but the AFL's Teamster Union affiliate won representation rights for virtually all of the state's cannery workers, with the help of employers who welcomed the Teamsters as a conservative alternative to the militant CIO organizers.

The organizing of field workers was left to a few small, independent, racially-based unions. The most prominent of these organizations, formed by Filipino asparagus pickers, made one of the few attempts to form a grass roots union by setting up a food cooperative and otherwise bringing its members together for more than strikes. The union even managed to get an AFL charter in 1940, but soon disappeared in the face of grower opposition and AFL indifference.

There were still hopes, however, that field workers would be organized. For the national concern that had been aroused by the violence in California's fields raised the possibility that they might be brought under the federal labor laws that had made it possible for other workers to conduct successful organizing drives. A strong move in that direction was made by the U.S. Senate's Committee on Education and Labor under the chairmanship of Robert M. La Follette Jr., the Wisconsin Progressive who had been a leader in the passage of the National Labor Relations Act and in investigations into violations of workers' rights.

Inspired in part by John Steinbeck's poignant description of the Dust Bowl Refugees in his extremely popular novel, *The Grapes of Wrath,* and by vivid and detailed accounting of the Associated Farmers' activities in a book by Carey McWilliams, *Factories in the Field,* the La Follette Committee conducted a series of hearings in California in late 1939 and early 1940. The committee's report, based on testimony and records from the Associated Farmers, government and law enforcement officials and others, detailed the "shocking degree of human misery" among farm workers and thoroughly exposed the violent tactics used by the Associated Farmers in carrying out the organization's openly admitted policy of taking the law into its own hands.

The committee charged the Associated Farmers with "the most flagrant and violent infringement of civil liberties" through use of espionage, blacklisting, strikebreaking, brutality and "sheer vigilanteeism." It concluded that because of the activities of the organization and local law enforcement officers, "The civil rights of strikers, unions, union organizers, outsiders and many of the agricultural laborers in California to speak, assemble, organize into unions and bargain are repeatedly and flagrantly violated."

The report recommended that the Labor Relations Act be extended to farm workers. But though the committee made a strong case for extending the law as a way of guaranteeing constitutional rights in rural areas and of easing the violence that had prompted its investigation, the report came too late. It was not issued until October of 1942. By then, public concern had disappeared. World War II was raging; many farm workers, including most of the Dust Bowl Refugees, had been drafted into military service or gone off to better-paying jobs in war plants. The concern now was for growers, who were demanding replacements for the departed workers as essential to the war effort. Growers got the replacements through a government program that brought masses of compliant Mexicans across the border, raising formidable new obstacles to the attempts to organize and better the conditions of farm workers.

The bloody struggles of an entire decade had ended in failure.

3

Revolt in the South

California wasn't the only state torn by farm labor conflict during the 1930s. A fierce struggle also was being waged in the cotton fields of Arkansas and several other southern states, under the leadership of socialist union organizers.

Those who worked in the southern fields were as desperately poor, oppressed and disorganized as the farm workers of California, and the organizers as dedicated to radical change as the Communist organizers in the Far West. But the peculiarities of southern agriculture placed them in a different relationship to the dominant landowners in their states. Many of the workers were not migrants or hired employees; they were tenant farmers and sharecroppers, with close ties to the land they cultivated, at great profit to the owners—planters, as they were called in the South—but at very little profit to themselves.

The tenant farmers and sharecroppers finally rose in protest during the Depression, when great numbers of them were driven off the land and from the communities that had been their homes for many years. Hence the southern union organizers, backed by the Socialist Party of Norman Thomas, did not stress the goal of a classless society as the way to improve conditions, but the goal of "land for the landless."

The southern agricultural system, which had developed around cotton, the dominant crop, was a direct outgrowth of the plantation system of the pre-Civil War era. After emancipation, the black laborers who had done most of the work as slaves had no money to buy land of their own and few opportunities to take other work or find housing off the plantations. This enabled the plantation owners to in effect substitute one form of slavery for another.

The black laborers, and some poor whites, were put to work on the plantations as sharecroppers, turning over up to half the cotton they cultivated in exchange for the use of the land and in partial payment for food, housing, supplies and equipment. The sharecropper's "wage" was his share of the crop, and what little he made from that was largely spent in plantation stores that charged exorbitant prices and on rental fees for the necessities provided by planters.

Sharecroppers were perpetually in debt to the plantation owners; they bought their food and supplies and rented their farming equipment on credit, at interest rates that ranged from 10 percent to as high as 40 percent. Sometimes they had to give up a part of their share in the crop as well to meet their debts. Most of them owned little more than a few pieces of furniture, a stove, cooking utensils and the clothes on their backs.

Some sharecroppers owned their equipment, but they also were usually in heavy debt to landowners, as were the tenant farmers who simply rented or leased the land they cultivated. The situation was at least as bad for hired workers, who made up only a relatively small part of the South's farm labor force.

The situation got even worse after a decline in cotton prices in the late nineteenth century forced many small white farmers to give up their holdings and turn to sharecropping and tenant farming. The ravages of soil erosion and the boll weevil further limited the possibilities for profitable farming, but poor families continued swarming into the cotton fields—more than 200,000 of them in the 1920s alone. The Cotton Belt, which stretched from the Carolinas to Texas, became the South's most densely populated area. The Great Depression sent cotton prices plunging, yet still they came, driven from cities where small businesses were failing by the hundreds, banks were closing, manufacturers shutting down. Warehouses filled with unsold cotton; poverty, disease and desperation were rampant. One investigator told of

one woman, her name was Ollie Strong, she died begging for a cup of coffee. She was the mother of 11 children. . . . I have seen her hack cross-ties and haul them 15 and 20 miles to sell them so she could get herself and the children something to eat. . . . She chopped cotton on various plantations when she was with child. . . . She went to picking when she was swelled so large she couldn't stoop over. She would have to crawl on her knees so as to be able to pick. . . . When she died there wasn't anything to eat at all in the one-room pole cabin. The last thing she called for was a cup of coffee, but there wasn't any.*

Hopes for easing the misery rose in 1933, after President Franklin Roosevelt set up an Agricultural Adjustment Administration to try to combat the effect of the Depression on farmers. The AAA offered

* Donald H. Grubbs, "The Southern Tenant Farmers' Union and the New Deal" (unpublished Ph.D. dissertation, University of Florida, 1963), p. 5.

benefit payments to growers of cotton and six other basic commodities who would limit their crop plantings and thus create a scarcity that would drive up prices. Some cotton planters plowed under up to half their acreage in 1933, prices rose, and the income of individual plantation owners as much as doubled. But though helping landowners, the program only worsened the condition of those who worked on the land.

In an attempt to sign as many cotton planters as possible to acreage reduction contracts, the AAA required them to turn over only 15 percent of their benefit payments to tenants. It was so small a share that tenants commonly referred to it as the "poverty payment." Sometimes tenants didn't even get that, since they were not represented on the local committees that worked with AAA agents to implement the program. Furthermore, the tenants' usual income was reduced or cut off altogether when their landlords took acreage out of production in accord with the government contracts.

Planters needed fewer people to work their land because of the reduced acreage and further lessened their need by using the government payments to buy tractors and other equipment to mechanize operations on the acreage that remained in production. Many planters simply evicted their tenants, even though that was prohibited by the government contracts, and met their reduced labor needs with hired employees who were not eligible for a share of the benefits or with desperate sharecroppers who would sign away their rights to a share.

The organized protest against these and other planter abuses began under the leadership of two young white socialists, H. L. Mitchell and Clay East, in the little Arkansas town of Tyronza. Mitchell, a former sharecropper who ran a floundering dry cleaning shop, and East, who operated a gas station next door, had long opposed the landlord-tenant system that caused such misery and kept so many of those who worked on the land from owning land themselves.

The system was especially harsh in eastern Arkansas, where large plantations were not developed until the beginning of the twentieth century, after the cutting of forests in the rich delta near the Mississippi River and the construction of flood-control levees. Many of the plantations were in the hands of lumber firms, insurance companies, corporations and other absentee owners, and there was little of the paternalism shown by the planters whose families owned the plantations in other areas of the South, where the system had been a way of life for more than a century. Tradition meant little to the Arkansas landowners; they were strictly businessmen. They wouldn't hesitate to evict tenants who did not keep up the pace demanded by "riding bosses" who roamed the plantations as overseers for the landlords. They could always find another tenant to do the work, or, preferably, replace him with a machine.

Many of the Arkansas sharecroppers and tenant farmers lived in the crudest of cabins, built of cracked green lumber, some partly roofless, some set on stilts to keep them above the rivers and streams that swelled and washed up through the floorboards during heavy rainfall. The staple diet was fatback, cornbread and molasses; there was little space to grow vegetables, since cotton planters demanded every foot of arable land. Illness was chronic. Children had to work the fields and had little time to attend the schools, which were generally in a state of near physical collapse for want of care by plantation owners and local authorities.

The fact that conditions on the Arkansas plantations were even worse than those in most other places, and the lack of a long tradition of worker submissiveness to landowners, caused more unrest in Arkansas than in other cotton-growing areas. The attempt by Mitchell and East to give some organized direction to the unrest began in 1932, when they formed a socialist group in Tyronza to protest actions taken against a group of tenants by the owner of a large plantation nearby. The tenants were so desperately poor the plantation's manager had advanced them credit for groceries on the basis of more acres than they were actually cultivating. The manager claimed they could not survive otherwise; but when his action was discovered by the former cement company attorney who owned the plantation, these "surplus" tenants were evicted.

Mitchell and East discussed their concerns with Norman Thomas when he came through Arkansas during his 1932 campaign for President and the three men later conceived the idea of forming a Southern Tenants Farmers' Union with the financial backing of the Socialist Party. The STFU came into being in July of 1934 at a meeting of some twenty black and white sharecroppers in an abandoned schoolhouse outside Tyronza. The founders adopted a constitution that attacked the "small ruling class who depend on exploiting the working class by rents, interest and profits," and members later issued a statement declaring that:

Poverty and misery have existed in our midst for months and years. We have seen our children and our children's children go to bed night after night without food. We have taken our children from school because they have no food. We have seen our women grow old before their day because of the grinding toil the landlords have forced upon us. We are hungry tonight, but we will eat the grass of the fields rather than take the miserable charity of those who have dispossessed, disinherited and enslaved us. We want jobs—not charity. We are willing to work. We want work. It is we who have produced the wealth of this land. It is we who have made Cotton King.

No specific plans were laid out, but the STFU promised that the organization would do what its members felt was necessary to protect sharecroppers, tenant farmers and other "tillers of the soil" from the abuse of planters and the local authorities who served the planters' interests, to provide relief for evicted tenants and to try to reform the Agricultural Adjustment Administration, whose policies had caused so many evictions.

The STFU was open to all tenant farmers, sharecroppers and hired workers—black or white—even if the member couldn't afford the initiation fee of 25 cents and dues of 10 cents a month. Many tenants and workers were frightened of joining the union—especially blacks. They had to be convinced, as an STFU organizer noted, "that the white man would not kill them if they joined." The fears were well founded, for union activity and interracial activity of any kind were extremely dangerous in the South. The fact that East was the town constable of Tyronza and a deputy sheriff eased the fears somewhat, but Mitchell warned that STFU members should "hold their meetings secretly and not let the landlord know who belongs and who does not." Members also decided to carry firearms, although they later adopted a policy of nonviolence as a safer course.

Very few of the STFU's members were committed socialists, and some were not even fully aware they had joined a union. The concept of unionism was foreign to them, and some thought at first that the STFU might be a new church. This impression was reinforced by the black preachers and young white seminarians who were among the STFU's early leaders; they led members in union songs adopted from hymn tunes, and their speeches rang of pulpit oratory. It was an effective organizing device among the church-oriented workers, and within a year, the STFU had signed up 25,000 members in Arkansas, Oklahoma, Texas, Missouri and Mississippi.

Educating their unsophisticated members became an important concern of the STFU's leaders, who published a widely circulated newspaper and conducted adult education courses. Mitchell insisted that members understand, above all, the difficulty of the struggle facing them. "Tell them," he instructed an organizer, "they cannot expect to get something without running the risk of losing—nothing is ever gained without a struggle." Mitchell was as determined to develop a true rank-and-file organization. "Never promise the workers that the union is going to do something for them," he advised. "Let them join the union to do something for themselves." But though the STFU developed membership participation, and secondary leaders from the rank and file, Mitchell served throughout the union's history as its principal officer.

The STFU functioned essentially as a protest movement, providing backing for Norman Thomas and others in their attempts to reform federal farm programs. "While we were not pure and simple Marxists," said Mitchell,

I think we had absorbed enough to consider that the plantation system and the U.S. Department of Agriculture—especially the Cotton Section of the AAA—were one and the same or an extension of each other. The statement that the government is the executive committee of the capitalist class was almost proven.

Mitchell's conviction was reinforced by a survey of 500 sharecropper families in Arkansas and two neighboring states that was conducted by a group of sympathetic university students. One-fifth of the families were found wandering over the land, pulling household goods behind them in makeshift carts, living in tents, abandoned shacks, corncribs and cotton storage sheds, seeking work or heading for towns where they could get relief payments from the same federal government whose farm policies had caused so much of their distress. For they all had been evicted from plantations as a direct result of the AAA's acreage reduction program.

The STFU began pressing strongly for reforms after discovering in January of 1935 that the Arkansas planter whose eviction of "surplus" tenants three years earlier had led to the first protests by Mitchell and East was now evicting tenants who belonged to the STFU. The planter was acting with the approval of local AAA agents, who told him he could evict any individual tenants as long as he replaced them with other tenants.

The STFU tried to fight the evictions in a local court, but the court refused to hear the union's pleas on grounds that tenants were not parties to the government contracts. So Mitchell and other STFU representatives took their protest directly to the AAA's national director, Chester Davis, in Washington, D.C. They argued that the local AAA position on evictions was an open invitation for planters to deny government benefits to tenants who had a legal right to them and to crush the union by displacing any tenant who supported it. Davis wouldn't act, but some prominent members of his legal staff who tried to overrule him managed to have an investigator sent to the Cotton Belt to document the abuses charged by the STFU. The investigator returned with "one long story of greed" on the part of plantation owners. She reported that the AAA's contract provisions on evictions and on the distribution of benefits to tenants were "openly and generally violated."

But the report was suppressed by Davis, who had earlier played down similar reports from his field agents and refused to publicly acknowledge that the AAA program was doing any harm. Davis, who had been feuding with the critics on his staff for some time on many issues, finally had them fired by going to Secretary of Agriculture Henry Wallace and complaining that they were endangering the program by raising irrelevant "social concerns." Wallace conceded that AAA policies were aggravating the problems of tenant farmers and sharecroppers and that the situation "had provided a fertile soil for Communist and socialist agitators." But he didn't want to risk upsetting a program that was helping shore up the country's badly sagging farm economy.

The STFU's protests nevertheless put the Department of Agriculture on the defensive and brought attention and support to tenant farmers and sharecroppers, partly through lobbying efforts in Washington, D.C., by some of the AAA staff members who had been fired. Norman Thomas helped raise the issue to the level of a national debate through his radio programs, speechmaking and constant dialogue with President Roosevelt and other liberals in the Democratic Party who listened closely to Thomas' ideas in devising their New Deal programs to try to overcome the country's deep economic depression.

The national attention, however, prompted a reign of terror in Arkansas against the STFU and its supporters—"damn yankee radicals," as they were frequently called in the southern communities whose political, economic and social systems were dominated by plantation owners. Planters identified STFU members, sometimes by boldly opening their mail, and began evicting them by the hundreds. The evicted union members suffered extreme hardship, often being denied even relief payments. Mitchell's chief aide, the Reverend Howard Kester, told, for instance, of a sharecropper and his wife who had been evicted from an Arkansas plantation for union activity:

They were living on a raft upon which some rough lumber had been gotten together for a house. They were a young couple and their first baby was already overdue. There was a cot with a few worn quilts, an oil can with one end knocked out for a stove, two boxes for seats, some boards laid across a barrel for a table and some broken bits of dishes. The mother wore her *sole* dress. "The baby's coming and we haven't anything for it," the mother told me. When the baby came, there was no doctor, no midwife, no one but the father and mother to welcome it and try to give it comfort. In Harrisburg not ten miles away the Federal Emergency Relief had its headquarters. Six miles away was Marked Tree with its planters, preachers and general townspeople. When some used clothing was given to this family, the Rev. Abner Sage, Pastor of the Marked Tree Methodist Church and secretary of the planters' union, raised a howl of protest.*

Hooded Ku Klux Klan members and other vigilantes rode through the Arkansas Delta beating STFU organizers and supporters. Homes were dynamited and riddled with machine-gun bullets. STFU meetings were broken up. Churches, schools and other union gathering places were padlocked, stuffed with hay or burned to the ground, forcing STFU members to meet outdoors in the presence of hostile witnesses, including law enforcement officers who jailed some organizers for months at a time on such charges as "criminal anarchy." One town even prohibited the outdoor meetings. The reprisals finally forced Mitchell and East to flee across the Mississippi River into Memphis. Other organizers followed them, sometimes as fugitives on the run, hiding with friends by day, traveling fearfully along back roads by night until they could reach the safety of Tennessee.

The terrorism increased the STFU's national support, and when the local attacks subsided in a few months with the help of private intervention from President Roosevelt and an Arkansas senator, union organizers were able to return to Arkansas and wage their first strike. That came in the fall of 1935, among hired workers in three east Arkansas counties. Just as the cotton was ripening, the STFU posted handbills urging pickers to stay out of the fields until planters raised the pay rate of 50 cents for every 100 pounds of cotton picked. Some 4000 pickers, most of them nonmembers, heeded the union's call and there were virtually no pickers in the fields for ten days. Planters would not agree to negotiations, and local authorities forced thousands of pickers to work by cutting off relief payments, but planters nevertheless raised the pay rate to 75 cents per 100 pounds, in some cases to $1.

This was interpreted as a victory for the STFU, and over the next two months the union was able to establish more than thirty new locals throughout the Cotton Belt. The STFU gained more national attention and local worker support when it exposed a flagrant example of peonage. Northerners were critical enough of the common practice of

* Howard Kester, *Revolt Among the Sharecroppers,* New York, Covici-Friede, 1936, p. 44.

hiring out gangs of convicts to do farm work for the profit of southern sheriffs and planters, but many were outraged when the STFU discovered a deputy sheriff who had arrested thirteen black strikers for vagrancy and then put them to work for several weeks on a project of his own. The union's complaints to the Justice Department forced court action, and the deputy was fined and sentenced to two years in jail. Still more attention came from a newsreel documentary on the STFU, distributed nationally as part of the popular *March of Time* series.

The union's success stirred its enemies into action again, beginning in early 1936. There was a rapid increase in the evictions of STFU members; law enforcement officers joined and sometimes led planters and vigilantes in raids; dynamite was tossed into a tent colony of evicted sharecroppers; a witness to the brutal breaking up of a union meeting was murdered. The union called another strike, setting up an unusual line of pickets who marched through plantations singing and calling for others to join them; but the planters had anticipated this strike, and easily crushed it through terrorism and intimidation.

The new wave of violence died down after Arkansas' governor, under pressure from federal intervention in the peonage case, set up a commission to investigate the problems of tenant farmers and sharecroppers. The governor, albeit with great reluctance, allowed two STFU representatives to sit on the commission, which endorsed some of the union's reform proposals. A federal commission was created after President Roosevelt was reelected by a huge margin in the fall of 1936 and so felt less need to conciliate southern conservatives. Roosevelt also set up the federal Resettlement Agency and Farm Security Administration to deal with the problems of the rural poor who had been bypassed by the early New Deal programs, and modified the AAA's acreage reduction program so that tenants got 25 percent of the government benefits. The payments were sent directly to them rather than through the planters, who sometimes withheld their shares.

The modification of AAA rules, however, gave planters an even greater incentive to replace tenants with paid employees, to increase mechanization and to expand their holdings. The consolidation of small plots into large units, combined with severe soil erosion and drought, which created a huge Dust Bowl area covering several states, drove thousands of tenant farmers and sharecroppers off the land. Some left the South to head for California's fields; others joined the stream of migrants who harvested crops up and down the East Coast, and some left farm work entirely to live in the black ghettos of northern and western cities.

The new federal agencies were forced to shift their emphasis from trying to keep tenants on the land to creating migrant camps for the uprooted, and the STFU found itself dealing largely with hired farm workers. The union's membership continued growing, although the STFU engaged in little direct action aside from a few sit-down strikes that raised pay in some cotton harvests, and still depended almost solely on church organizations, socialist labor groups, the American Civil Liberties Union and other outsiders for financing, publicity and legal work.

By 1937, the STFU had 30,000 members in seven states and was eager to add to its strength by affiliating with the newly emergent CIO, even though the price was merger with the CIO's farm industry union—the United Cannery, Agricultural, Packing and Allied Workers of America—which was active in California. Mitchell hoped his organization would be able to operate as an autonomous regional unit within the CIO union, but the union's president, Donald Henderson, centralized all operations under the tight control of himself and his fellow national officers. They regarded the STFU's approach as idiosyncratic and too regionally oriented, and their radical aims were often at odds with those of the STFU. "Those fellows," Mitchell complained, "were a lot more interested in whitewashing the Stalin purges and fighting the Spanish Civil War than in organizing farm workers."

Henderson abolished local control; STFU dues went directly to the national union office, and all major decisions came from there. Members who had been carried on the STFU's books even though they couldn't afford to pay dues were dropped and the union generally became a cold bureaucratic organization run from afar. Henderson soon began to undermine the STFU leaders, and after he suspended some of them for not following orders during demonstrations against the eviction of sharecroppers from Missouri plantations in 1939, Mitchell left the CIO to try to operate the STFU independently. During the eighteen months of affiliation with the CIO, however, thousands of unhappy members had left the organization and only 40 of the STFU's original 178 locals were still active.

The STFU had only a few hundred members left by 1941, and that, said Mitchell, "does not constitute a trade union; there is no basis for trade unionism in southern agriculture with conditions such as prevail." The union became more active during World War II, when Mitchell arranged contracts for several thousand workers who took temporary jobs on truck farms in New Jersey and other northeastern states that were short of agricultural manpower. Mitchell developed a working relationship with the AFL's Meat Cutters Union, which was organizing workers in some of the northern farm areas, and this led the STFU into an affiliation with the AFL after the war and a few more organizing drives in the South.

But the AFL was no different from the CIO. It, too, lacked the will to effectively back the formidable task undertaken by the STFU. Thus southern farm workers would remain virtually defenseless, for nothing short of full commitment by the established labor movement could conceivably establish a union strong enough to long withstand the awesome power of the plantation owners who controlled every phase of life in the rural South.

The Southern Tenant Farmers' Union had served an important purpose nonetheless. Its struggles had stirred the national conscience profoundly and, among other things, had led to creation of the La Follette Committee, which investigated the abuse of workers' rights throughout the country. Ironically, the committee never managed to bring its investigators into the South; but in alerting the nation to the plight of the sharecropper and tenant farmer, the STFU prompted other action that made the harsh life of southern "tillers of the soil" a little less harsh.

4

Hawaii: The Great Exception

There seemed to be little hope that farm workers anywhere could be organized on a permanent basis. The Wobbly organizers in the Far West had been unable to do it, the Communists in California had failed, and now the socialist organizers of the Southern Tenant Farmers' Union had failed as well.

Yet there was one area where outside organizers did not fail. Workers on the sugar and pineapple plantations of Hawaii were organized by the CIO, and gained an economic and political status rarely achieved by workers in *any* industry.

Hawaii's agricultural system was no different from that in the South, in that it was dominated by powerful plantation owners. Nor was Hawaii's farm labor force much different from that in California. It, too, was made up largely of penniless workers who were imported from poor countries and purposely kept apart from all but their fellow nationals in an attempt to keep them from joining in a movement to demand better conditions. But there was one extremely important difference between Hawaii and the areas where farm labor organizers had failed. Hawaii was surrounded by water.

The Hawaiian planters depended on sea transport to get their sugar and pineapples to market. Further, the planters owned most of the stevedoring firms that supervised the loading of the produce and everything else that was shipped from the eight major islands that made up Hawaii. Once the CIO set out in the late 1930s to organize the longshoremen who worked for the stevedoring firms, as an extension of its organizing drive among mainland dock workers, it was inevitable that the CIO also would try to organize the laborers who worked in the fields for the same employers.

The CIO could not pass up the opportunity to put together a unified force to confront the unified force of the longshoremen's employers. Organizing the field workers was not an easy task, but it could be done by using the great leverage available to the CIO in Hawaii. For if planters balked at the demands of their field workers, longshoremen could simply refuse to handle their sugar and pineapples; and if they didn't handle it, the produce would not leave the islands.

There had been attempts to organize Hawaii's farm workers before the coming of the CIO; the workers had formed a number of independent unions over the years, and had a long history of protesting their working and living conditions, dating back to the first plantation strike in 1841. But the Hawaiian farm workers' unions, organized along racial and ethnic lines and active only in limited geographical areas, were no match for the plantation owners, who controlled almost every segment of Hawaii's economy.

Most of the control was exercised by five major companies—the so-called Big Five—which were established in the nineteenth century by missionaries and others from Europe and the U.S. mainland. They arranged the marketing of produce and otherwise acted as plantation agents for other white settlers, who acquired most of the islands' arable land in 1850 by convincing Hawaii's king and local island chiefs to grant it to them in huge individual parcels for commercial development of the sugarcane that grew wild in the rich volcanic soil. They began large-scale cultivation, and turned Hawaii into a one-crop economy, during the U.S. Civil War, when disruptions curtailed the output of sugar plantations in the American South and opened the United States to large quantities of Hawaiian sugar.

Gradually the Big Five assumed control of the Hawaiian sugar plantations, and began growing pineapple as well when it was found to be ideally suited to the island areas that were too dry for sugar cultivation. Through interlocking directorates and similar devices, the five companies came to function as a single combine that dominated the whole of Hawaiian life. The companies owned the canneries in which pineapple was processed, they owned sugar mills, irrigation companies, steamship lines, farm equipment manufacturers, utilities, banks, insurance firms, newspapers. The economic well-being of many areas was based entirely on the companies' operations; churches were dependent on them for support; most politicians were employees of the companies or at least loyal members of the Republican Party, which was synonymous with the Big Five in Hawaii.

The companies' large-scale farm operations required far more workers than were available among Hawaii's natives, and the plantation owners very early turned to other areas for labor, transforming Hawaii into what became known as "the world's melting pot" of races. The imported workers came in an unending stream—more than

400,000 of them between 1850 and 1930. They were brought in from China, Japan, Korea, the Philippines, from Madeira and the Azores Islands, from Puerto Rico, Spain, Germany, Russia, Norway.

The imported workers came first as contract laborers who were bound by law to remain on the plantations where they lived in crude accommodations; their pay, hours and primitive working conditions were determined unilaterally by plantation owners, and they were subject to the whims of overseers who walked among them brandishing whips. Contract labor was outlawed when Hawaii was annexed to the United States in 1898, and thousands of workers left the islands to work in California's fields. But there were as many thousands to replace them, and ways to keep them working on the planters' terms; for there were few other places in Hawaii where the imported workers could find jobs or living quarters.

Plantation owners purposely recruited workers of diverse backgrounds, for "by employing different nationalities," as a planters' trade journal noted, "there is less danger of collusion among laborers, and the employers, on the whole, obtain better discipline." To try to guarantee that there would be no "collusion," planters created a caste system on the plantations, allocating work assignments and setting varying pay rates according to nationality. Housing was provided on the same basis. "On my plantation," a Japanese sugar worker recalled:

The Portuguese *lunas* [overseers] lived along the roads in the company town. Japanese, who did the hoeing, lived in the next row of shacks. Filipino cane cutters were in barracks in the last row. On top of the hill the white plantation manager lived in a big house.

The system closely united the workers of various nationalities among themselves; they formed organizations and waged dozens of strikes in the years immediately following annexation. But because the system kept nationalities apart, employers were able to defeat the workers' bids for better pay and conditions by evicting strikers from the plantations and replacing them with members of other national groups, often at slightly higher pay.

Most of the strikes were called by Japanese workers; as a consequence, planters greatly increased the importation of Filipinos—to the point that by the 1920s Filipinos dominated the plantation labor force and could not be so easily replaced when they, too, began waging strikes. Growers defeated their efforts, however, by calling on local law enforcement agencies. In 1924, for example, police killed 16 of some 1600 Filipinos who struck plantations on the island of Kauai, during demonstrations in which 4 policemen also were killed. The strike was broken after eight months when local judges sentenced sixty of the strike leaders to jail terms of up to four years each in connection with the demonstrations.

Strikes broke out periodically over the next dozen years; but the strikers, having no support outside their immediate area or outside their own national group, were invariably defeated. Hawaii's farm workers obviously needed a leader to pull them together into a single multiethnic organization to confront the united employers who so easily played them off against one another. That leader finally appeared in 1936. His name was Jack Hall, a tall, dour sailor who would launch one of the most remarkable organizing campaigns in the history of American labor.

Hall, the son of a miner, had gone to sea immediately after being graduated from a southern California high school in 1932; it was the only job he could find in that darkest year of the Great Depression. But Hall—then only sixteen—found that conditions were immeasurably worse in Asia, where he first touched land. The brutal poverty he saw among the Asian masses sickened and angered the young sailor and, Hall later recalled, "determined which side of the fence I was on." He began fighting on that side in 1934, as a member of the Sailors Union in the San Francisco general strike that led to unionization of the West Coast's waterfronts.

Hall returned to sea when the San Francisco strike ended, but was irretrievably drawn back to union activity after landing in Honolulu during a maritime strike in 1936. He handled much of the strike publicity for the Sailors Union and soon was caught up as well in the organizing campaigns being waged by the International Longshoremen's and Warehousemen's Union, which was chartered by the CIO in 1937.

That year, Hall led a longshoremen's strike on Kauai that brought the ILWU its first Hawaiian contract, then led CIO farm union organizers from the mainland in a campaign among the island's plantation workers. The success of the strike by the longshoremen—many of them friends and relatives of plantation workers—was an effective organizing tool; within two months Hall had signed up 3000 workers and persuaded Harry Bridges and other ILWU officers that the newly organized workers and all other plantation workers should be brought into the ILWU, if only to enhance the bargaining strength of longshoremen.

It was no great chore to persuade workers who did onerous hand labor for less than 50 cents an hour that they were being exploited and needed organizational help, but it was difficult to persuade them to join a multiethnic union. Hall talked with the workers endlessly, often in meetings that were held in secret, outside the closely guarded plantations. Hall, a tough, plainspoken man with a reputation for scrupulous honesty, stressed the basic message of working class solidarity. Over and over he told the workers they could not achieve the unified strength necessary to combat exploitation by employers if they continued to remain apart because of ethnic differences. "Know your class," Hall pleaded, "and be loyal to it."

Hall proved his case to the satisfaction of many workers in a strike by Filipino longshoremen at the port of Ahukoni in 1938. The ships the Filipinos normally loaded and unloaded were diverted to Port Allen, where most of the longshoremen were Japanese, because employers were certain Japanese would not support a strike by Filipinos. But thanks to Hall's efforts, none of the longshoremen at Port Allen would work. It was, said Hall, "the first clear case of workers walking out in support of another group in the islands even though it was made up of another race."

The ILWU's first farm victory came shortly afterward with the signing of a contract at a pineapple plantation on Kauai. But the crucial breakthrough came later that year when the ILWU set up a political organization, the Kauai Progressive League, to elect a pro-labor candidate against an incumbent who also happened to manage a sugar plantation. This led to the creation of similar organizations on other islands, and to other election victories that gave the ILWU political power as potent as its economic strength.

The union's organizing drive was curtailed with the outbreak of World War II in 1941 and the imposition of martial law on the strategically located islands. The military regulations, which virtually prohibited union activity and froze plantation workers in their jobs, were eased in 1943 under pressure from the ILWU and others, and the union quickly won contracts for workers on the major sugar plantations in the Hilo area.

In 1944, after Hall became the ILWU's regional director in Hawaii, he persuaded the islands' other unions to join with the ILWU's political organizations in a drive to register workers to vote in that year's election. The new voters helped elect a substantial number of candidates to the territorial legislature and give Hall the backing to win passage in 1945 of an Employment Relations Act that granted Hawaii's plantation workers the legal rights to unionization denied farm laborers on the mainland. Union representatives also won passage of legislation granting such benefits as unemployment and job-injury insurance to farm workers, secured positions on government regulatory

agencies and, in 1946, led an election campaign that broke fifty con-
secutive years of Republican control in Hawaii's legislature.

The ILWU's legislative effort was coordinated with a massive organizing campaign in the fields, in pineapple-processing plants and in
many other segments of Hawaiian industry, agricultural and non-
agricultural alike. The drive brought 30,000 new members into the
union over a period of just eighteen months—6 percent of Hawaii's
entire population—and formal recognition from hundreds of employers, including, by mid-1946, all but a very few of the islands'
sugar and pineapple planters.

The union was tested almost immediately by the sugar planters,
whose rejection of the ILWU's contract demands in the fall of 1946
prompted an industry-wide strike. The union had prepared carefully
for a walkout by stockpiling rice, potatoes and canned milk in camp
kitchens set up throughout the islands, planting vegetable gardens and
forming committees to supply other food by fishing nearby waters and
hunting down wild goats and pigs in outer island areas. Employers also
had prepared, by recruiting 6000 workers in the Philippine Islands,
on the assumption that memories of Japan's occupation of the Philippines during World War II would make the workers hostile to the
ILWU because of its large Japanese membership. But most of the
workers signed ILWU pledge cards while sailing to Hawaii, thanks to
Filipino stewards aboard the ship. The stewards, members of a CIO
union closely allied with the ILWU, passed out the cards in the ship's
mess hall, sometimes exchanging an extra helping of food for a worker's signature. The Filipino workers were greeted at the dock in
Hawaii by musicians from the ILWU, presented with leis and taken
off to a round of parties; when the strike broke out two weeks later,
they were on the picket lines with the islands' 22,000 other sugar
workers.

The planters were hard-pressed to find local strikebreakers, and
because the ILWU had organized longshoremen, they could not have
shipped their sugar from the islands in any case. Employers nevertheless held out for seventy-nine days, attempting to force strikers back to
work by a variety of devices, including intimidation by planter allies
in local law enforcement, who arrested hundreds of strikers for violating restrictive antipicketing injunctions.

Planters finally decided to settle after the federal government announced an increase in its subsidy to sugar producers. They met most
of the ILWU's demands, ending racial discrimination in job assignments, setting up machinery for workers to press grievances and raising basic pay by 20 cents an hour from the previous rate of 46.5

cents. The raise actually was 1.5 cents more than strikers had demanded, but was granted partly because planters had agreed to a demand to abolish the so-called perquisite system through which the ILWU said workers "had been cheated for years, by receiving part of their earnings in bad housing, inadequate medical care and so on." The ILWU considered that demand as perhaps the most important one of all, for under the perquisite system:

Everything used or needed by the worker was owned by the boss—the land, house, water, heat and power and all other services. The workers were often the complete victims of the company store. They were hardly a step above slavery, as they were forced to pay over and over again for things which remained the property of the employers. Out of this strike they received sufficient wages to pay for their own goods and services, to buy what they want, and where they want to. It means that the worker, not his employer, will decide what his needs are. It also means these workers will receive freeholder's title to their homes, which means that the homes will become their own and they will no longer be a victim of the employer's whim.

"Congratulations," said ILWU President Harry Bridges in a telegram to the sugar workers. "Hawaii is no longer a feudal colony."

The union struck the pineapple industry in 1947, but ended up with less favorable contract terms because of its relative weakness in that industry, which used many part-time temporary workers in processing plants. These workers, mainly housewives and students, made up almost 40 percent of the work force, and very few of them were ILWU members. In seeking to keep these relatively conservative workers from turning to the union, their employers launched an attack on the radicalism of the ILWU's leaders, and other employers soon joined in what became a major campaign to discredit and weaken the union everywhere by picturing it as Communist-dominated.

It was true enough that Hall and other ILWU leaders had worked with the Communist Party or been members themselves; but they had shifted into politically orthodox channels after firm establishment of the ILWU gave them the standing to work effectively within the two-party system. They were open to heavy attack nonetheless. For the near-hysterical concern with Soviet expansionism just after World War II created a climate in which employers and their political allies could seize on any association with communism—past or present—as supposed evidence of treasonable motivation. Hence the publisher of the Honolulu *Advertiser,* Lorrin Thurston, described the 157-day strike by Hawaiian longshoremen in 1949 as the work of political radicals whose purpose was "crucifying Hawaii." Thurston asserted that the ILWU leaders' "every move . . . for 15 years tallies exactly with Communist manuals and their teachings," and noted that their names were included on "every Communist list, as issued by the Un-American Activities Committee of the House of Representatives."

The committee came to Hawaii in 1950, shortly after the strike ended. Sixty-six Hawaiians, including most of the ILWU's chief officers, were summoned to explain why they had been named as Communists by witnesses at previous committee hearings. More than half of those summoned refused to testify, and the Hawaiian press launched a strident campaign against them.

The campaign came to a climax in October of 1951 when federal agents arrested Hall and six officers of the tiny Hawaiian Communist Party on charges that they had illegally "conspired to advocate overthrow of the government by force and violence." The government's motivation for arresting Hall was indicated by two agents from the Federal Bureau of Investigation who told Dave Thompson, the ILWU's education director in Hawaii, that the charge against Hall would be dropped if Thompson would persuade Hall to lead the union's Hawaii division out of the ILWU. Thompson scoffed at the proposal, had the union's public relations director secretly record his conversation with the FBI men and played it on radio programs broadcast throughout the islands by the ILWU.

At the trial, Hall refused to answer specific questions about Communist Party membership, spoke proudly of his youthful radicalism, discussed his later belief that "socialism isn't practical"—and was found guilty with the six others in June of 1953, fined $5000 and sentenced to five years' imprisonment, the maximum penalty under the law. Hall remained free while ILWU members conducted an intensive campaign to overturn the conviction on appeal. Finally, five years later, the U.S. Supreme Court granted the appeal, agreeing that Hall's constitutional rights had been violated.

There were strikes and other disputes after that, but, as the ILWU noted, "it was the last major attempt by the Hawaiian economic establishment to bust the union." The ILWU not only assumed a commanding position in Hawaii's economic life; it also became the most important political force in the islands, forming a coalition with the Democratic Party that gave the union as much influence as the employers' Big Five had exerted previously through the Republican Party. It was a rare politician who was elected without ILWU support and, as a consequence, the government and legislative programs in Hawaii became among the most worker-oriented and progressive anywhere in the fields of health, education, welfare, labor and social services.

Under the circumstances, employers usually preferred to cooperate with the ILWU, and the union eagerly accommodated them—as long as it meant bettering the pay and conditions of ILWU members; for the union didn't seek to overthrow the system, but to reform it for the benefit of working people.

The ILWU's success in winning higher pay and benefits for plantation workers pushed employers to mechanize their operations to increase productivity and reduce the work force. Rather than oppose this development, the ILWU encouraged it, just as the union would do later in dealing with longshoremen's employers on mainland docks. The ILWU felt it was futile to take the traditional trade union approach of "fighting the machine"; it saw no reason why work should not be as easy and efficient as possible, if, as in Hawaii, employers could be persuaded to grant special benefits to compensate for the loss of jobs caused by the shift to streamlined methods.

This approach was particularly appealing on the plantations, where many of those who did the unskilled hand labor that was being abandoned were aging Filipinos who had long wanted to return to their homeland, but had never been able to earn enough to do so. Under the seniority provisions of the ILWU's contracts with planters, those older workers would be the last to be laid off in the reduction of jobs. But the planters wanted to retain as many of the younger, more adaptable workers as possible to man the labor-saving equipment that had been brought onto the plantations. Hence ILWU negotiators, led by the union's brilliant secretary-treasurer, Lou Goldblatt, were able to win agreements that offered extra pension benefits, lifetime medical care, free transportation home and other inducements to workers who would retire before age sixty-five. Some of the older workers received as much as $16,000 in severance and pension payments for voluntarily leaving the plantation work force. Not all of those who left the plantations did so voluntarily, and not all of them were older workers; but all who left received at least some severance payment.

The mechanization of the plantations cut the work force to less than 20,000 by the 1960s, almost two-thirds below what it had been at the end of World War II just fifteen years earlier. But at the same time, stoop labor was virtually eliminated, and the plantation workers became far and away the world's most highly compensated agricultural laborers. No longer were there gangs of workers wielding machetes and carrying loads of sugarcane and pineapples on their backs. Specially designed bulldozers, cranes and other equipment did the heavy work, and those who operated the equipment received pay and benefits virtually unheard of among farm workers elsewhere. The Hawaiian workers got such things as employer-financed medical and dental care, sick leave, paid holidays and vacations, pensions, overtime pay and wages that ranged up to more than $6 an hour by the 1970s.

The plantation workers, furthermore, had put together an extremely democratic union structure whose main characteristic was rank-and-file participation. ILWU members throughout Hawaii, whatever their occupation, are in a single huge local of more than 25,000 members; but each plantation has its own unit within the local, and no less than one of every eight members serves as a unit officer, shop steward or on one of the committees set up by each unit to deal with such matters as medical care, pensions, welfare, political action, education and publicity. Communication among units is close, and members have developed a strong loyalty to the union; the ILWU has its own radio programs, publishes several newspapers, conducts workshops and classes and provides counseling in a wide variety of personal as well as job-related subjects, operates island-wide athletic leagues, and holds conventions twice a year, with decisions subject to membership ratification. Retired members also keep close to the ILWU through active pensioners' clubs that are represented at conventions and in other union affairs.

When Jack Hall, the tall sailor from the mainland who helped start it all, died prematurely at the age of fifty-five in 1971, people all over Hawaii stopped work to show their respect, and a memorial service tantamount to a state funeral was held in Honolulu's International Center. It was an appropriate tribute; for in winning their struggle, the Hawaiian workers transformed an entire society, from a virtually feudal territory controlled by a few huge financial interests into a modern pluralistic state with the most racially and ethnically mixed political leadership in the world. The workers brought democracy to the islands, as Governor John Burns noted at the memorial service, and profoundly influenced "the life of every solitary citizen in Hawaii."

But despite its internal unity and external power, the ILWU has not prevented Hawaii's plantation owners from once again turning to cheap labor. Because of the union, the companies can no longer import such labor; but they have been able to move their operations to areas where it is still available. The Hawaiian planters began doing this in the 1960s, establishing pineapple plantations in such places as the Philippine Islands, Taiwan, South Korea, Thailand, Malaysia and South America, where pay is less than 20 cents an hour and there are no union restrictions and generally far fewer government regulations to disturb them.

Rather than use their Hawaiian plantation profits to expand agricultural operations on the islands, the plantation owners have been putting them into these plantations abroad, and into a wide array of nonagricultural ventures in Hawaii and elsewhere around the world. Further, they have found that some of their plantation lands in Hawaii can be used more profitably for hotels, golf courses and similar enterprises because of a tourist boom.

As a result, there has been a severe cutback in Hawaii's plantation acreage, especially in the pineapple industry. About 40,000 acres of pineapple were grown in Hawaii in 1976, as compared with 73,000 acres in 1950, and Hawaii, which grew almost three-fourths of the world's pineapple then, now grows less than one-third. In 1975, pineapple growing was completely abandoned on two of Hawaii's major islands, Kauai and Molokai. The effect on Molokai was especially serious, since fully one-third of the island's 5200 people had worked full-time or seasonally on pineapple plantations and in processing plants, and there were few other sources of employment on the island for them.

The ILWU has won increased severance payments for the several thousand plantation workers who have been displaced so far, higher pay and benefits for those who have retained their jobs and union contracts for many of those who have been forced to shift to hotel work and other service occupations. But the union also has vowed to fight what it sees as "the phasing out of agriculture and the unrestricted development of tourist facilities and condominiums which are springing up all over Hawaii." This not only exposes workers to unemployment and "the precarious ups and downs of the tourist industry," but also threatens the viability of Hawaii's economy. "The question is," says ILWU Vice President George Martin, "is agriculture going to be the fundamental industry in Hawaii? Or are they going to make it into another Miami?" The plantation owners, President Harry Bridges promises, will not be allowed "to pick up and go elsewhere and leave the workers to struggle for themselves just because the pickings are better elsewhere."

The ILWU has sought to carry out the promise by negotiating severance payments designed to make it increasingly expensive for employers to phase out their Hawaiian agricultural operations, by encouraging the organization of workers on foreign plantations and by lobbying Congress to raise the trade barriers for foreign-grown pineapple and to otherwise "inhibit and discourage the transfer of American jobs overseas." But the union has been unable to halt the employer exodus from Hawaii; for the Hawaiian plantation owners are strictly profit-oriented, and as long as there's greater profit to be made elsewhere, they will continue shifting operations. "Our only emotional attachment," as the president of one company says, "is to our stockholders' needs."

The outcome of the ILWU's ironic struggle against employers who have reduced workers' job opportunities largely because of the union's success in helping those workers win unprecedented pay and benefits remains in doubt. In the meantime, however, thousands of workers will continue to be employed, and they will continue to stand as an extraordinary example, as incontrovertible evidence that dignity and a decent life can be won by those who harvest the food that sustains us all.

5

"Strangers in Our Fields"

Braceros, they were called—literally, men who worked with their arms. They began crossing the border from Mexico in 1942, and eventually there were hundreds of thousands of them, an army of contract laborers moving swiftly, quietly and efficiently through the fields of California and the great American Southwest, returning home with earnings only dreamed of in their dusty, poverty-ridden towns and villages.

The braceros came on the demand of their North American employers, worked under regulations written and enforced by the growers and government officials, and were returned to Mexico when no longer needed. The regulations provided only minimal pay and protections and, moreover, were frequently violated. But the bracero dared not complain; that would virtually guarantee him a quick trip back across the border, where thousands of other desperately poor men waited anxiously to take his place. Waiting, too, were moneylenders who provided the "fees" often passed to Mexican officials to help them decide who among the thousands should be sent north.

The braceros, imported under a program set up by the U.S. and Mexican governments, partly in hopes of controlling the unregulated hiring of Mexicans by U.S. growers, were supposed to be a *supplemental* work force, hired only when there was a legitimate shortage of U.S. workers. But the easy availability of such cheap labor proved too great a temptation for growers, as well as for their allies in government, who found braceros a welcome substitute for resident workers who could not be sent away after harvests and thus required expensive community services. In reality, the braceros became an *alternative* work force, through a constantly expanding program. For twenty-two years they crossed the border—4.5 million of them—to take the jobs of U.S. citizens who might demand better pay and conditions, and to raise a virtually insurmountable barrier to farm unionization.

Few other groups of U.S. employers enjoyed such privileges as the bracero program granted growers; most other employers had to compete solely in the domestic market for their workers, attracting them, if necessary, by raising wages, agreeing to unionization and making other concessions. But the year of 1942, when the program began, was no time to quibble; there was a war to be won, and food was a major weapon on the home front. The military draft and the lure of higher-paying jobs in war plants had taken many workers off farms, and no one wanted to endanger any harvest because of a shortage of workers, whatever the reason for the shortage.

By then, California's growers were planting more than 130 crop varieties, many of them grown nowhere else, and many growers shifted from crop to crop to meet market demand. Plantings of most crops remained large; they were brought to maturity and shipped to market as quickly as possible, and workers still were paid mainly on the basis of how much they picked rather than according to how many hours they worked. It was a system, in short, that could continue to exist only if growers could continue to recruit a large and steady supply of laborers willing to work hard and fast for short periods at low pay.

When the Dust Bowl Refugees who had been the most important segment of the farm labor force began going off to military service and war work, growers turned to schoolchildren, conscientious objectors who were assigned farm labor in lieu of military service, Japanese-Americans who had been put in government internment camps, soldiers from rural training bases and a variety of other hastily-recruited workers, including Mexicans who slipped across the border illegally.

The federal government responded quickly to grower pleas for a stabilized labor force; by mid-1942, an agreement was reached with the Mexican government, which was under heavy economic and political pressure to find work for its masses of unemployed and seriously underemployed citizens and to protect those who were already working on U.S. farms as aliens without legal protection.

The agreement promised that no braceros would be imported unless there was a legitimate shortage of domestic labor; if growers in one area were short of workers, they would have to seek U.S. workers from other areas before calling for Mexicans. The braceros' food, housing, medical care and transportation from Mexico and back were paid by the U.S. government; housing was to be at least equal to that available to domestic workers; pay was to be at the prevailing rate for domestics or at least 30 cents an hour; braceros were to be provided work or the equivalent in pay for at least three-fourths of the one- to six-month period for which they would be hired, and they would not be required to make personal purchases strictly at grower-owned stores. The U.S. government also promised there would be no discrimination against the workers and, as proof, initially barred growers in Texas from importing braceros because of widespread discrimination against Mexicans in that state.

Mexican authorities were pleased. Foreign Secretary Eziquel Padilla praised the bracero program for providing "an opportunity to earn high wages, a noble adventure for our youth."

Growers, who hired almost 13,000 braceros during the first few months of the program, seemingly had no reason to complain. The government did all the recruiting and paid all the costs of the program; growers had only to provide the workers' pay. But growers protested that the federal agency that operated the program, the Farm Security Administration, was much too worker-oriented; for the FSA not only insisted on strict adherence to the terms of the bracero agreement, but also insisted on minimum standards for the U.S. migrants who were recruited to meet farm labor shortages. Grower allies in Congress and the Department of Agriculture had administration of the bracero program transferred to the War Manpower Commission (which largely ignored the protective regulations that had been enforced by the FSA) and won enactment of legislation that in effect stopped domestic farm workers from leaving their home counties for the duration of the war.

The program grew rapidly, and despite protests from the Mexican government and union and liberal groups in this country, very little protection was afforded Mexican or domestic workers. Program administrators relied on the word of growers in determining if there were legitimate shortages of domestic workers and in determining the prevailing wage rate for workers. Growers were supposed to be denied help if they employed illegal aliens, but many continued using both legally and illegally imported Mexicans, providing pay and conditions that were well below the standards originally set by the Farm Security Administration.

By 1945, growers in California and Texas alone were employing some 50,000 braceros, and objected strenuously when the State Department proposed discontinuing the program at the end of World War II in 1946. Growers had become accustomed to this huge, compliant work force; they did not want to offer the inducements necessary to attract an all-domestic work force, and were not much interested, at any rate, in hiring men who might have learned something about union organization from their experiences elsewhere. Nor did growers want to cut back their ever-expanding crop plantings to accommodate a smaller work force.

"We are asking for labor only at certain times of the year—at the peak of our harvest," explained a spokesman for growers in California's San Joaquin Valley, "and the class of labor we want is the kind we can send home when we get through with them." Local authorities heartily agreed. So did the growers' powerful congressional allies. The bracero program was renewed through 1949. Administration was shifted to the Labor Department, but day-to-day functions were left mainly to state and county agencies whose interests matched those of the growers.

A key duty of the government agents was to ascertain that employment of braceros by particular growers would not lower the pay of domestic workers, deny them job opportunities or otherwise have an "adverse effect." But many bracero users commonly offered wages so low that a sufficient number of domestic workers would not apply; then, having created an artificial shortage of workers, the growers successfully applied to the government for braceros, and were allowed to pay them at the artificially low rate they had offered domestic workers. Some growers even turned down domestics willing to work at the low rates in order to get the maximum number of more easily managed braceros. Others gave domestics the worst possible jobs in hopes they would quit, or found excuses to lay them off, especially if they moved to strike or take other concerted action to try to get better pay and conditions. The willingness of government agents to condone such employment practices, despite their obvious "adverse effect," gave growers an invincible weapon against union organizers.

Organizers from the old Southern Tenant Farmers' Union nevertheless set out in 1947 to attempt the seemingly impossible. They moved into California's fields, armed with the support of the AFL, which had chartered their organization in 1946 as the National Farm Labor Union and authorized the California drive on an experimental basis. As if the odds weren't heavy enough, the new union picked as its first target the giant DiGiorgio Corporation, probably the strongest foe of unionization among California growers. H. L. Mitchell and other leaders of the NFLU were convinced, however, that wresting union recognition from DiGiorgio would give lesser growers a powerful incentive to go along or face battle with a giant killer.

Mitchell and Hank Hasiwar, a former auto workers' organizer from New Jersey who headed the NFLU's California effort, settled on the strategy after touring the state to seek support from local labor councils. They got the support, and Hasiwar, a husky war veteran, had no great difficulty signing up employees at DiGiorgio's main ranch in Arvin, near Bakersfield.

The Arvin Ranch spread across 11,000 acres of Kern County, the headquarters of a corporate operation that generated $18 million a year in gross revenue from the sale of fresh fruits and vegetables, wines and processed foods. DiGiorgio virtually owned the town of Arvin, and its grape vineyard, plum orchard and winery there were among the world's largest. More than 800 people worked year-round on the ranch, many of them migrants from Oklahoma, Texas and Arkansas. Another 1600 workers were called in at the autumn harvest peaks, most of them Mexican-Americans or braceros.

Hasiwar concentrated on the full-time employees, and by September of 1947, two months after he began organizing at DiGiorgio, he had signed up a majority. They formed their own NFLU local, elected officers and framed a set of demands designed primarily to give the employees some control over their working lives. The workers, paid at the area's generally prevailing rate—a minimum of 80 cents an hour—did demand a 10-cent increase; but more than that, they demanded a union contract that would base hiring on seniority rather than on the unilateral decisions of DiGiorgio supervisors and would set up machinery for them to press grievances against DiGiorgio.

DiGiorgio wouldn't even recognize the existence of the employees' union, much less listen to their demands, despite attempts by the local labor council and state and federal mediators to arrange meetings between union representatives and Joseph DiGiorgio, the corporation's aging, Sicilian-born founder and principal officer. DiGiorgio's only response was to fire some members of the NFLU, precipitating a strike on October 1 by most of the other members.

More than 1000 pickets spread out along the twenty miles of roads that surrounded the huge Arvin Ranch, drawing out Anglo and Mexican-American workers alike. The 130 braceros on the ranch halted work in sympathy, and unionized winery workers and Teamster produce truck drivers refused to cross the picket lines.

DiGiorgio struck back fast. The Mexican consul was summoned from Los Angeles to join the Kern County sheriff and a representative of the U.S. Department of Agriculture in a conference with the idle braceros, who were told, in effect, to return to work or be deported. The agreement under which the braceros had been hired said they could not be used as strikebreakers, but two days after the strike began they were back at work, escorted across the picket lines by government officials. "After all," one of the officials explained, "it was our job to see that the [Mexican] nationals got work."

AFL President William Green and other labor representatives protested to union allies in Congress, and the braceros eventually were taken out of DiGiorgio's fields and put to work elsewhere. But that was six weeks later. By then, DiGiorgio had recruited several hundred workers from Texas, neglecting to inform them that a strike was in progress until they arrived at the ranch, where they, too, were escorted across the picket lines by government agents. The strikebreakers were housed in camps on DiGiorgio property, where NFLU organizers could not reach them; if they tried, they'd be arrested for trespassing. DiGiorgio also filled in for strikers with illegal aliens and local workers sent by friendly growers nearby or by the state's Farm Placement Service, despite its rules against dispatching workers to struck farms. Additionally, most of DiGiorgio's Mexican-American employees returned shortly after the strike began, since organizers had made no particular effort to bring them into the union.

DiGiorgio got its wine-making and produce deliveries resumed through a curious ruling by a National Labor Relations Board examiner. He held that while farm workers were exempt from the provision of the Labor Relations Act that guaranteed the right to collective bargaining, they were covered by a new provision against secondary boycotts, which had been put into the law just a few weeks earlier through the Taft-Hartley Act. The examiner said it was perfectly legal for field workers to refuse to do work assigned them by DiGiorgio and otherwise refuse to handle DiGiorgio products, because they were the primary parties to the dispute. But secondary parties—truck drivers, winery workers, members of other unions or the public generally—could not be asked to do the same. The NFLU later got the ruling overturned by the full Labor Relations Board, which said farm workers were exempt from all provisions of the Labor Relations Act and its amendments. But by then the strike was virtually over.

The strike dragged on for more than two and a half years, with the support of unions from all over the state, and from church, student and liberal groups; they saw the NFLU as an underdog to a corporation that had become a major symbol of oppression to them because of its long history of fierce antiunionism. The supporters came in car caravans from Los Angeles and San Francisco to join the picket lines, boycotted DiGiorgio products, formed national and statewide support committees headed by prominent citizens and donated more than $250,000 in money, food and clothing to add to the $250,000 provided by the AFL.

DiGiorgio attempted to counteract prostriker publicity generated by the support groups by engaging in an extensive public relations campaign. One consequence was that there was little of the violence that had marked prewar farm strikes; calling in sheriff's deputies and vigilantes from the Associated Farmers was no way to woo public opinion. The relative calm of the strike was shattered once, however, by a gang of unidentified gunmen who fired into a room where the NFLU local's president, James Price, was conducting a meeting. Price was wounded seriously, but no one ever captured the gunmen or discovered their motivation.

DiGiorgio issued pamphlets describing the supposedly superior living and working conditions of its employees and claiming that most of them were neither union members nor on strike. The dispute was attributed to "outside agitators"—and, said Joseph DiGiorgio in a throwback to the grower tactics of the 1930s, "this agitation is Communist-inspired by subversive elements." DiGiorgio called on the state senate's Un-American Activities Committee to back the allegation, but the committee cleared the NFLU of subversive taint, as had investigators from the House Un-American Activities Committee. Grower forces tried to link the NFLU to the Communist-dominated CIO farm industry union with which the Southern Tenant Farmers' Union had merged before affiliating with the AFL and changing its name. But NFLU President H. L. Mitchell had broken with the CIO union, of course, and, like so many other AFL leaders of this period, was as strong in his denunciations of left-wing CIO leaders as were employers and members of legislative committees.

DiGiorgio fared much better in hearings conducted later in the strike by a subcommittee from the House Education and Labor Committee, whose members included an ambitious young California Republican, Richard Nixon, who was about to launch a successful race for the Senate with strong conservative backing against a prolabor Democrat, Helen Gahagan Douglas. The subcommittee had been sent to California to investigate the strike as part of a broader purpose of determining whether to recommend extension of collective bargaining rights to farm workers. But Nixon's ruthless examination of union witnesses turned the hearings into a trial, designed to convict the NFLU and other farm labor groups of the crime of "outside agitation" against DiGiorgio and Nixon's other corporate allies in agriculture.

James Price testified in vain that he, the president of the striking union local, had been employed by DiGiorgio for more than a decade, as had the others on the local's executive board and many of those on strike. It was not "outside agitation" that had prompted them to strike, said Price, but low wages, poor working conditions and the authoritarianism of DiGiorgio.

But, Nixon demanded, were the conditions at DiGiorgio any worse than elsewhere in agriculture? Why was DiGiorgio singled out? How could a corporation be faulted for following the highest standards in its industry? DiGiorgio was still operating with full work crews, so how could anyone challenge the corporation's declaration that its workers did not want to unionize or strike?

Nixon also artfully drew testimony from growers implying that union organizers used violent tactics. Grower witnesses told Nixon that, yes, they had formed the Associated Farmers after outbreaks of serious violence. They didn't say the violent acts had been committed by growers, of course, because Nixon was careful not to ask them *who* had been violent.

"Why is it," Price asked the subcommittee, "that if the farming industry, the Associated Farmers, if they have got the privilege to have an organization, why is it that the farm workers, the laborers, the guy that does the old heavy-heavy, why hasn't he got the privilege to have an organization?"

The subcommittee answered Price's question in its report four months later:

Agriculture labor has been exempted from all labor relations [laws] ever written. The evidence before the subcommittee shows that it would be harmful to the public interest and to all responsible labor unions to legislate otherwise. The evidence shows that a strike of any serious proportions in agriculture would choke off interstate commerce in necessary foodstuffs, would cause incalculable harm to the public, and would antagonize public opinion in the cause of trade-unionism. . . . The exemption of agriculture labor from the Labor-Management Relations Act is sound. . . .

The subcommittee report was largely a rebuttal of charges of mistreatment of farm workers made against DiGiorgio and other agricultural corporations in a widely distributed film, *Poverty in the Valley of Plenty*, which was made for the NFLU by a group of Hollywood unions. DiGiorgio had made similar rebuttals in filing a libel suit against the union and others for producing and showing the film, and the subcommittee's well-publicized report helped considerably in the corporation's campaign to convince the public that DiGiorgio had been unfairly attacked. By the time the subcommittee report was issued, in March of 1950, the DiGiorgio strike was over for all practical purposes; most strikers had drifted away and there was just one lone picket at the Arvin Ranch. The AFL insisted it was time to back off; it neither wanted to prolong a losing strike nor to finance an expensive fight against the libel suit, especially now that the suit was backed by a congressional report. The NFLU, its treasury depleted, agreed to an out-of-court settlement that required the union to destroy all copies of the film and officially call off the strike in May, 1950.

Actually, the strike had been doomed from the start. The breadth of outside support was unusual, and it helped set a pattern that would recur in farm labor struggles over the next three decades. But though the outside support would prove decisive in later disputes, it was woefully short of what was needed to defeat DiGiorgio in this strike. Pleas by outsiders for economic justice could not cut off DiGiorgio's unlimited supply of workers or halt the delivery and sale of the produce they harvested throughout the strike. The outsiders could not match the economic and political influence of DiGiorgio and its grower allies in the Associated Farmers, especially in the political atmosphere of the period, which had spawned the Taft-Hartley Act and other devices to weaken organized labor. The NFLU's supporters weren't just fighting DiGiorgio; they were bucking a strong popular movement to diminish the power labor had gained in the 1930s, now that unions, freed from the economic constraints of World War II, were using that power to militantly press new demands everywhere.

The AFL, in any case, provided precious little help. A quarter-million dollars was a pitiful sum when pitted against DiGiorgio's millions; Hasiwar, as a local grower noted, was sent out "with a popgun to shoot elephants." The NFLU could not even pay strike benefits; strikers had to take jobs elsewhere to sustain themselves. Even those who managed to find work in the immediate area could picket and engage in other strike activities only on a part-time basis. This prevented the deep involvement essential to create a lasting, firmly-rooted union. The workers had not built their union local; they had formed it at the suggestion of Hasiwar and his fellow organizers. And when the outsiders left, few members had the commitment to carry on alone.

After the DiGiorgio strike collapsed, the NFLU began concentrating on the Mexican-Americans whose participation was absolutely necessary if an effective farm workers union was to be put together. But this undertaking also was seriously underfinanced and, lacking a dramatic confrontation such as the DiGiorgio strike, did not attract the public support that had previously gone to the union. It was essentially a one-man operation—the one man being an unusual labor leader named Ernesto Galarza, who had become the NFLU's director of research and education five months into the DiGiorgio strike.

Galarza, a slight, sharp-featured man then in his early forties, had come to the NFLU after resigning in anger from the Pan American Union in Washington, D.C., where he had worked for eleven years.

He protested that the organization, formed by the South American republics "to further peace and understanding" among the countries of the hemisphere, was acquiescing in the exploitation of Latin American workers by U.S. interests.

But though deeply concerned with the problems of working people —especially Mexican-Americans—Galarza had no union experience and little in common with farm workers beyond sharing their language and ethnic background. He was a scholar, probably the only labor leader in the country with a Ph.D. Galarza had grown up in a California *barrio* after his family left Mexico in the exodus of 1910, and had worked on farms during summers as a teenager. But he had left that behind long ago to head off to college on a scholarship and eventually to Columbia University for his doctorate in Latin American affairs. Galarza was primarily an intellectual whose weapons were words, and he ultimately would attempt to accomplish with writing what most union leaders tried to do through economic action. Initially, however, he was determined to assume an activist's role with the NFLU.

Galarza's determination was fierce, almost fanatic. It shone out of the piercing eyes that glinted under his heavy brows. His sharp tongue spared few who opposed what he thought right for the farm worker, including AFL leaders whose declarations of support were backed by very few dollars and who often counseled caution and compromise. To Galarza, they were "the labor fakirs back east." His constant complaints against growers, politicians, government officials and uncooperative labor leaders brought him as many enemies as friends. His friends pictured Galarza as a lone, courageous champion of farm workers' rights; but his critics described him as a tempermental maverick incapable of the delicate compromises necessary in building an organization.

During the period in which he was helping lead the DiGiorgio strike, Galarza also had led a strike by several thousand cotton pickers that blocked grower attempts to cut pay to the previous year's level, and helped vineyard workers win pay increases. But his efforts following the DiGiorgio strike were thwarted by the bracero program. In 1950, for instance, several thousand tomato pickers in the San Joaquin Valley struck under the NFLU banner, only to be replaced by some 2000 braceros who were escorted across their picket lines by deputy sheriffs and state highway patrolmen.

Galarza moved south to the Imperial Valley in early 1951 in hopes of curtailing grower use of illegal aliens and other Mexicans; they crossed the nearby border in such great numbers that growers abandoned the piece-rate system of payment for a straight hourly rate that was barely enough for U.S. workers to live on, but which Mexicans would accept gladly. Galarza's forces made citizen's arrests of illegal aliens and otherwise alerted government agents to their presence; but there was an unlimited flow of other Mexicans to take their place with a minimum of government interference.

The availability of so many destitute foreigners willing to work under virtually any conditions, and the eagerness of growers to hire them, not only undermined the position of U.S. workers; it threatened the existence of the bracero program, which, although also hurting domestic labor, at least provided minimal protection to Mexicans. The program actually had been halted for six months in 1948 when the Mexican government withdrew its cooperation because of the treatment of braceros by cotton growers and U.S. officials in Texas. The growers, well aware that thousands of Mexicans were waiting anxiously in Juarez for bracero permits from their government, set the picking rate for braceros at $2.50 per 100 pounds, even though the Mexican government demanded a $3 rate as a condition for permitting Mexicans to take the jobs. U.S. Labor Department representatives approved the lower rate, and when the Mexican government continued to balk at issuing bracero permits, other U.S. officials opened the border at Juarez. Some 6000 Mexicans streamed across the border during the five days the United States kept it open; they were arrested as they crossed into El Paso and turned over to cotton growers who were waiting there to hire them. Not long afterward, the pay rate fell to $1.50 per 100 pounds.

The program was resumed in 1949 after U.S. authorities agreed to protect the illegal workers by certifying them as braceros, and Congress renewed the program through 1950. It was described as a "temporary measure," but the outbreak of the Korean War in 1950 changed that status. Using the same rationale they had when the program was begun in 1942, growers argued that an alleged wartime shortage of able-bodied U.S. workers required creation of a firmly established and greatly expanded program. They got what they wanted from Congress in the form of Public Law 78, passed in mid-1951 over the strong objections of organized labor and approved by Mexican authorities in talks with U.S. grower interests and State Department officials from which Galarza and other union representatives were barred.

Mexico had made its approval contingent on the United States tightly closing the border to illegal aliens. U.S. officials assured Mexican authorities as well that providing growers with an increased supply of braceros would deter them from employing illegal workers and thus discourage the workers from slipping across the border. But growers continued to employ illegal aliens in growing numbers, and the illegal traffic was not shut off. It was so heavy that would have been impossible anyway, even if the U.S. government had fulfilled its promise to tighten border policing.

Cutting the flow of illegal aliens was especially difficult because Congress, in passing legislation in 1952 that was supposed to help curb the traffic, virtually exempted growers from being penalized for hiring workers who came across the border illegally. Growers were made subject to fines and loss of bracero help if it could be proved they knew the status of illegal workers when they hired them, but it was a meaningless provision since there was no requirement that growers determine a worker's status before hiring.

The agreement with Mexico was further weakened and its standing as a bilateral pact further undermined when Congress amended Public Law 78 to sanction the practice of hiring Mexican workers without their government's permission. The amendment specifically allowed U.S. representatives to unilaterally recruit braceros if Mexican authorities did not move fast enough to suit them in filling particular grower orders.

In one major instance, in fact, U.S. authorities actually allowed growers to openly hire illegal aliens, in response to the continued reluctance of Mexican authorities to grant permits to braceros who were offered pay their government considered too low. That was in 1954, when some 3500 Mexicans were allowed to cross the border at Calexico to work for California growers. As it had done in the similar situation in Texas six years earlier, the Mexican government withdrew from the bracero program and ordered all emigration halted. The order was lifted after the U.S. Attorney General mounted a campaign that led to the arrest and deportation of more than one million aliens.

Galarza quickly discovered that the bracero program under Public Law 78 would offer no more protection for U.S. workers than it had prior to the law's passage, for the program was still administered by grower-oriented state and county agencies. He returned in 1952 to the Imperial Valley fields where, in the previous year, the unchecked flow of braceros and other Mexican workers had defeated the NFLU's attempts to increase the pay and job opportunities of U.S. workers. This time, the union got half the local workers to strike for a pay raise; but growers had purposely ordered a surplus of braceros and parceled out the surplus Mexicans among struck employers, even though this practice was prohibited by Public Law 78.

Galarza concluded that farm workers could not form a successful union or otherwise improve their condition unless the bracero program was abolished, or at least drastically reformed, and he set out to do just that—but by publicly documenting the program's abuses rather than through orthodox union activity. He would call no more strikes, Galarza said, because he could not in good conscience subject strikers to the virtual certainty of losing their badly needed jobs to braceros. Galarza had little choice but to abandon active organizing anyway; the AFL, always extremely hesitant to move in agriculture, was now providing very little support of any kind. AFL leaders had never had much faith in the idea that farm workers could be organized, and had now lost confidence in Galarza as well.

Although generally inactive in agriculture outside Hawaii since the 1930s, the CIO retained an interest in organizing farm workers and was becoming active again. Its vehicle was the Packinghouse Workers Union, which had been given the jurisdiction of the Food, Tobacco and Agricultural Workers Union when that organization was expelled from the CIO in 1951 on charges that it was controlled by Communists. The Packinghouse Workers attempted to organize shed workers whose operations had been shifted into the fields, but also was thwarted by the bracero program and soon followed the NFLU in making abolition of the program its primary goal. Organizers from the Packinghouse Workers collected thousands of affidavits from U.S. workers who claimed they had been displaced by braceros or simply turned down for jobs by growers who candidly told them "we're hiring Mexicans this year." When government officials ignored the affidavits, the union staged a series of demonstrations and brief strikes aimed at mobilizing public opinion against these and other violations of Public Law 78.

But the public paid scant attention to either Galarza or the Packinghouse Workers, and although open violations of the law mounted, the bracero program continued expanding rapidly. The Korean War emergency had long since ended, but growers only needed to claim they were facing a labor shortage that threatened a crop, and in came braceros regardless of the availability of U.S. workers. Braceros were employed in more than twenty states, making up nearly one-third of the country's overall farm work force, more than 20 percent of the harvest work force in California and the Southwest. Their most serious effect was in those crops requiring intensive hand labor; 40 to 80 percent of the workers in the lettuce, tomato, asparagus, strawberry and melon harvests were braceros.

Growers of these crops began recklessly expanding their acreage and overproducing because of the easy availability of braceros. The widespread use of braceros also froze farm pay for several years at a time in several areas, or even lowered the rate, and forced thousands of domestic workers to seek jobs elsewhere. This had a severe impact on rural merchants who relied heavily on the patronage of local workers, for braceros rarely strayed from their isolated farm camps.

When the charges of abuses against U.S. workers failed to prompt action, Galarza turned to documenting abuses against the braceros themselves. Helped by a grant from the Fund for the Republic, he conducted a four-month inspection tour of more than 150 bracero camps in California and Arizona. Galarza's report, issued in 1956 under the title *Strangers in Our Fields,* detailed massive violations of the bracero program's regulations on pay, food, housing, transportation and other matters. It charged that illegal profits were being made by grower associations, insurance agents, health care and food concessionaires and others, and claimed the federal government had not even tried to curb the abuses, since it had only fifteen compliance officers in the two states, where nearly 100,000 braceros were living and working.

The report got broad public attention—and a stinging rebuke from government officials. Ed Hayes, the chief of California's Farm Placement Service, called in representatives from grower associations and the Labor Department, then issued a point-by-point refutation of Galarza's charges. Hayes described them as "a pack of lies." Federal officials, including Secretary of Labor James Mitchell, were equally harsh.

Yet even this was a victory for Galarza, since the government had never before responded so strongly to his charges; it kept the issue before the public and led to reforms, despite the official denials of abuses. The Labor Department beefed up its compliance staff; regulations on bracero housing were tightened and more than 400 units closed or ordered cleaned up and repaired; the braceros were specifically prohibited from driving tractors or displacing U.S. workers in other semi-skilled work, as Galarza showed they had been doing. Additionally, the government closed the camp stores from which concessionaires were profiting at the expense of braceros and local merchants, and California's attorney general clamped down on agents who had been charged with bilking braceros in selling life and medical insurance.

Bracero users even increased their hiring of domestic workers because of government pressure. But they frequently hired domestics to supplement rather than replace crews of braceros and so limited the earnings of domestics, since most were paid on a piece-rate basis. Growers also continued to set pay at artificially low levels with gov-

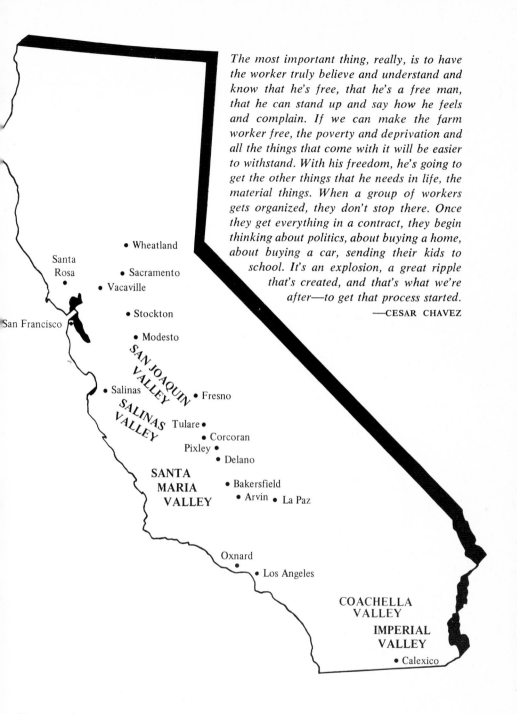

The most important thing, really, is to have the worker truly believe and understand and know that he's free, that he's a free man, that he can stand up and say how he feels and complain. If we can make the farm worker free, the poverty and deprivation and all the things that come with it will be easier to withstand. With his freedom, he's going to get the other things that he needs in life, the material things. When a group of workers gets organized, they don't stop there. Once they get everything in a contract, they begin thinking about politics, about buying a home, about buying a car, sending their kids to school. It's an explosion, a great ripple that's created, and that's what we're after—to get that process started.

—CESAR CHAVEZ

Farm workers struggled up and down the state of California for nearly a century attempting to organize a union of their own. (*Adamson & Walton, Inc.*)

California growers helped defeat early attempts to organize farm workers by importing thousands of virtually defenseless Chinese and Japanese workers beginning in the 1870s. By 1900, Japanese made up the bulk of the work force in the labor-intensive crops that have made California preeminent in farming. (*History Division, Los Angeles County Museum of Natural History*)

ABOVE: The many Asians employed by California growers early in the twentieth century were forced to accept abysmally poor conditions, until, with other farm laborers, they joined in protests by the Industrial Workers of the World. The protests drew national attention after the Wheatland Riot of August 3, 1913. It broke out when a posse moved in on these workers as they met to demand improved conditions on the hop ranch where more than 2800 of them lived in ragged tents or in the open. (*Archives of Labor History and Urban Affairs, Wayne State University*) BELOW: In 1915 the Industrial Workers of the World formed the country's first broadly based farm union, the Agricultural Workers Organization. Government and employer opposition ultimately destroyed it, but the union gave farm workers a rare opportunity to express their collective will and at least temporarily win better pay and conditions. (*Archives of Labor History and Urban Affairs, Wayne State University*)

The 1933 cotton strike was one of the most violent in farm history. Here, a grower posse prepares to ambush a group of strikers in Pixley, California, on October 10, 1933. Two strikers were killed and eight wounded in the attack. (*Courtesy of the Bancroft Library*)

A Communist-led farm workers' movement arose in the 1930s and, with it, the massive California cotton strike of 1933. Pickets roved throughout the state's San Joaquin Valley, often using the piercing notes of a bugle to call workers from the fields. More than 15,000 answered the call. (*Courtesy of the Library of Congress*)

Gains won in California's farm strikes of the early 1930s were eroded by an influx of penniless migrants later in the decade. They competed desperately for jobs at whatever conditions growers provided, living in make-shift roadside camps as they moved from harvest to harvest in battered automobiles. (*Dorothea Lange photo, courtesy of the Bancroft Library*)

Pat Chambers (*left*), of the Cannery and Agricultural Workers Industrial Union, with aides during the 1933 cotton strike, helped lead California farm workers in nearly 50 strikes between 1932 and 1935. (*Courtesy of the Bancroft Library*)

ABOVE: The Southern Tenant Farmers' Union was led by (*left to right*) H. L. Mitchell, Howard Kester, J. R. Butler, and other socialists dedicated to securing land for the tenants and sharecroppers who toiled in poverty on the huge holdings of plantation owners. (*Southern Historical Collection, University of North Carolina*) BELOW: Many of California's migrant workers came from southern states. Those who remained behind, as tenant farmers and sharecroppers, struggled with conditions as bad as those of the migrants. They tried to overcome them by forming the biracial Southern Tenant Farmers' Union in 1934. (*Southern Historical Collection, University of North Carolina*)

Jack Hall, the tough sailor who brought Hawaii's ethnically divided plantation workers into their extremely successful union in the 1940s. It helped transform Hawaii from a feudal territory into a modern pluralistic state. (*ILWU*)

Plantation workers in Hawaii were the exception—they were organized effectively by the International Longshoremen's and Warehousemen's Union. This forced employers to provide machinery to help them cut sugar cane and do other work that previously required back-breaking hand labor. (*ILWU*)

ABOVE LEFT: Creation of the bracero program in 1942 raised an insurmountable barrier to farm unionization outside Hawaii, enabling growers to import millions of poverty-stricken Mexicans to take the jobs of U.S. citizens who might demand better conditions. Union organizer Ernesto Galarza (*right*) led a long fight against the program. (*Southern Historical Collection, University of North Carolina*) ABOVE: Father Thomas McCullough laid the groundwork in the late 1950s for the California farm workers' movement that captured international attention a decade later. (*Reprinted, by permission, from Joan London and Henry Anderson,* So Shall Ye Reap, © *1970 by Thomas Y. Crowell Co.*) LEFT: The drive that finally brought the promise of lasting unionization to all farm workers began in 1965 with a strike in the grape vineyards around Delano, California. (People's World)

The California grape strike quickly drew support from Walter Reuther of the Auto Workers Union, who marched in Delano between strike leaders Larry Itliong (*left*) and Cesar Chavez in 1965. (*Ron Taylor, Fresno* Bee)

Cesar Chavez dramatized the cause of striking California vineyard workers by undertaking a twenty-five-day fast in 1968. He broke the fast by sharing a piece of bread with Senator Robert Kennedy at a Mass near the struck vineyards in Delano. Chavez' wife Helen is at Kennedy's right. (*Fresno* Bee)

Cesar Chavez' fledgling United Farm Workers Union relied heavily on nation-wide boycotts waged against the produce and products of struck growers by the union's urban supporters. (*UFW*)

LEFT: "Miracle" in Delano. Cesar Chavez preparing to sign the contract that granted union rights to California vineyard workers in July, 1970. With Chavez are Auxiliary Bishop Joseph Donnelly of Hartford, Connecticut, who helped arrange the settlement, and John Giumarra, Sr., the state's leading grape grower. (*Fresno* Bee) ABOVE: In 1970 the Teamsters Union began signing "sweetheart contracts" with growers in hopes of breaking the United Farm Workers Union. This prompted a series of major strikes by the UFW and violent confrontations with Teamster "guards," such as these men bearing down on a UFW picket in Arvin, California, in 1973. (*Rick Tejada-Flores,* El Malcriado) RIGHT: The United Farm Workers Union faced rough treatment from law enforcement officers, including Kern County deputies who arrested strikers during demonstrations at vineyards in Lamont, California, in 1973. (People's World)

LEFT TO RIGHT: Richard Chavez, Fred Ross, Cesar Chavez, and Dolores Huerta of the United Farm Workers Union, seeking support for the nationwide Gallo wine boycott in 1974. (*Cathy Murphy, UFW*)

Some of the 15,000 adherents of the United Farm Workers Union who marched into Modesto, California, in 1975 to demand a law which finally promised collective bargaining rights to California's farm workers. (*Jim Kunz,* El Malcriado)

Deputy sheriffs face an armed citizens' posse that blocked union organizers from entering a Stockton, California, tomato field during the United Farm Workers' campaign for votes in the union representation elections guaranteed by California's new farm labor law in 1975. (*Erhardt E. Krause, Sacramento* Bee)

It took the United Farm Workers Union just 29 days to gather nearly 720,000 signatures on petitions for a 1976 ballot initiative designed to strengthen California's farm labor law. (*Los Angeles County Federation of Labor*)

ernment approval, often in consultation with fellow growers but never in consultation with worker representatives.

Frustrated and near exhaustion, Galarza began issuing a series of strident press releases and open letters to California's governor, Goodwin Knight, which protested alleged violations and made personal attacks on state officials and others, including labor leaders whom Galarza charged with cowardice. Galarza's insistent pressures helped force the state to correct some of the violations he exposed and helped prompt an investigation of the state's Farm Placement Service. The probe showed that officials had been accepting produce and other gifts from bracero users and discriminating against domestic workers. One official was fired and Chief Hayes and two other top officials resigned. Hayes immediately became the chief executive of the Imperial Valley Growers Association, a major bracero user. Galarza was fighting on another front as well, waging a jurisdictional dispute with the Packinghouse Workers Union, the former CIO affiliate that had retained an interest in farm labor organizing after the AFL and the CIO merged in 1955.

But by now, Galarza's union, renamed the National Agricultural Workers Union, barely existed. The NAWU held no contracts, had very few members, and Galarza, its sole representative in California, had made many powerful enemies inside and outside the labor movement. By 1959, as Galarza said, the union had "no money, no organizers, no support." AFL-CIO President George Meany suggested that the NAWU merge with the Packinghouse Workers; but rather than join their old rival, Galarza and NAWU President H. L. Mitchell merged what was left of their organization into a former AFL affiliate, the Meat Cutters Union, which had done some farm organizing in the East. Galarza went off to try to organize in Louisiana; but others continued attempts to organize California's farm workers despite the barrier of the bracero program.

Galarza's efforts to end the program helped mobilize opponents who came together in 1959 for a major lobbying effort in Congress, led by the AFL-CIO. The congressional effort had begun quietly some years earlier, largely through James Vizzard, a Jesuit priest who headed the Catholic Rural Life Conference, and Arnold Mayer, the Meat Cutters' Washington lobbyist. Vizzard and Mayer spent several years lining up support from urban congressmen who could be reached solely by appeals to economic justice since they had no powerful grower constituencies to worry them.

Vizzard and other Catholic representatives devoted as much attention to President Eisenhower's Secretary of Labor, James Mitchell, also a Catholic. Mitchell responded with reforms that made it increasingly expensive for growers to use braceros, although he was hampered by threats from grower allies in Congress to transfer jurisdiction of the bracero program from the Labor Department to the Immigration and Naturalization Service if he went too far. Mitchell nevertheless was able to do such things as require growers to meet government standards for the pay and conditions of the domestic workers they had to seek from state placement agencies to be eligible to use braceros.

Reforms continued under the Kennedy Administration, helping drop the employment of braceros from the peak of almost 500,000 in 1959 to about 200,000 in 1962, most of them employed in California. . The most important of the changes required growers to pay a set, predetermined government rate to domestic workers to be eligible for braceros. Opponents of the bracero program believed, however, that nothing short of terminating the program could provide adequate protection for U.S. workers. Whatever the provisions of the program, exploitation was unavoidable as long as growers were exempted from competing for their workers exclusively within the same high-standard economy as other U.S. empolyers.

Opponents finally got their chance in 1963, when serious unemployment among U.S. workers provided the pressure needed to kill the bracero program outright. It had become politically dangerous to argue for a foreign labor program at a time when more than four million U.S. citizens were looking for jobs. Grower allies in Congress nonetheless sought a two-year extension of the program, and when the House rejected the extension bill and opponents in the Senate insisted on an amendment that would have made the program unacceptable to growers, they had little choice but to accept defeat. The most grower supporters could salvage was a temporary one-year extension, granted with the understanding that the program would expire after that, at the end of 1964. Grower allies agreed to it in exchange for Senate opponents dropping an amendment that would have required growers to provide domestic workers the same minimum pay, free housing and transportation and guaranteed hours of work they had to provide braceros. Grower allies and opponents alike warned growers that the extension, approved by Congress just twenty-seven days before the program would have expired in 1963, was granted primarily to give them time to make plans for securing an all-domestic labor force.

But California's bracero users made almost no effort to attract domestic workers. They insisted it was the government's job to find

domestic workers, and they would accept only those who were as willing as the braceros to work strictly on growers' terms—but without
even the minimal guarantees provided the braceros. Union and government representatives argued that even unemployed U.S. citizens
could not be attracted if pay and conditions were not improved. Most
of them lived in urban areas; they took for granted such things as
union representation, fringe benefits, social insurance coverage and
guaranteed hours of work. Yet they were being asked to take jobs that
provided none of these things and that might in some weeks pay them
less than they could get in unemployment insurance benefits. They
were being asked to work under conditions so primitive that, as California's Public Health Department reported, there still was "an almost
universal lack of toilets and handwashing facilities." Most also would
have to leave their families behind, since growers had built little housing save single-men's barracks during their twenty-two years of reliance on braceros.

Labor Department officials argued that growers could well afford
to improve these conditions. They prepared studies showing that even
doubling pay would add no more than a few cents to the retail price
of most produce and have an equally inconsequential effect on the
growers' outlay for labor, since that amounted to less than 10 percent
of their overall costs. Actually, according to surveys of unemployed
workers in Los Angeles and smaller cities near agricultural areas, it
probably would have taken no more than a 25 percent increase in pay
to attract large numbers of U.S. workers.

Yet growers insisted that no improvements could be great enough
to attract U.S. workers, because "Americans won't do stoop labor."
Their argument became the theme of a campaign to force the government to continue supplying them Mexican workers. It was a racial
matter, as Jack Bias, manager of the San Joaquin Valley's principal
grower association, explained at one of dozens of hearings on the demands for continued Mexican help. "Those of Mexican nationality,"
Bias declared earnestly, "do this type of work better because of their
short stature." Robert Fouke, speaking for California's Chamber of
Commerce, assured Labor Department hearing officers that "the majority of young people and the unemployed either are incapable of
performing the physically demanding work or are totally disinterested
in engaging in such employment." Similar testimony was voiced by
witnesses from banks, railroads, canneries and other interests with
heavy financial stakes in agriculture. Their chief political ally, Republican Senator George Murphy of California, introduced a bill to revive the bracero program after he, too, declared that Mexicans

preferred farm work because "they are built closer to the ground."

Union witnesses attacked the peculiar reasoning not only as outright nonsense and blatant racial prejudice, but also as an admission of extreme exploitation. For the grower spokesmen were arguing that they needed Mexicans to harvest U.S. produce because, although the task was vital to the country, it was too degrading for U.S. citizens to perform for themselves. As a matter of fact, as one AFL-CIO witness noted, U.S. workers had done "stoop labor" in agriculture long before the braceros came and were working as well at much more difficult jobs. "Why do Americans work cleaning out the city sewers?" the union witness asked. "Why do Americans work as cement masons, when 75 percent of the work is down on the knees? Why do Americans work as garbage collectors, as roofers handling hot tar all day?"

The answer was self-evident. But California growers were strongly determined to have Mexican help, and rather than improve pay and working conditions, they openly spoke of how bad conditions were, in hopes of further discouraging U.S. workers. Jack Bias told a hearing, for instance, that "I would rather dig ditches" than do the farm work offered by the growers he represented. Government officials nevertheless tried to recruit domestic workers who would accept the jobs during the 1965 harvest, which was to be the first without braceros since 1942.

State officials allowed groups of convicts to spend their days in the fields on work-furlough programs and ordered able-bodied welfare recipients to take farm work on whatever terms growers offered or lose their benefits; and although there were 400,000 unemployed Californians, Employment Department representatives searched for workers throughout the country. In addition to migrants from southwestern states, they recruited American Indians off reservations in the Dakotas and teams of vacationing high school athletes from the Midwest. In some areas of California, school authorities delayed the start of the fall term so local students could continue working in the fields.

California growers were provided with several thousand workers from out of state and through local farm placement offices, but protested they were neither numerous enough nor efficient enough to fill in for braceros, sometimes protesting under circumstances that angered even the usually very cooperative government recruiters. The Labor Department raised particularly strong complaints against an Imperial Valley grower who rejected 1800 recruits as "unacceptable" before they had even been put to work, and against the state's largest strawberry grower. Although claiming that his crop was "rotting in the fields," the strawberry grower turned away more than 1000 workers, on the excuse that he didn't have time to do the paperwork required to "process" the recruits.

The grower was typical of many in California who had formerly used large numbers of braceros; they overplanted on the gamble they would get cheap imported labor and were prepared to plow under part of their crops with great fanfare if they didn't get it. That would have caused them no great loss; indeed, it would have tended to increase the price for their commodities. But the Labor Department could not resist pressures from politically expedient officeholders in both parties and from an uninformed public that was outraged at the idea of destroying food, even such obviously unessential food as strawberries. Midway through the 1965 harvest, the department was forced to set up an "emergency program" for importing Mexican workers under the immigration laws.

But the Labor Department acted only after President Johnson's Secretary of Labor, Willard Wirtz, did his utmost to enlighten the public about the actual state of affairs. Wirtz took a whirlwind tour of California's fields with a planeload of reporters in tow, popping up unannounced at farms to ask embarrassing questions and point to conditions many newspaper readers and television viewers associated only with the dim past recorded by John Steinbeck in *The Grapes of Wrath.* At one stop, Wirtz stood in the center of a field, surrounded by workers, looking out over tall rows of asparagus that covered the land in all directions. "Where," he asked the grower, "are the toilets?" The grower, genuinely incredulous that the question would even be asked, explained that "there are none." In Salinas, Wirtz paid a surprise visit to a farm labor camp at breakfast time, finding conditions that "make me ashamed anything of this kind exists in this country . . . looking at the food, I wonder how anyone can eat it!" In another camp, Wirtz walked away from the communal bathroom shuddering. "Did you see it?" he asked a reporter. "God!" The Council of California Growers acknowledged that Wirtz had exposed "filthy, disgraceful conditions" and, although it claimed the conditions were atypical, joined the Labor Secretary in warning growers to clean up the situation or lose their chance for imported workers.

Strengthened by the publicity given his tour, Wirtz ruled that growers could get imported workers only if they recruited widely for domestic workers and offered them the same guarantees the Labor Department would require them to provide the Mexicans. That included pay that was 40 to 60 cents an hour higher than the $1 that had last been required under the bracero program. The reluctance of growers to seek imported help under these restrictions and the reluctance of

Wirtz to approve their requests greatly curtailed the hiring of Mexicans under the government program. California growers, who had employed 128,000 braceros in 1964, hired only 21,000 Mexicans under the new program in 1965 and only 7350 in 1966, when the program was all but halted because of grower reluctance to call for help on the Labor Department's terms. Yet the "disaster" growers said would follow termination of the bracero program failed to materialize.

Growers had warned that wages and prices would skyrocket and that worker shortages would force many of them out of California, severely cut back production and income and greatly reduce the work force. It turned out a bit differently, however: pay rose a modest 15 to 20 percent over the two years after the bracero program ended, prices remained stable, the number of workers increased slightly and production and income rose steadily. The profits of the California growers dropped about $75 million in 1966 from 1964's record level, but gross income reached a record $3.95 billion and production increased to 37 million tons, well above the average for the previous five years.

Despite their loud grumbling, growers had done what union and government spokesmen had foreseen in arguing to end the bracero program. Forced to attract new workers, they improved housing and working conditions as well as pay, adopted new management practices and generally made their operations more efficient to help offset the higher costs. There was much less worker turnover than in the years of widespread bracero use, and an increased use of workers from areas in the immediate vicinity of farms. Those workers, reported James Bennett, the state's deputy director of agriculture, "actually picked more than braceros." Among "the many adaptations of work practices" reported by the state Employment Department were those that enabled growers to increase the number of women workers by 10,000 and greatly ease the onerous methods used in harvesting tomatoes, the state's largest crop. Tomatoes had been picked almost entirely by hand, but by 1966 machines were being used to harvest 80 percent of the crop, and although this cut down the number of workers picking tomatoes, new and expanded operations in other crops more than made up for the job loss.

Even with the improvements that came after the end of the bracero program, the pay and conditions of domestic farm workers still were far behind those of most other U.S. workers, and attempts to catch up were undermined by continued grower reliance on Mexicans. For though growers were forced to hire more domestics, they also hired masses of illegal aliens from Mexico as well as Mexicans who were allowed to enter the country legally on temporary work permits. This gave growers a major weapon in their fight to block the unionization of farm workers. But powerful forces had been brought onto the workers' side during the long struggle against the bracero program, and they were in the fight to stay.

6

The Coming of the Union

It began quietly, the move toward the self-organization farm workers had to have if they were to realize their full potential as human beings. It began, not through trade unionists or radical organizers, but through a Roman Catholic priest. Thomas McCullough was his name. It was he who laid the groundwork for the movement that would some day capture international attention, as he went about his duties of ministering to those who lived in the ramshackle farm labor camps and communities in the sprawling agricultural region around Stockton, California, about eighty miles east of San Francisco. McCullough became convinced that the spiritual and material needs of the workers, most of them Spanish-speaking Catholics, could not be met without organization generated from within. He naturally felt this was the job of union organizers, but when they ignored his pleas for help, McCullough became an organizer himself.

That was in 1958. McCullough formed the Agricultural Workers Association, with the initial goal of simply building a sense of community among the thousands of demoralized, disorganized and isolated farm workers. The basic tool was the house meeting. One worker would hold a meeting in his house with a half-dozen others, get two at that gathering to hold similar meetings at their homes, and later bring all participants together to discuss matters they agreed on and actions they might take. Within a year the AWA had a set of officers and plans for committees to deal with the whole range of the workers' basic concerns. There were to be committees on employment, but also on social and educational activities, housing, health and welfare, political action, community service and other matters beyond the traditional union concerns. The plans even envisioned a food cooperative, with AWA members growing their own vegetables.

The Agricultural Workers Association didn't get far beyond the planning stage, however. For in 1959, the AFL-CIO's national leadership announced it would move into farm labor organizing on a broad scale, despite the continued existence of the bracero program. The AFL-CIO would bypass the National Agricultural Workers Union, which had been struggling in California with minimal support and little success in organizing; it would set up a well-financed, well-directed Agricultural Workers Organizing Committee to do the job started by the AWA in the absence of such a major union effort.

Pressures for the AFL-CIO action had been mounted for several years by religious spokesmen such as McCullough, and liberal citizens' groups and legislative committees whose investigations of farm labor invariably concluded with recommendations for a major farm union drive. AFL-CIO President George Meany was constantly appealed to by organized labor's liberal allies, most forcefully by Eleanor Roosevelt and other prominent members of the most active of the citizens' groups, the National Advisory Committee on Farm Labor. The labor federation's AFL faction of craft union leaders had resisted, however, and those leaders controlled the federation through Meany, a former Plumbers Union leader who had headed the AFL before it merged with the liberal industrial unionists of the CIO. The conservative AFL men insisted that the AFL-CIO could not handle a task of such magnitude. But the CIO faction, headed by President Walter Reuther of the United Auto Workers Union and other leaders of the AFL-CIO's Industrial Union Department, finally pushed through a proposal for "an all-out drive to organize farm workers."

That came at the AFL-CIO's Executive Council meeting in San Juan, Puerto Rico, in February of 1959. Meany and the other former AFL leaders were openly pessimistic; they suggested that if an organizing drive was to be undertaken, it might be waged more profitably among the nonunion public employees and other white-collar workers who now outnumbered the craftsmen and blue-collar production workers who dominated organized labor. Meany argued that such a campaign might at least begin paying its way within a reasonably short period, while it might be many years before the farm workers could put together a self-sustaining organization. But there was heavy pressure, in any case, to add to the AFL-CIO's dwindling proportion of the country's work force, if only to keep the growing nonunion segment from undermining the organized workers whom the AFL-CIO leaders represented. They were persuaded, ultimately, that if the AFL-CIO could meet this internal pressure for organizing, while at the same time meeting the insistent and major demand of its liberal political allies that it be done in agriculture, it was worth a try.

Just a year before, the AFL-CIO had drawn heavily on those liberal supporters to defeat a major attempt to enact a "right-to-work" law in California that would have greatly weakened union strength by barring contracts requiring employees of unionized enterprises to join the unions that bargained for them, and the AFL-CIO would need these allies for future political battles. So by the winter of 1959, delegates to the federation's national convention were expressing "faith in the simple proposition that agricultural workers can be organized" through a resolution that had been put before them by the unanimous vote of their executive council.

If the organizing was to be done, it probably would have to start in California. Here was the country's greatest concentration of agricultural wealth, its highest percentage of farm workers and its most intensive use of mechanized operations. The state also had more of the corporate farms that dominated the agricultural economy everywhere, under control of the same banks, insurance firms and other financial interests that fought the AFL-CIO on many fronts. If California was the place, the election of a liberal state administration and legislature in 1958 for only the second time in sixty-four years provided the opportunity. This lessened the temptation of labor leaders to employ their traditional gambit of gaining concessions from conservative, rural-dominated legislatures in return for promises to ignore farm workers. It also presented labor leaders with a governor, Democrat Edmund G. Brown, who had been elected with their strong support, and who was not as eager as his predecessors to help supply growers with the braceros and other unorganized workers whom they had used to fight off unionization. Nor was it likely, in the changed political climate, that growers could easily resort to the violence they had used against so many previous union organizers.

The AFL-CIO set up the headquarters of its new Agricultural Workers Organizing Committee—AWOC—in the center of Agricultural Workers Association activities in Stockton, and Father McCullough was called in for the initial planning. He and others in the AWA assumed AWOC would build on the foundation they had begun to lay down. They readily dissolved the Agricultural Workers Association, and one of the AWA's chief organizers, a creative, energetic young woman named Dolores Huerta, joined the AWOC staff.

McCullough urged AFL-CIO representatives to concentrate on the relatively stable workers in the settlements on the fringes of the cities and towns throughout California's valleys. They were the permanent, skilled workers who were essential to agricultural operations, a more likely base for a successful union than the smaller group of migrant workers who drew the bulk of union and public attention. McCullough, Huerta and others in the AWA also had these admonitions for the AFL-CIO: "Organize around the felt needs of the people; let them choose their own spokesmen; don't be maneuvered into premature strikes."

The AFL-CIO organizers set up operations in the battered old Labor Temple in Stockton, its scarred, deep brown walls reeking of a past when meeting rooms were filled with men planning onslaughts against employers who now accepted them on the mere showing of a union card. The dingy atmosphere of the barren, neglected rooms did not dampen the organizers' spirits. On the contrary; in stirring memories of militancy, it *heightened* enthusiasm. "This is really exciting, this is the old days!" declared Franz Daniel, the assistant director of organization for the national AFL-CIO, as he sat beneath a display of faded union banners near his cluttered desk on one hot, muggy afternoon not long after he was sent from the AFL-CIO's modern, well-appointed headquarters in Washington, D.C., to help launch AWOC.

Like the other men who would direct AWOC, Daniel, a tall, personable Southerner, was a veteran of the industrial organizing campaigns waged by the CIO, and determined that the CIO victories in the factories would now be repeated in the fields. "We're out to do it, whatever it costs, whatever time it takes!" promised one of the chief AWOC organizers, Lou Krainock, a craggy-faced survivor of numerous picket line battles who had been educational director of the Packinghouse Workers Union. Daniel echoed Krainock's promise. He insisted that the new organizers were "just as emotional and indignant" as the unsuccessful organizers from individual AFL and CIO affiliates and independent unions who had preceded them into the fields. "But," Daniel added, *"we're* going about it realistically. This means having time and resources."

It would take "at least five years" to build a basic union structure, in the estimation of Norman Smith, who was appointed as AWOC's executive director by the AFL-CIO's national director of organization, Jack Livingston, an old friend from Smith's days as an organizer for the Auto Workers Union. Smith seemed to be the very prototype of the veteran union organizer—a stocky, gray-haired man of sixty-one in rumpled work clothes, with an arresting rolling gait, full of pragmatic wisdom and tales of the old days, always ready with a bit of plain but emotional rhetoric. He had most recently been a supervisor at the Kaiser Steel mill in Fontana, near Los Angeles, far south of the fields and orchards of Stockton. But Smith had thirty-five years in the labor movement behind him, and the experience had made him tough, smart and realistic.

"Look," he explained in a gravel voice, "we're working at one of the toughest organizing jobs anyone ever attempted, and I was in from the beginning at General Motors. The farm communities are hostile against the workers, and against us. The workers are shifting, always on the move. They've been pushed around so long they don't know they have a right to expect anything different."

Smith looked up, his voice rising as it always seemed to rise when he talked of how it *was* or how it *should be*. "You know . . . believe me! Most of these people have had so little chance for schooling we literally have to teach them they're entitled to the rights other Americans take for granted. I mean it! Believe me!"

The initial planning was sound, based on the essential recommendations of the Agricultural Workers Association. Organizers were to concentrate on creating local branches, thus building a base of permanent workers; they were to train organizers and leaders from the fields, and stress political education. Further, Henry Anderson, AWOC's brilliant young research director, was laying out plans for an entire program strikingly like that used later by the forces of Cesar Chavez.

But AWOC's deeds proved to be far different from AWOC's plans. The vital advice of the Agricultural Workers Association was ignored in practice, and soon Father McCullough went on to more customary church work and Huerta resigned from AWOC in disgust to work elsewhere on building a community of farm workers. The problem was that Smith could not forget the CIO. He was told that agriculture was different, and he *knew* that agriculture was different; but he and his organizers nevertheless acted as if they were organizing auto workers.

Industrial workers generally are concentrated in relatively small plants, work together in relatively close quarters and enter and leave at set hours through a few easily accessible gates. An organizer can be reasonably certain he will be dealing with the same workers every day, workers who are legally protected from intimidation by anti-union employers, and who see unions as a fact of life in the community around them. Organizers are often denied access to industrial workplaces, but an organizer can easily conduct his business just outside the plant gate—and effectively, if he has the oratorical talents of a Norman Smith.

Smith and his seventeen organizers wandered over the San Joaquin

Valley around Stockton for a time, seeking out such large groups of readily accessible, prounion recruits. They discovered, however, that the valley's farm workers were scattered in small crews throughout large, isolated farm holdings, working irregular hours and frequently changing employers. Growers could—and did—tell them to stay clear of AWOC; in any case, the Mexican-Americans and Filipinos who dominated the valley's farm labor force tended to think of unions as distant outside organizations, run by and for Anglo workers who spoke a different language, had different problems and came from a different culture.

Sometimes Smith found no workers at all; they were hidden from view, far beyond the "no trespassing" signs that few growers allowed organizers to pass. The organizers rarely even tried to reach the workers at their homes during nonworking hours; at best, they held widely advertised meetings at which Smith and others sought to win members with the oratory that had been effective in other times and other places. It yielded few results at this time and in this place. So Smith, ignoring the advice of his research director, turned to the one place where farm workers *were* gathered for easy access. That was the office of the state's Farm Placement Service, deep in Stockton's extensive Skid Road.

Labor contractors came there daily, before dawn, to fill their yellow buses with enough bodies to meet the manpower demands of growers who relied on them for help during the peak harvest seasons. Smith and his aides also were there before dawn each day, even before the contractors pulled in to seek recruits and haul them off to the fields. But though AWOC's organizers found large numbers of workers, they hardly were the basis for a union. They were mostly single men, down-on-their-luck transients looking for a day or two of work, perhaps nothing more than the price of their next bottle of cheap fortified wine. Few of them felt any permanent attachment to the farm labor force, in Stockton or anywhere else, and not many were willing or able to pay even the meager dues of $2 a month required for AWOC membership.

AWOC also waged a series of strikes against smaller growers, aimed at taking advantage of the high labor requirements and short harvest seasons in California. This made growers vulnerable to brief strikes that could all but wipe out a crop—providing most of their employees honored the picket lines and kept others from replacing them in the fields. Growers responded predictably to the AWOC strikes by quickly calling for the state Employment Department to help them get braceros to replace strikers. But Governor Brown's new administration reacted differently from its predecessors. Brown's director of employment, backed by decisions of a Brown majority on the state Supreme Court, ruled that farms being picketed were involved in legitimate labor disputes, even though the pickets might be organizers seeking union recognition, rather than unionized employees demanding contracts. That, said Employment Director Al Tieburg, prohibited him from certifying to the federal government that braceros should be sent to such farms. Nor could Tieburg allow dispatch of resident workers to the farms through the Employment Department's Farm Placement Service, which previously operated as a compliant employment agency for growers. Growers turned to Secretary of Labor James Mitchell, but Mitchell upheld the state's interpretation of the law, despite heavy pressure on him from other members of President Eisenhower's Cabinet.

AWOC's first major strike was waged in 1960 at a cherry ranch, Podesta Farms, near Stockton. Like many of the 100 or so strikes that were to follow that year, it involved one of the few crops that were dominated by Anglo workers. Those were the fruit crops such as cherries, peaches and pears that required fewer workers than most other fruit and vegetable crops, generally paid better, and gave workers the chance to work off ladders instead of bending and stooping constantly under the direct rays of a summer sun that raised temperatures to 100 degrees and more during the workday. Also like most of the early AWOC strikes, the strike against Podesta was not called by AWOC, but by the workers themselves. They summoned the organizers after they had struck on their own, and they sought help only in winning a pay raise. They did not even demand union recognition or a contract that would have established a union at the ranch. Podesta fought hard, recruiting more than 1000 growers, housewives, students and others in a well publicized campaign to "save the cherries." But they were too late; the cherries needed picking on the very day the regular workers struck. The farm lost most of the $100,000 crop and eventually did grant a slight pay increase in the hope of avoiding future problems.

Although there were other losses, few other growers suffered nearly as much from any of the other strikes. At most, they, too, had to grant slight pay increases. Some escaped entirely by calling for the braceros and unorganized domestic workers who still were available to influential growers who pushed hard enough in the right places. They could get friendly local judges to block government refusals to send them strikebreakers and allow them to complete their brief harvests before higher courts overturned the local rulings. Other growers got manpower without government aid by forming associations through which they pooled their workers for dispatch to struck members.

Such actions enabled growers generally to maintain a strong position against the organizers, but many felt that more should be done. They saw AWOC as the most serious threat yet to their nonunion status, for the organizers were backed by the entire AFL-CIO. This meant farm employers might be faced with a genuine challenge to their great economic and political strength, which had been sufficient to counter previous union campaigns.

John Zuckerman, a powerful Stockton grower who headed two of the new employer associations, described it as no less than "the spearhead of a movement carefully planned, carefully executed and calculated to bring all agriculture under the domination of organized labor." Similar warnings came from the Farm Bureau Federation and other influential farm groups, and growers heeded them.

They turned to the law, no longer secure in mere exclusion from the National Labor Relations Act. They wanted protection from what the AFL-CIO threatened to do in spite of the exclusion. Grower groups proposed state legislation that would have required a ninety-day "cooling-off period" between the calling and carrying out of a strike; this would have effectively blocked any farm strike, since very few harvests lasted as long as ninety days.

Growers also wooed public opinion. They set up a statewide public relations organization to try to counteract the widespread publicity the strikes were giving to the complaints and demands of their employees and AWOC's organizers. Grower spokesmen began issuing news releases, appearing at press conferences, speaking before service clubs. Zuckerman insisted that "organized labor has no place in agriculture; the tactics which labor leaders employ in industry would destroy agriculture." Growers contended that pay and working conditions were not really bad, and that the costs of any improvement would have to be passed on directly to the consumer, because they worked on small profit margins, and were at the mercy of retailers and other middlemen. Besides, they asserted, their employees didn't *really* want to be unionized; it was the idea of outside "agitators and labor parasites," declared Zuckerman in one of his appearances before the press, clad in jodhpurs and a properly creased military shirt.

"If we, as farmers and employers, accept the union as bargaining agent," declared President Louis Rozzoni of the California Farm Bureau, "we are taking away the individual laborer's right of choice

—his right to freedom of work. This is a struggle for the right of a farmer to deal directly with his employees—a stand for free enterprise."

There wasn't much evidence, however, that such arguments had any important impact in California, a highly unionized state whose citizens had heard similar rhetoric from urban employers before they succumbed to unionization. Actually, the growers' decision to join the public debate may have *helped* AWOC, if only because it magnified the organizers' activities, and identified growers with the "right-to-work" advocates who had been beaten decisively in a statewide election less than two years before. But power, not rhetoric, was the deciding factor in the new union-grower battle, and although growers were quite correct in sensing that their power was being eroded, they still had more than enough to continue fending off unionization.

AWOC nevertheless managed to score a victory against the Di-Giorgio Corporation, one of the few major growers the union struck. It was a minor victory, but symbolically important. DiGiorgio granted part of AWOC's pay demands after a week-long strike at the corporation's pear ranches, the country's largest, in Sutter and Yuba counties, north of Stockton. Some of the other struck growers who argued successfully that they needed braceros did so by claiming they were required, not for the illegal purpose of replacing strikers, but because there was a general shortage of domestic labor in their areas. They backed the arguments with evidence that they had sought and received braceros in recent strike-free harvests. But DiGiorgio was denied braceros on grounds they hadn't been employed on the pear ranches at any time during the previous two years. The corporation did convince a federal district court to order the state to dispatch domestic workers from its Farm Placement Service offices, but AWOC pickets forcefully convinced the recruits to seek work elsewhere, and Di-Giorgio decided it would be less bothersome to settle with the strikers.

DiGiorgio pickers who had been earning a flat 75 cents to $1 an hour were granted $1.10 plus 10 cents for every box of pears they picked. It wasn't much of a settlement (AWOC had been demanding $1.25 an hour and a union contract), but any kind of union settlement with DiGiorgio was a breakthrough. Smith argued that AWOC couldn't hold out for more because it did not have enough money to support the strikers for long, or enough strength to continue checking the flow of strikebreakers.

Cutting the flow of braceros soon became AWOC's principal concern. AWOC representatives and groups of members appeared regularly before legislative committees to argue that braceros were not needed, and Smith's last strike was devoted chiefly to illustrating that point. It came in January of 1961, after the major harvests had concluded in the Stockton area. AWOC might better have used the time and effort to organize the permanent workers who remained in Stockton during the off-season; but Smith moved operations south to the Imperial Valley, where California's winter lettuce harvest was starting with a work force consisting largely of braceros, plus other Mexicans who commuted across the border daily to try to find work at 70 to 90 cents an hour.

As in Stockton, AWOC concentrated on the farm placement offices where masses of unemployed workers gathered in hopes of signing on with labor contractors. Organizers circulated daily through the anxious, frustrated crowds of more than 4000 job seekers in these human cattle pens known by such names as *El Hoyo* (the hole). They found many recruits who were eager to join AWOC in picketing fields where braceros stooped over long rows of lettuce, doing work they had sought. The law hadn't given them the work, but maybe the union could. They picketed, under the hostile eyes of more than 500 regular and special deputies, providing ample evidence that local workers *were available*. The picketing, and some highly publicized demonstrations at camps where braceros were housed, finally compelled the federal government to heed AWOC's complaints, and some braceros were sent home. But Arthur Goldberg, who had succeeded Mitchell as Secretary of Labor when the Kennedy Administration took office, insisted that nothing could be done about removing the rest of the braceros "pending study"; by the time the study was completed in March, the harvest also was virtually completed.

Internal union bickering had just about broken the strike before then anyway. AWOC operated jointly with the Packinghouse Workers Union, which was organizing in the lettuce-packing sheds where the Meat Cutters Union also claimed jurisdiction. By then, too, the National Agricultural Workers Union had completed its merger with the Meat Cutters and was still claiming jurisdiction over field workers. Representatives of the NAWU and the Meat Cutters complained formally to Meany about the "raiding" tactics of their rivals. Midway in the strike, Meany summoned leaders of the conflicting AFL-CIO unions to Washington, D.C., and threatened to "cut the whole thing off" if they didn't stop squabbling; when they didn't, Meany ordered AWOC to pull out of the strike.

AWOC threatened to carry the struggle north to the Salinas Valley during the summer lettuce harvest, and picket farms owned by some of the same growers who had been picketed during the winter harvest in the Imperial Valley. The threat set the precedent for a far more serious interunion conflict, which would preoccupy organizers in the years to come.

Bud Antle, then the Salinas Valley's largest lettuce grower, feared AWOC picketing might endanger his supply of braceros, who did most of his field work. So he turned to the Teamsters Union, which was not an affiliate of the AFL-CIO, represented truck drivers and some other Antle employees and was the only major union in the state that supported the bracero program (for fear that any shortage of field workers would curtail the work opportunities of Teamster members in processing plants). The Teamsters signed a contract that did very little for field workers, but gave Antle and the union the protection they sought. The contract covered only a small number of the relatively few local workers in Antle's fields and none of the braceros; it promised that the Teamsters would help Antle "in obtaining foreign supplemental workers," and gave Antle the right to hire and fire workers without consulting the union, and the unilateral authority as well to decide how many workers should be used for any particular operation, how they should do the work and how their performance should be judged. It was enough to keep AWOC from picketing Antle, since the law would recognize the field workers as already being under a union contract, whatever its provisions, even though some were excluded and none had been consulted either before or after the contract was signed.

Only one other lettuce grower took the AWOC threat seriously enough to sign a Teamster contract. The rest of the growers were infuriated with Antle for breaking ranks. They forced him out of the local grower association, which he had once headed, and continued their nonunion operations as always. The other growers eventually would turn to the Teamsters, but nine years later, in response to a genuine union threat. The present threat, they correctly surmised, would never be carried out. By the time their harvest was in full swing, AWOC was gone, disbanded in June of 1961 at the insistence of George Meany.

AWOC's leaders pleaded for more of the "time and resources" they had been promised. Franz Daniel argued they had not been at it long enough to get beyond the stage of merely "creating a climate in which collective bargaining might someday be established," much less come up with the self-sufficient organization that Meany was demanding. Meany had been told it would be a slow process, and he had granted the organizers only about half the money and manpower they claimed they needed. But Meany was angered over the jurisdictional fighting with the Meat Cutters Union, and impatient over the lack of substantial results.

AWOC had been operating for twenty-six months and had spent about a half-million dollars of AFL-CIO funds, yet it had struck only a little more than 100 of California's 45,000 farms, had won no contracts, had signed up no more than 4500 members from a potential of more than a quarter-million, and was getting only relatively slight help from a supposedly sympathetic state administration and legislature. Even Smith's staff was complaining about his slow, deliberate operations; his hit-and-miss organizing and failure to develop a successful blueprint for a stable union or to develop rank-and-file leaders and take other steps to attract workers who were highly suspicious of the outsiders who asked them to risk their scarce work opportunities by striking and joining a union; his inability to grasp the need to do something *with* instead of *for* the farm worker.

But the AFL-CIO campaign was not a total failure. The general indifference of workers and public alike was being broken down, however slowly. AWOC's strikes and strike threats helped raise average pay in several regions to $1.10 an hour or more from the previous average of 80 to 90 cents, and bring workers $11 million more in pay overall. It also helped speed attempts to mechanize back-breaking hand-labor operations; prompted some growers to provide health, education and housing programs and job accident insurance; and aided in bringing farm workers under the state's disability insurance program for off-the-job injuries. Further, AWOC's activities helped cut the flow of braceros and made it more difficult for growers to argue for continuance of the bracero program.

Meany nevertheless looked on the organizing campaign as a business proposition. He was convinced that the AFL-CIO was not getting a quick enough or large enough return on its investment, comparatively slight though it might be, and he did not believe Smith could ever produce a proper return. Smith could have been replaced with an imaginative director who better understood farm labor organizing, but that also would have been expensive, and Meany was in no mood to take further risks. He ignored Daniel's plea that the AFL-CIO seize the "opportunity to renew its youth and reassert its claim to the idealism of man's duty to his brother and to society." Ignored, too, were the pleas of the liberal critics who had originally urged the AFL-CIO to undertake a major farm labor campaign. "Sadly," said writer Paul Jacobs, "one must conclude that the AFL-CIO has very little spirit left for dealing with problems which are not easily soluble in the old ways."

Norman Smith was bitter; he may not have shown enough understanding and imagination, but he had put considerable energy and great dedication into the campaign. "When we went into this program," he told an interviewer, "it was with the understanding that it would be a long educational program." However, Smith added, *"Mr. Meany is a very practical businessman."*

The AFL majority on the labor federation's executive council readily agreed with Meany's judgment that the council had been correct in its reluctance to approve the campaign in the first place. The council ratified his decision with no debate whatsoever. Reuther and his CIO colleagues saw no practical point in arguing; they had been given their chance and, if the campaign wasn't yet a failure by their measurements, it was by those of Meany, and Meany ran the AFL-CIO.

But the AFL-CIO did have something for its liberal allies. The AWOC campaign had proved once again, Meany told them, that farm unionization could not come about without legal reforms. So the AFL-CIO would join its friends in a renewed drive to get Congress to terminate the bracero program and bring farm workers under the Labor Relations Act. The federation's allies were not satisfied; they were aware that the AFL-CIO *always* preferred lobbying to organizing, in farm labor or any other field, and that the lobbying would be weakened by the compromises AFL-CIO lobbyists were still willing to make to win improvements in laws that covered urban workers. But they had no alternative; the half-loaf offered them by the AFL-CIO was immeasurably more than anyone else was offering at the time, and they meanwhile could mount new pressure to try to get the AFL-CIO to lobby *and* organize.

The AFL-CIO transferred AWOC's membership to the Packinghouse Workers and Meat Cutters. Those unions were busy organizing in their customary jurisdictions; but Henry Anderson and some other former members of the AWOC staff grabbed at the chance to try out their grass roots techniques, now that they were freed of the AFL-CIO's discipline and the restrictions of old-line organizers who ignored their proposals. Most of them were living on unemployment insurance payments and had very little money; yet they managed to put together a loose organization of college students and other young volunteers from outside organized labor to begin what Anderson called "the slow process of building structures of communication and trust and mutual aid among farm workers, without asking them to run before they could walk."

The volunteers, working largely with funds solicited from student groups, churches, individual unions and political organizations, went into farm workers' homes to talk about such basic concerns as learning English, setting up child care centers and converting vacant lots in the rural slums to playgrounds. The volunteers called meetings for discussion rather than oratory, helped farm workers set up a half-dozen "area councils" under their own local leaders and attempted to connect the councils through a newsletter. They tried to reach braceros by leafletting their camps, and even called one strike, an unsuccessful effort against brussels sprouts growers in Santa Cruz County, south of San Francisco.

The efforts culminated in a statewide conference in December of 1961, which brought together 200 farm workers and supporters to try to develop a comprehensive organizing plan. But the conference made what Anderson would later judge a fatal decision. He tried unsuccessfully to get the support of Walter Reuther and the AFL-CIO's Industrial Union Department, and, lacking that, conference participants assessed themselves $2 each to help send four representatives to the AFL-CIO's national convention in Miami Beach, Florida, later that month to ask Meany to revive AWOC.

Their plea was addressed to a packed, emotional session of the AFL-CIO convention by Maria Moreno, a farm worker who described near-starvation conditions that were a daily fact of life for her and her twelve children in the citrus groves of Tulare County. She told of boiling greens to make meals, of entire days in which the family lived on soup made from potato peelings, of a nineteen-year-old son who passed up this pitiful fare so his younger brothers and sisters could have more. It was a dramatic climax to months of heavy pressure that had been put on Meany by Reuther and others inside the AFL-CIO, in company with liberal Catholic leaders such as James Vizzard and others who worked closely with the federation in Washington. Meany, backed by the enthusiastic endorsement of convention delegates, promised to revive AWOC immediately and give its organizers "as much money as needed."

The AFL-CIO did provide another half-million dollars, yet even that was largely wasted; it turned out to be not much more than a sop for Meany's liberal critics. For Meany's primary concern still was to put the farm labor effort on a sound business footing. The new version of AWOC was to be a highly centralized operation with little worker input; it would be run by cautious AFL men who supported Meany's views without question; men who, while having little of the idealism and militancy of the CIO men who had operated AWOC previously, did have the same general ignorance of the problems facing them. They would try to organize farm workers as if they were Anglo building tradesmen.

Smith was replaced as AWOC's director by Al Green, a gruff, florid-faced, cigar-chomping veteran of many years as an organizer for the Plasterers Union in rural California. For the previous twelve years Green also had been western regional director of the AFL-CIO's Committee on Political Education, and so in close contact with the congressional lobbying staff that Meany considered the AFL-CIO's most important unit.

AWOC was placed directly under the AFL-CIO's state Labor Federation and the local Labor Councils that were answerable directly to Meany. Green fired Anderson and sent away his volunteers, making it known that the organization would be run by AWOC officials at the top, not the farm workers at the bottom. Maria Moreno was made an organizer, but she soon was fired for allegedly keeping inadequate dues records, the "area councils" of workers that the volunteers had helped establish withered away, and Green began concentrating on signing agreements with labor contractors. He was following his practice with the Plasterers, where he got subcontractors who did work for primary building contractors to require their employees to join the union.

Labor contractors who balked at AWOC's demand were picketed, but few resisted, and Green signed up 136 contractors, including most of those in the northern end of the San Joaquin Valley. In doing so, however, he ignored the many permanent farm workers who did not work through contractors, and angered many of those who did. For in practice, Green's system meant that many workers had to pay AWOC dues before they could board a contractor's bus. They often got higher pay in exchange, since AWOC's agreements with the contractors called for them to seek larger fees from growers and in turn pay the workers more; but more often than not, the workers perceived AWOC as merely an organization that forced them to pay dues in order to work. It built no loyalty among them, and certainly not among the general run of farm workers. Many considered labor contractors to be parasites, supplying bodies to growers for a fee, deducting their own large fees from the workers' sparse earnings, and exploiting them further by charging exorbitant prices for transportation, housing, food and even water. Some contractors also lent money at loan-shark rates and added even more to their take by offering liquor and wine and prostitutes.

Henry Anderson, arguing for creation of union hiring halls in a research paper prepared for AWOC before Green took over, noted that contractors did very well even without the extras. He cited a "typical contractor" in the Stockton area who supplied six apricot growers with 225 pickers during the 1959 harvest. The growers paid the contractor 45 cents for each of the average of twenty-four boxes of fruit picked by each member of his crews daily, and the contractor in turn paid each picker 27 cents a box. The contractor took deductions for job injury insurance, Social Security and the like from his share of the 45 cents per box, along with the pay for nine foremen and checkers who worked for the contractor directly, and paid for gasoline and the upkeep of his buses. Even after that he made $671 a day in net profit. The "typical contractor" did almost as well in the peach harvest, where he supplied 100 pickers. He got 23 cents a box from the peach growers, paid his crew members 13 cents a box, and netted $550 a day. This meant that more than two-thirds of the growers' labor costs in the two crops covered payments to the contractor, not to the workers.

Cesar Chavez, who was by then becoming active in efforts to bring farm workers together, expressed a common feeling by declaring that "I would rather there be no union at all than to recognize the rotten contractor system."

But though farm workers objected, Anderson noted that growers were pleased because Green's system allowed them to avoid recognizing the union; labor contractors were pleased because they could keep their profits, and Meany and Green were pleased because it enabled AWOC to get dues-paying members with a minimum of effort.

Green spent much of his time arguing against the bracero program in the legislative hearing rooms that suited his experience much better than the fields, since he had far more rapport with legislators than with farm workers. However, Green's use of AWOC as a supplier of manpower through labor contractors enabled grower witnesses to challenge AWOC on the growers' terms. The overriding issue became simply whether AWOC could supply enough workers to meet the growers' alleged labor shortage. If the braceros were to leave, as Green demanded, said the growers, then AWOC had the responsibility to supply domestic workers to replace them. Like Norman Smith before him, Green argued repeatedly that the workers would be available if pay and conditions met union standards. But he couldn't very well argue the deeper issue, that growers should have the same responsibility as other employers to recruit their own workers, and so Green's arguments became obscured by the simple demand for manpower to avoid the specter of "rotting crops" which agricultural spokesmen constantly invoked.

Even a supposed AWOC ally, Governor Brown, demanded angrily that the AFL-CIO "put up or shut up" on its claim to have enough available workers. That was to become typical of Brown's position after he was elected to a second term in 1962. He had made it more difficult for growers to use braceros as strikebreakers during his first years as governor, but he supported the grower-sponsored bill that would have blocked farm strikes and he meekly allowed the state legislature to kill bills he had proposed at the AFL-CIO's urging for a state minimum wage in agriculture and for creation of a "fact-finding commission" on farm labor. Yet Green, again drawing on his previous labor experience, transformed AWOC into an arm of the AFL-CIO's Committee on Political Education in 1962 by putting virtually all of its efforts into Brown's successful reelection campaign against Richard Nixon. AWOC claimed it registered more than 7000 farm workers to vote and delivered 15,000 votes to Brown.

AWOC, however, didn't get much in immediate returns for abandoning organizing to work for the governor. Brown, already thinking of a third term and the interest of growers and their powerful allies in a strong conservative candidate to oppose him, began supporting grower requests for braceros. It was reluctant and temporary support, Brown explained; but it was important support nonetheless. Brown even authorized the use of state prison inmates to help Stockton asparagus growers alleviate a supposed labor shortage; and he came out against the state minimum wage he had once proposed for farm workers. Brown adopted the California growers' argument that a national minimum was needed to protect them from "unfair competition," yet knowing all the while that the size and diversity of their crops gave them an overwhelming competitive *advantage,* and that Congress was not about to enact a national minimum in any case.

Even after the AFL-CIO was able to use its political strength effectively, to help kill the bracero program, AWOC did not take advantage of the situation. Tom Pitts, who then headed the AFL-CIO's state Labor Federation, declared hopefully that "at long last, some of the major obstacles to the organization of domestic farm workers appear to be on the verge of crumbling." But Green went on with his activities among labor contractors, at one point operating jointly with Teamster officials who were organizing produce drivers and shed workers in citrus-growing regions.

The Teamsters also got involved through Lou Krainock, who had gone to work for the International Longshoremen's and Warehousemen's Union after leaving AWOC's organizing staff. Krainock persuaded the ILWU to try a joint venture with the Teamsters, in hopes that the Teamster potential to control the transport of produce along California's highways would give organizers the same leverage that the ILWU's control over seagoing produce had given that union in organizing Hawaii's agricultural workers. But the Teamsters quickly dropped out of the project and the ILWU had neither the strategic position nor the financial resources to continue it.

The effective organizing was going on elsewhere, outside the rigid structure of the AFL-CIO and the Teamsters. Cesar Chavez and others were laying the basis for the campaign that would at last bring collective bargaining into agriculture, and the AFL-CIO and the Teamsters Union with it.

7

"When That Damn Eagle Flies . . ."

"I had some ideas on what should be done. No great plans; just that it would take an awful lot of work. A gamble? Sure it was. But I had seen *so much* injustice, and I knew that organization was the key to changing it. *Someone* had to do the organizing."

It was not the methods of AWOC that guided Cesar Chavez in his gamble. "That's not *organizing*," he said contemptuously, this organizer so unlike the hundreds of organizers who had come before: a stocky, sad-eyed, disarmingly soft-spoken man, shining black hair trailing over the edge of a face brushed with traces of Indian ancestry; a man who talked of militance in calm, measured tones; a devout Roman Catholic; an incredibly patient man who hid great strategic talent behind shy smiles and an attitude of utter candor.

Chavez' ideas did not come from union headquarters in the East; they came from his own experience in the orchards, vineyards and the cotton and vegetable fields of the West, from his own daily life. Inspiration came from his fellow *campesinos;* he was, like them, the victim of the injustice pressed down on the poor and unorganized. Ideas came, too, from men and women outside organized labor who tried to help these farm workers help themselves, from the few inside labor who also understood, and from activist philosophers who offered workable substitutes for the weapons of money and power.

Chavez was one of those in the stream of migrants who moved endlessly from crop to crop, up and down the central valleys of California, adapting to "working conditions that few other Americans would accept . . . because we were powerless to defend ourselves." They worked in open-air factories where temperatures soared to 115 degrees in the summer and plunged to freezing in the winter, driven by poverty and a piece-rate system that focused their interest almost solely on picking as much as possible, as quickly as possible. The migrants accepted a job-injury rate three times that of U.S. workers outside agriculture, and countless humiliations—"the big humiliations of labor camps and being looked down upon as 'dumb Mexicans' . . . the little humiliations of no toilets, no mobile sanitary units in the fields." They accepted child labor, "because otherwise our families couldn't live"; and, in the off-season, they accepted "poverty and handouts or hunger" because they had no unemployment insurance. The death rate of the migrants' babies and their mothers was 125 percent higher than the rate among other Americans; the migrants were twice as likely to get flu or pneumonia, even more likely to suffer from tuberculosis. Other Americans lived to age seventy on the average, but the migrants' life expectancy was forty-nine years.

"I went through a lot of hell," Chavez recalls, "and a lot of people did." Life had started differently for Chavez; he and his family lived on their own small farm, not in wealth, surely, but in an independent manner only dreamed of by most farm workers. The Chavez family had a few horses, some cows, and raised grain, alfalfa, vegetables and watermelons on their eighty acres in the Gila River Valley about a dozen miles north of Yuma, Arizona. Chavez' grandfather had acquired the land in 1899 when he came into what was then the Territory of Arizona as a homesteader seeking some better fate than awaited him as a *peon* in Mexico. It had been just another section of sage and mesquite, but the elder Chavez irrigated it, planted the land and built a sturdy home.

Chavez has never forgotten the cool adobe house in the midst of the hot desert climate, the horses he and his brother Richard and his cousin Manuel curried with the care demanded by a watchful father; climbing a big shade tree with Richard and Manuel, learning the tenets of Catholicism from a devout grandmother. But his was a short-lived childhood, cut short, like so many, by the Great Depression. When the property tax bill fell due in 1937, his father Librado could not pay it or the bills for irrigation water. Chavez would later recall bitterly that others—Anglos—got loans to meet such emergencies. But his father did not get a loan. County authorities foreclosed, the farm was sold at auction, and Librado Chavez, his wife Juana, ten-year-old Cesar and their four younger children did the only thing they could do. They, too, became migrant laborers.

The family moved west into California, stopping first in the lettuce fields of the Imperial Valley. They exchanged their thick-walled adobe home for a wooden shack in a labor camp, one room lit by a single bare globe overhead, with a chipped enamel sink, rusted kerosene stove and four narrow beds. For six weeks the family worked in the fields, taking lettuce from the ground by means of an instrument of torture known as *El Cortito*—an eighteen-inch hoe that kept them bent double, scurrying over the fields like spiders, pausing only for a quick lunch of the bologna sandwiches and Coke that were the staples of the farm workers' diet. They were to be paid at the end of the six-week harvest; but "we were green . . . oh, were we green," says Chavez, and when the harvest ended, they got nothing. The crew leader who hired them had disappeared.

There was no farm work to be had in the winter, so the Chavez family moved to a rented house in the Mexican section of Brawley, in the heart of the valley, taking what few odd jobs they could find. Chavez and his brother did their part by gathering wild mustard greens from ditches for their mother to cook, fishing in canals and shining shoes on the edge of Brawley's "Anglo Town." There was just enough to live on; there never was much more. "We thought that always you had to suffer and be hungry," Chavez recalls. "That was our life." There were many times when the entire family made $1 for a day's work, "maybe $2 if things went right"; times when Chavez and his brother walked to school barefoot through the winter mud; a succession of decaying labor camps with communal outhouses and single water taps serving whole groups of families, or sometimes no more shelter than a tent, or a bridge overhead.

Chavez also remembers he and his father being turned away from restaurants with notices specifying "White Trade Only" and "No Dogs or Mexicans Allowed," and a movie theater manager who had him escorted out by the police for refusing to leave a seat in the "Anglo section."

It was no different in the schools; teachers were not prepared for the migrant children who drifted in and out of their classrooms as their families moved from crop to crop. Migrants were treated as backward for not being fluent in English, taught it was "dumb" to speak Spanish and were often relegated to segregated schools. "The Anglos had their schools and we had ours," says Chavez. "I didn't mind this too much. But I always remember that we got the pencil stubs, the worn-out books." Chavez attended more than sixty of these schools before finally dropping out for good at age fourteen. He turned to public libraries. It was there that he began learning of the men, the ideas and the historical events that would shape his thinking, his future and the future of many others.

Chavez especially would not forget the Mexican Revolution, Gandhi, Thoreau, Saint Francis of Assisi and Saint Paul. It was not mere intellectual exercise. Chavez was training himself, not just how to think, but how to act. Hence he would describe Saint Paul as "a terrific organizer who would go and talk to the people right in their homes—sit there with them and be one of them."

Chavez learned in the fields as well. He watched as his father, his uncle and others experienced the hopeless frustration of the disorganized, poorly supported strikes of the late 1930s. Chavez enlisted in the Navy at seventeen, one step ahead of the draft board, at the tag end of World War II. After service in the South Pacific, he returned to the fields, in time to carry a picket sign himself for the first time, during a strike in the Tulare County cotton fields near Corcoran in 1946. He says he "would have died right then if someone had told me how and why to die for our cause; but no one did. There was a crisis, and a mob, but there was no organization, and nothing came of it all. A week later everyone was back picking cotton in the same fields at the same low wages." Chavez took part in the other cotton strikes in the area in the late 1940s, learning some of the tactics he would later employ: the use of support from outside unions and urban clergy, students and prominent liberals, the caravans of strikers and strike supporters to the picket lines, the daily rallies and meetings.

Chavez was married during this period, to Helen Fabela, the daughter of a former colonel in Francisco Villa's revolutionary army, whose family had settled in Delano to work in the vineyards. Chavez had met her during one of his migratory stops in Delano before the war and they were married two years after his return to civilian life. Characteristically, their short honeymoon was spent touring the California missions, whose tranquility, historical presence and buildings so like Chavez' boyhood home would draw him back frequently for reflection.

After marriage, the couple joined Chavez' brother Richard and his wife and Chavez' parents in a sharecropping venture on a strawberry farm just outside San Jose, about sixty miles south of San Francisco. But that undertaking soon was abandoned, Chavez and his brother tried working for a summer as loggers in the Pacific Northwest and then settled in the East San Jose barrio, known mockingly as *Sal Si Puedes* ("escape if you can"). His brother turned to carpentry, but Chavez returned to farm labor, in the fruit orchards outside San Jose.

Chavez was one of those in the barrio and surrounding fields who drew the attention of a Catholic priest, Donald McDonnell, who was trying to bring Mexican-Americans together in the same way his colleague, Father Thomas McCullough, had in the Stockton area preceding the formation of the Agricultural Workers Organizing Committee. McDonnell, said Chavez, "sat with me past midnight telling me about social justice and the Church's stand on farm labor, and reading from the encyclicals of Pope Leo XIII in which he upheld labor unions. I would do anything to get the Father to tell me more about labor history. I began going to the bracero camps with him to help with Mass, to the city jail with him to talk to prisoners—anything to be with him so that he could tell me more about the farm labor movement." Chavez learned quickly. McCullough, a frequent visitor to the area, found him "more realistic than anyone I'd encountered about the necessity and capacity of workers themselves to own their own union and support it."

McCullough later tried to persuade Chavez to join the AWOC staff. But by then McDonnell had brought him into contact with a master organizer named Fred Ross who set him out on a far broader path. Ross, tall, spare, quietly but deeply dedicated, began working with migrants in the same year that the Chavez family left Arizona to join the migrant stream. Ross worked with the federal government's Farm Security Administration and then, living in near-poverty himself, with such private organizations as the American Friends Service Committee in a variety of projects among the poor in urban and rural areas.

Saul Alinsky, who had created the Industrial Areas Foundation in Chicago and similar organizations elsewhere to help the poor organize themselves, hired Ross in 1952 to help carry out the program in California, through a new group called the Community Services Organization, or CSO. Ross began organizing Mexican-Americans into political blocs that could demand improvements in the woefully inadequate community services provided them. Once those in a particular community were strong enough to run their own CSO chapter, Ross moved on to another community. The basic premise, that self-organization was the key to social change, appealed strongly to McDonnell, and when Ross appeared in San Jose, McDonnell suggested that Chavez might be a valuable helper.

But though Chavez might also support the CSO premise, he distrusted "this *gringo*," as he called Ross; he might be yet another of those pesty sociologists who were always trying to document the Mexican-American's poverty. Ross had to call at Chavez' house in Sal Si Puedes three times before Chavez would talk with him; and even then, Chavez wasn't sure. He finally agreed to arrange a meeting between Ross and barrio residents, but mainly to subject the gringo to the heckling of his equally suspicious neighbors. There was very little heckling, however; for Chavez quickly discovered that Ross "was making a lot of sense . . . that this man was not like the other Anglos; when he discussed our troubles he did not lie or minimize.

He told the truth, and we all recognized it as the truth. . . . He knew the problems as well as we did."

Soon Chavez was serving as a CSO volunteer, first at night after working all day in the apricot groves at 48 cents an hour, then full time while drawing unemployment benefits. Chavez signed up more than 4000 barrio residents in a voter registration drive and helped others become citizens so they also could vote. He worked closely with Ross, "observing the things Fred did, because I wanted to organize. . . . I was impressed by his patience and understanding of people . . . this was a tool, one of the greatest things he had."

Ross also was impressed, by what he saw as Chavez' drive and enthusiasm, deep commitment and attention to details, his "good sense about people" and, especially, "the intensity of his loyalty to the Mexican poor." Ross convinced Alinsky to hire Chavez as a CSO organizer at $275 a month, took him on an organizing tour of outlying farm areas, and then assigned him to a CSO chapter in the nearby community of Decoto.

Chavez' first big test came shortly afterward when he was assigned to Oakland, a large industrial city in the East Bay Area across from San Francisco. Chavez arrived fresh from the fields, a slightly built twenty-five-year-old who looked closer to seventeen, standing only five-foot-six, shy, quiet-spoken—and *damned* frightened. But he walked the streets of the city, talking to Mexican-Americans who couldn't find work, who couldn't read or write, who didn't vote, who needed medical care. He organized house meetings, trying to reach these suspicious strangers through genuine concern and understanding, boyish humor and simplicity, trying to convince them that they must "start pushing themselves, on their own initiative." Chavez worked very hard at it. He tape-recorded meetings, playing back the tapes to discover just what it was that had made the people laugh, "why they were for one thing and against another." But though he learned some valuable lessons, Chavez remained uneasy in the barrios of industrial Oakland. After four months, he returned to the fields, registering Mexican-American voters throughout the San Joaquin Valley, organizing classes in citizenship and naturalization, setting up CSO chapters, and helping the Spanish-speaking deal with indifferent government bureaucracies they neither understood nor trusted. Chavez helped bail people out of jail, helped them get welfare payments and driver licenses, helped settle their immigration status.

Chavez worked in the valley for five years, but his most dramatic work was in southern California, with CSO members who worked in the citrus groves around Oxnard in the Los Angeles area. Braceros had taken many of the citrus jobs, depressing pay to as low as 80 cents an hour and forcing many local workers into the area's carrot fields, where pay had always been even lower. Chavez, armed with a $20,000 grant from the Packinghouse Workers Union, moved into the area in 1958 to try to get the citrus jobs back for the local workers. They could not be hired without first getting dispatch slips from the state's Farm Placement office and presenting them to members of the local growers' association. But the state office was in Ventura, twelve miles from the fields, and it didn't open until 8 a.m. By the time local workers got dispatch slips and returned, braceros had been assigned to most of the citrus jobs, since local workers had not been available when the morning picking started. Growers were then free to meet their obligation to the state by hiring those with dispatch slips for work in their carrot fields. Chavez found that even those local workers who managed to get citrus jobs were subjected to pressures that frequently forced them to quit or be fired, for not keeping up with the exceptionally fast pace set by young braceros on grower orders.

CSO members filed more than 1000 formal complaints with the state, and Chavez took crews of local workers into the groves for sit-ins, calling in reporters and Labor Department inspectors to witness this evidence that local workers *were available*. Growers sometimes did fire braceros on orders of the federal inspectors and replace them with local workers, only to return to bracero labor after the inspectors were gone. After four months, however, the pressures forced the placement service to open an office much nearer to Oxnard. Then Chavez turned to the sort of media demonstration that would become one of his primary tactics in later years. Workers marched from Oxnard to the new placement office, got job dispatch slips and then piled them up for burning in front of newspaper photographers and television cameramen who had been alerted to the demonstration.

That convinced the state to agree that workers could be hired by the growers directly, at the edge of the fields. Chavez then set up what amounted to a hiring hall nearby, dispatching CSO members much as the state had, often at the request of growers who were compelled to raise pay by as much as 20 cents an hour now that braceros were not readily available. The campaign created something that might have been built into a genuine farm workers' union. But CSO's directors ordered Chavez to turn the operation over to the Packinghouse Workers, and the union let it die.

Yet, while not interested in operating a union, the CSO directors were extremely interested in the leadership qualities Chavez had displayed. They immediately called him to Los Angeles to become the CSO's general director, overseeing twenty-two chapters in California and Arizona. The CSO also hired an assistant director, Dolores Huerta, the former AWOC organizer who was working in the Stockton area with Fred Ross; and that marked the beginning of a collaboration that would have a profound impact on agricultural union organizing.

Huerta shared Chavez' belief in "grass roots organizing with a vengeance," and generally agreed on tactics. But where Chavez was shy, she was bold and outspoken. She had to be if she was to assume the leadership to which her commitment had drawn her. Mexican-American men did not easily grant leadership to women, most certainly not to frail, beautiful women like Huerta. She was less than five feet tall; straight, jet-black hair drawn back from high, Indian cheekbones draped to her shoulders; she had large, deep brown eyes. But Huerta was frail only in appearance and, if not entirely indifferent to her beauty, single-mindedly dedicated to doing the work she felt to be utterly essential, whatever the cultural imperatives to the contrary. Besides, when she was a child her mother had been divorced, "so I never really understood what it meant to take a back seat to a man."

Huerta's family also had been in farm work, but after the divorce, she, her mother and three brothers and sisters ran a small hotel in Stockton. Huerta left at eighteen in 1948 for the first of three marriages, bearing the first of ten children before also going through a divorce and entering college in Stockton. Huerta earned a teaching credential, but scarcely used it. She had met Father McCullough while doing Catholic charity work; that led to her work in the short-lived Agricultural Workers Association, her brief affiliation with AWOC and a decisive association with Ross. It was he who finally convinced her "that the status quo *could be changed.*"

Huerta was not particularly impressed with Chavez when Ross introduced them in 1955, but impressed enough to be persuaded to become his chief aide four years later. Chavez would quarrel with her frequently; that was inevitable, given Huerta's temperament and the harsh discipline Chavez imposed on himself and his close associates. But they were always headed in the same direction, and though Chavez was not wholly immune to the Mexican ideal of male supremacy, he was not the traditional *macho* leader by any means, and he marveled at Huerta for being "physically, spiritually and psychologically fearless . . . absolutely."

Huerta was assigned to the state capitol in Sacramento as the CSO's full-time lobbyist. It was an unfamiliar task, but during two years in

Sacramento Huerta helped push through an impressive amount of legislation. She was instrumental in passage of bills that extended social insurance coverage to farm workers and aliens, liberalized welfare benefits and, among other matters, required that drivers' examinations be given in Spanish as well as English.

But Huerta soon realized that legislation "could not solve the real problem" of Mexican-Americans. Many of them were poverty-stricken farm workers, and what they needed was not government aid passed down from above to try to ease their poverty, but some way to escape that poverty. The way out, Huerta concluded, was farm labor organizing.

Chavez had reached the same conclusion, and assumed the CSO would move in that direction as a natural outgrowth of its early work among the Mexican-American poor in farm communities. In meeting after meeting, Chavez pleaded for "action, not just legislation." But the CSO's board of directors showed no more interest than when it had abandoned the promising organizing base Chavez had established in the citrus groves before becoming general director. The organization continued moving in another direction, in accord with the concerns of the professional and semiprofessional people who had come to dominate the CSO. They preferred projects such as registering urban Mexican-American voters who would elect Spanish-speaking Democrats to help Huerta press for legislative reforms in Sacramento.

Finally, Chavez presented a formal proposal for an organizing campaign at the CSO's statewide convention in 1962. When the plan was rejected, Chavez rose from his chair and unemotionally announced, "I resign." Chavez had been the CSO's general director for two and a half years, an organizer for seven and a half years before that and, as he later recalled, "I was heartbroken—the CSO was my school, where I learned how to organize."

The CSO, Chavez was certain, had become "too middle class," too urban an organization. The CSO's members "didn't have the heart and courage that were necessary if something was to be done for farm workers. They said it was not their problem; that it should be done by labor—but labor wasn't doing it."

Chavez was determined to return to the fields, to work among *his* people. "I really wanted to organize," he said. "I felt that if I didn't try, I couldn't live with myself. And I think I'd learned my lessons; I had a real lot of confidence." AWOC quickly offered Chavez an organizer's job, but he was planning his own campaign.

Huerta remained behind in the CSO, but soon she joined Chavez in the fields, along with another of his CSO aides, Gilbert Padilla.

Like Chavez and Huerta, Padilla was in his early thirties at the time, a thin, curly-haired, mustachioed man with a deceptively casual manner. Chavez had met Padilla in 1957 when Padilla was working as a foreman in the San Joaquin Valley's cotton fields, and had brought him into the CSO's leadership four years later. Padilla also became a key leader of the farm labor movement that was beginning to germinate. He left most of the speechmaking to Chavez and Huerta, but he, too, would become skilled at improvising tactics and gaining the trust and support of farm workers. Padilla and his parents had been migrants most of their lives, and his plain words made clear to farm workers that he *felt* their problems and had realistic plans to try to overcome them.

Chavez decided to center his organizing activities in Delano, where his wife Helen had been raised and where his brother Richard was working regularly as a carpenter. The $1200 Chavez had saved from his $7200-a-year salary as the CSO's general director wouldn't last long with eight children to feed, and Richard's presence was assurance that his family would always have food and shelter. Chavez worked briefly with his wife and eldest son Fernando in the local fields, but only until he had laid out a rudimentary program for a new organization he called the Farm Workers Association.

The term "association" was chosen carefully. A union would arouse the suspicion and probable opposition of growers, workers and AWOC officers alike. It might someday become a union, but only after Chavez built a solid foundation—slowly, cautiously and quietly. "You cannot build a union," he believed, "until the members who must do the real work understand what all this means, what kinds of acts are involved. They must, first, be able to articulate their own hopes and goals."

Chavez drew a map encompassing eighty-six farming towns scattered over the San Joaquin Valley between the Delano area and Stockton 200 miles to the north, climbed into a battered 1953 Mercury station wagon and set out to enlist "a small nucleus" of members for his FWA. Because of the nature of the organization, he would seek membership from whole families rather than individual workers. The families, which often worked as units, also would be treated as single dues-paying units. Chavez traveled the valley towns for six months, sometimes in company with his brother, his cousin Manuel, his three-year-old son "Birdie" and Huerta.

The FWA organizers passed out thousands of questionnaires that asked farm workers what *they* wanted and explained that the FWA "is a group of workers who have come together for the purpose of conducting a survey among farm workers. . . . This is not a union and we are not involved in STRIKES." The FWA's recruiting literature carried out this theme. Appeals were not based on the dogma of organized labor, which was considered foreign and suspect in the fields. They relied, rather, on the Roman Catholic Church. It was the one institution that was known and supported by virtually all of the workers and by many of their employers. The FWA's original "Statement of Purpose" was largely an explanation that the organization was following the encyclicals of Pope John XXIII, which praised farm workers and their efforts to organize. The statement spoke not of labor-management confrontation, but of "our desire to work together with all Christians under the guidance of conscience and right reason, to create to a high degree that just economic order which we believe all Christians desire."

Nevertheless, only about 100 workers responded to the FWA's questionnaires. Their Church might have become more liberal under recent Popes but, just as in Mexico, they continued to accept whatever the *patron* chose to give them. *It had always been that way.* Even those who returned questionnaires asked for no more than 10 to 25 cents an hour more in pay that ranged from 90 cents to $1.15 an hour, and such simple amenities as fresh drinking water on the job.

Chavez went to those who responded, to begin "educating them on the importance of organizing." He used techniques he had learned in the CSO, talking endlessly with them in the fields, in small grocery stores and in house meetings and cafes at night. What were their real needs and desires? How far would they venture in trying to meet them? What were the possibilities? What actions did they fear? How many people would *they* organize?

There was no deep philosophizing, no appeals to prominent community leaders or any other outsiders, no publicity—just a lot of hard talking to individual farm workers and small groups of workers. Chavez operated basically on the theory that "the main thing in convincing someone is to spend time with him . . . and the harder a guy is to convince, the better leader or member he becomes. When you exert yourself to convince him, you have his confidence and he has good motivation."

The FWA organizers taught by example as well. They demonstrated the value of organization by performing personal services, as the CSO had done in rural areas. Among other things, lawyers were found to help workers press wage claims, organizers helped them appeal traffic tickets and translated for them in court.

It was quite true, as Chavez repeatedly told the farm workers, that they would have to sacrifice if they were to build their own organization. Sacrifice was their only weapon; it was their substitute for money. They worked very hard all day, and had very little money. But the organizers also worked all day, often all night. They, too, had little money—so little they frequently had to turn to members for food, lodging and gasoline. Chavez himself had turned down the $22,000-a-year salary the Peace Corps offered him to become a regional director in Central America, and he insisted that the FWA accept no outside funds, including a $50,000 grant that had been offered by an admirer from the CSO days. It was crucial that farm workers rely solely on themselves at the start and build only as fast as their own resources would allow; otherwise, the organization would "get too far ahead of the people it belongs to."

FWA dues were purposely set at a relatively high figure of $3.50 a month, and regular payment was demanded as a condition of membership. Chavez' savings were going fast, and the FWA had almost no funds; but Chavez was seeking commitment more than financing, and was certain, in any case, that no amount of money could ever organize the poor. It required genuine sacrifice for farm workers to pay the dues, but precisely because of that, they would feel themselves an important part of the organization with the right to demand service, and with a deeply vested interest in its activities. Collecting the dues became a painful necessity to Chavez:

I went to a worker's home in McFarland, seven miles south of Delano. It was in the evening. It was raining and it was winter. And there was no work. I knew it. And everyone knew it. As I knocked on the door, the guy in the little two-room house was going to the store with a $5 bill to get groceries. And there I was. He owed $7 because he was one full month behind plus the current one. So I'd come for $7. But all he had was $5. I had to make a decision. Should I take $3.50 or shouldn't I? It was very difficult. Up to this time I had been saying, "They should be paying. And if they don't pay they'll never have a union." $3.50 worth of food wasn't really going to change his life one way or the other that much. So I told him, "You have to pay at least $3.50 right now or I'll have to put you out of the union." He gave me the $5. We went to the store and changed the $5 bill. I got the $3.50 and gave him the $1.50. I stayed with him. He bought $1.50 worth of groceries and went home.

Chavez said the experience "hurt me, but it also strengthened my determination. If this man was willing to give me $3.50 on a dream, when we were really taking the money out of his own food, then why shouldn't we be able to have a union—however difficult. . . . With the kind of faith this farm worker had, *why couldn't we have a union?*"

The organization was formalized later in that first year of 1962, at a convention that drew about 300 delegates—virtually the FWA's entire membership—to Fresno, in the heart of the valley. They elected Chavez director and Huerta and Padilla as vice-presidents. The most dramatic moment came when Manuel Chavez jumped to the stage, grabbed at a large piece of wrapping paper on the wall and unveiled a sixteen-by-twenty-four-foot banner. It was a symbol that was to become world famous—a red flag with a stylized black Aztec eagle in the center. Chavez wanted "to get some color into the movement, to give people something they could identify with." He turned to ancient history for a color combination the Egyptians had found to "crash into your eyes like nothing else"; chose a symbol of Mexico for the emblem, and had Manuel draw it with straight edges simply because his cousin had difficulty drawing it any other way.

"When that damn eagle flies," Manuel roared, "the problems of the farm workers will be solved!"

The farm workers were not ready to hoist their banner over a union yet, however. They had other priorities. As Padilla noted, "People didn't even have money for a decent burial." So a $1000 burial insurance program would come first, then a credit union to provide the low-interest loans that Anglo banks denied farm workers, and a cooperative so they could buy parts and tires for the broken-down autos that carried them to and from the fields.

That was almost more than the fledgling organization could handle. There was nearly a complete turnover in membership before the year ended, and by June of 1963, only twelve families remained, half of them related to FWA officers. But house meetings and other organizing efforts continued, and by 1964, the FWA had signed up 1000 families in seven counties. It was enough to make the FWA self-supporting, pay Chavez and Huerta $50 a week each, put Helen Chavez to work running the credit union full time at $40 a week, and prompt an ambitious name change. From now on, it would be the *National* Farm Workers Association, or NFWA.

Once the NFWA members put together a basic organization on their own, they began attracting outsiders, and Chavez sought and accepted their aid as long as it would be used in accord with the NFWA's precepts or under the NFWA's direct control. The most important outside help came initially from the Migrant Ministry, an arm of the National Council of Churches—a Protestant rather than Catholic organization. Growers had become wary of the expanding NFWA, and most of the valley's Catholic prelates and many priests were hesitant to risk offending such prominent financial supporters by aiding the organization. Their reluctance was shared by many local Protestant ministers, who also feared losing support. But Chris Hartmire, the eloquent young director of the Migrant Ministry, had no local congregation to worry him, and he saw the NFWA as an ideal vehicle to effectively carry out the task of helping farm workers which the Migrant Ministry had begun in 1920.

The Ministry operated child care centers, clinics, day schools and other educational and recreational programs, counseled farm workers, supplied emergency food and clothing, and lobbied for laws to improve living and working conditions. Hartmire, however, felt such charitable service was peripheral; it skirted the workers' central need to provide the services themselves. Hartmire based his activities on a belief that "farm workers want to be organized so they can have enough power to change their situation. They will not long tolerate programs that either evade the issue of power or get in the way of organizing." This meant the Migrant Ministry would have to join in an attack against growers—"men like us who happen to have too much power over the lives of their workers."

Hartmire's position drew heated opposition from the growers' ministerial and lay allies in local churches and repeated attempts to curtail, if not halt, the Migrant Ministry's activities. But though the Council of Churches did not provide major financial aid, it did give Hartmire a relatively free hand, and he was able to raise operating funds from a wide range of supporters in California and other states.

There was good reason for similarity in the views of Hartmire and the NFWA officers. He had been sharing their experiences since 1959, when he came to Stockton from the Union Theological Seminary in New York City to study community development. Hartmire worked with Chavez and Fred Ross in their CSO projects, lived in the small hotel operated by the Huerta family, and by the time he was named director of the Migrant Ministry in 1961, he was determined to move it in new directions. Hartmire sent some of the Migrant Ministry staff to study with Saul Alinsky in Chicago and readily hired a fellow seminarian, Jim Drake, who shared his views. Drake, a chunky, intense young man who was raised in one of California's major agricultural areas, was working nearby in a farm worker support project for the United Church of Christ, and he was eager to become involved more directly. So Hartmire assigned him to the NFWA, where Drake became the first of a series of youthful administrative assistants who served Chavez.

By 1964, the activities of the Migrant Ministry and the NFWA were virtually inseparable. In addition to paying Drake's salary as an NFWA staff member, the Ministry hired Padilla that year to work

with Drake and others on a community organizing project in Tulare
County, just a few miles north of Chavez' Kern County headquarters
in Delano, that was designed to bring new members into the NFWA.

The organizations were reluctantly drawn into strikes by workers
who sought help in getting pay raises at a small grape ranch and in
the commercial rose-growing area south of Delano. Raises were
granted after brief strikes, largely because they involved skilled workers who weren't easily replaced. But the NFWA wasn't strong enough
to demand that growers grant power as well as money by signing
union contracts. That would require a relatively large, securely-based
following with the experience, confidence and material resources to
wage lengthy strikes.

"The workers," said Chavez, "have to strike *and* be prepared to
hold out. I can walk through any field in the valley and start a strike.
It isn't hard. But we want to make it stick. The growers are powerful
and the workers have gotten the attitude of defeat. . . . We're going
to show them they can win."

The NFWA's leaders felt this process would take at least four or
five years and so remained convinced, despite the minor victories, that
they should avoid major strike activity.

The NFWA and the Migrant Ministry nevertheless did conduct a
well-publicized rent strike at a farm labor center operated by Tulare
County's Housing Authority. Ninety-five families of three, four and
more lived there, crammed into windowless wooden shacks, stiflingly
hot in the summer when the sun beat down mercilessly on the tin
roofs, almost unbearably cold in the winter. Water came from outdoor
taps near garbage stands between every fourth cabin; toilets, showers
and laundry tubs were in a grimy communal building.

The center, built by the federal government to give temporary shelter to Dust Bowl Refugees in the late 1930s, was condemned by the
county Health Department in 1965. But instead of closing it immediately, the Housing Authority raised the rents to finance construction
of a new center, demanding $25 a month for the one-room shacks
that had rented for $18. The families, however, continued paying $18
a month—into a trust fund set up by Drake and Padilla. They would
give the money to the Housing Authority only after the rent increase
was rescinded. Padilla led them in a series of demonstrations that attracted civil rights activists and other outside supporters, but did not
move the Housing Authority. It sued the families for the back rent.
After three months, however, the court ruled that the increase had
been imposed in "bad faith." Rent remained at $18 a month, the trust

fund was turned over to the Housing Authority and the NFWA won some new adherents.

The NFWA sought to strengthen the organization further through the federal government's antipoverty program. Chavez applied for a $500,000 grant from the Office of Economic Opportunity to train twenty NFWA members to conduct classes for their fellow farm workers and to help them in community development. They were to teach and advise workers in matters of personal finance, the rights and responsibilities of citizenship, developing such community projects as sewer and water systems, and also to set up a cooperative store and a garage where workers could learn to repair their own cars.

Part of the grant was approved by OEO Director R. Sargent Shriver, but the NFWA was denied use of the grant and the opportunity to build slowly outside the arena of labor-management conflict. A resurgence of activity by the Agricultural Workers Organizing Committee would force the NFWA into the most important strike in farm labor history.

8

"Strike or Crawl"

The Agricultural Workers Organizing Committee was virtually dormant, but did have several Filipino organizers who maintained close relations with the tightly knit crews of Filipinos who worked in major farm areas. The crews were composed mainly of the men, now aging bachelors, who had been lured to the state three decades earlier with the promise of work that would enable them to escape poverty in the Philippine Islands. Many had expected to earn enough to return home in a few years, others to establish families here by sending to the islands for brides or by marrying local women. But their lack of non-agricultural skills confined them to low-paying farm work, and discriminatory laws and practices limited the immigration of Filipino women, prohibited them from marrying Caucasians, kept them from buying land and barred them from integrating into the community at large. It made them among the most isolated of those groups of isolated foreign workers favored by California growers; but it also caused them to draw closely together.

The Filipinos lived together in farm labor camps that became their own well-organized communities. They formed extremely efficient work crews, directed by their own leaders, to travel the state doing the most highly skilled work in several crops. At times, they had formed their own unions, forcing concessions from growers who relied heavily on their skills and ability to outproduce most other crews.

The Filipino crews included a group based in Delano, which worked almost year-round in the vineyards, picking grapes as well as doing much of the specially skilled work of pruning and vine tying that preceded the harvest. The harvesting season for grapes was short; but growers, who often operated vineyards in several areas, planted them so they would mature at different times in different places, to assure them of an adequate work force and the highest possible market price. The picking season began in May, in the Coachella Valley, about 100 miles from Mexico. When those grapes were picked, the Filipino crews and others moved north to other vineyards as the later-maturing grapes became ready, finally ending up in the vineyards around Delano in September. The Coachella growers were under pressure to get their crop out quickly, before grapes in the other areas could mature, and they frequently called for braceros to speed the work.

The growers were under particularly heavy pressure in 1965 because of weather conditions that were causing grapes in northern vineyards to mature unusually early. The federal government had ruled, however, that growers could not qualify for Mexican help unless they offered domestic workers at least the $1.40 an hour they were required to pay the braceros. That was 15 cents more an hour than growers offered the Filipino crews when the Coachella season started. So the Filipinos demanded $1.40 an hour, and when the growers resisted, they struck under the AWOC banner. Unable to qualify for braceros to fill in for striking crews and anticipating they would want supplemental Mexican help later in the season, growers were forced to agree to the strikers' pay demands within ten days.

The Filipinos carried their pay demand north to the 400 square miles of rich vineyards that fanned out from Delano through northern Kern and southern Tulare counties. But braceros generally were not employed in this area; there was usually an abundance of poor, locally based pickers willing to work on the growers' terms. Those terms in September of 1965 were $1.20 to $1.25 an hour plus 10 to 15 cents for each box of grapes picked, *take it or leave it.* There were about 1500 Filipino workers, and they were an important part of the growers' work force; but they were critically needed only during preharvest operations. Should the Filipino crews strike over their demand for a base of $1.40 an hour, growers were confident they could find more than enough extra pickers among the 3500 Mexican-Americans in the harvest work force.

The growers easily forced the Filipinos back to work on the growers' terms after a brief strike in the Arvin vineyards, just south of Delano, and were certain they could do the same in the Delano area. Growers had an additional advantage there; the labor camps in which the Filipinos lived were their winter homes, located inside the vineyards and owned by the growers. The Filipinos decided to strike nevertheless, and called in Larry Itliong, the AWOC organizer who had led them in the Coachella Valley strike and who had been organizing in the Delano area for the past five years. Itliong was reluctant, but willing to help; for he understood the deep anger and frustration that motivated his fellow Filipinos. "They are getting older," he noted. "They

have been here in this country for a number of years and they had not
got anything to show for their labor, so what have they got to lose?"

Itliong, a short, wiry man toughened by years of organizing, had
come here himself in 1929 as a fifteen-year-old immigrant from the
Philippines, where his father operated a small farm. He lost three fingers from his right hand while working on a railroad siding, turned
to farm work and within a year was involved in an unsuccessful tomato pickers' strike in Washington State. After that he worked in the
fields of California, where:

I began to see minority workers being discriminated against in pay, being discriminated against in employment chances and not having any kind
of a right at all. This of course amazed me because while I was in the
Philippines we heard and read about the kind of government that this
country had and the kind of system that the United States has in a lot of
things that are beneficial to its citizenship. But I found out differently; that
if you are in a minority group, you don't have any kind of chance to help
yourself.

So from year to year I traveled all over the state trying to get a job that
I could make money on. In the meantime I had forgotten about going to
school. I never made enough money, and whatever money I made from
one job was not enough for me to live on until I got to the next job.

I learned also that other farm workers have the same kind of problem. I
began to learn the causes of the problems of the farm workers. I learned
that if you do not have any kind of an organization, if you have any complaint, your complaint is going to be heard in one ear and it passes through
the other ear. Like if you said to your employer that you wanted some
cold water while you are working for him during the hot season, he was
going to tell you that you must bring your own jug, he has no time to bring
any water to you.

Itliong did not have Chavez' intellectual and philosophical bent,
nor his deep distrust of outside unions and their orthodox tactics. But
he was as convinced as Chavez of the need for union organization,
and the depth of his conviction made Itliong a natural leader among
the Filipinos. He began trying to organize them as early as 1933, when
he worked with radical organizers in the Salinas Valley. He continued
to work in the fields, in canneries, aboard fishing boats and at a variety
of odd jobs up and down the West Coast; but he also worked as an
organizer periodically, notably among cannery workers in Alaska and
southern California. He was working in Stockton when AWOC got
under way and the former CIO men who ran AWOC readily hired
Itliong to try to organize the numerous crews of Filipinos in the area's
asparagus fields, and to work among Filipino workers generally.

The strike Itliong led in Delano for AWOC began more as a sit-in.

Despite their anger, the Filipinos were reluctant to picket the property where some of them had lived and worked for as long as thirty years, and to risk losing their homes for doing so. They simply stayed in the grower-owned camps at ten vineyards and refused to report for work.

How many actually took part in the work stoppage was never clear. Their employers, at any rate, refused to consider their demands. It didn't matter to the growers that the Filipinos had worked for them for decades without raising a serious complaint; that they had been "our boys," as the growers were fond of calling them. Nor did it matter that they were seeking no more than a pay raise of 15 to 20 cents. The growers would not negotiate with Itliong. Instead, they ordered the Filipinos to report to work or leave the camps. Those who ignored the order were forced out, their belongings piled on the roadways.

"One day they cut off the water, then the electricity and then, in another two days, the gas, and we had to cook outside," as one camp resident recalled. "Then they padlocked the doors and we had to sleep under the trees. . . ."

Some of the protesting Filipinos gave in to the pressure and returned to work. Others began picketing—up to 1200 by AWOC's reckoning; "a few hundred," according to growers. No striker picketed the particular vineyard where he worked, however; they still feared confronting their bosses directly.

The growers refused to publicly acknowledge the existence of a strike. They recruited Mexican-Americans to replace the strikers and continued the harvest uninterrupted, certain the picket lines would disappear within a few weeks for lack of support. Despite Itliong's activities, AWOC's primary interest was not in conducting strikes, but in adding to its dues-paying membership by organizing labor contractors in the area near AWOC's headquarters in Stockton, far north of Delano. Growers relied as well on animosity between Mexican-American and Filipino workers, caused in large part by the growers' practice of setting up separate camps and work crews for various racial and ethnic groups. It was a calculated attempt to keep the work force divided, and, as an AWOC strike leader noted, it fostered "suspicions, fear and racial hatred."

Chavez, however, didn't hesitate when Itliong asked him for help. The NFWA wasn't prepared to strike, but neither would it play the growers' game of divide and conquer. Three days after the AWOC strike started, the NFWA circulated leaflets urging its Mexican-American members to honor the picket lines. Yet if they weren't to work, Chavez and his members asked themselves, why shouldn't they make demands of their own? Their pay and working conditions were no better than those of the Filipinos, their aspirations no lower. If the Filipinos won, all workers would win; if they lost, it would strengthen the growers' power over everyone. Five days later, the NFWA's members did the inevitable. They voted unanimously to strike.

Nearly 1500 men, women and children crammed into every corner of a parish hall in Delano for the decision. The NFWA had only $87 in its treasury, was not at all certain AWOC would get AFL-CIO support for a prolonged strike, and Chavez, at least, remained convinced that his organization should put down deeper roots before striking. But circumstances forced the NFWA to toss aside its timetable. Chavez did not understate the enormous task ahead; but, whatever the odds, he believed the NFWA's members were now faced with "striking or crawling."

Emotions were high. The strike meeting was quite purposely called on Mexican Independence Day, and workers jumped up, one after another, to voice heated, excited words that linked their cause to that which had freed Mexico from Spain 145 years earlier. Others invoked the saints whose statues filled niches in the hall around them. But though they drew their inspiration from the revolutionary and religious traditions of the Mexican poor, they would draw on the decidedly non-Mexican tradition of nonviolence for their major weapon. Chavez insisted on it. Violence would subject the farm workers to counterviolence from overwhelmingly powerful opponents who could easily crush them, but who would be far less able to cope with nonviolent tactics. Chavez himself wasn't sure just what these tactics should be, but he knew that if the farm workers could not turn to violent methods, they would of necessity develop effective alternatives. If they were to win anything, Chavez felt, it would take at least ten years, and the use of nonviolence would give them the strength essential to wage such a lengthy struggle. It would force them to work hard, to master themselves, to be "resourceful, creative—and patient." The use of nonviolence also would give the farm workers a moral base to attract the outside support they desperately needed.

Chavez went first to AWOC to propose a joint strike. But Al Green was still running the AFL-CIO group, and he distrusted the unorthodox tactics of "that Mexican," as he frequently called Chavez. The distrust was mutual, and Chavez asked Green at least to sign an agreement that AWOC would not try to recruit NFWA members. Green wouldn't even agree to that; but, at Itliong's urging, he did agree that NFWA members and their families could eat at a commissary the AFL-CIO had set up for AWOC strikers. AWOC's members also got strike benefits from AFL-CIO sources, but the NFWA, of course, would have to get its financing elsewhere.

Green's refusal to agree to a joint operation meant there would be two strikes. AWOC would continue picketing the ten vineyards it had struck; the NFWA would honor the picket lines and call its own strike against the area's thirty other major grape growers. Chavez sent letters and telegrams asking each of the thirty growers to negotiate contracts that would set minimum pay at $1.40 an hour and cover "all the other conditions of work for your employees." A representative of the state Conciliation Service and a local priest also brought Chavez' request to the growers. But none of the growers would negotiate with anyone.

The NFWA had an advantage over those who had called strikes in other crops. The growers' system of bringing grapes to maturity at varying periods and the nature of grape cultivation itself provided greater work opportunities in the vineyards. Their employees generally were more skilled, earned more money and were less migratory than other farm workers. The vineyard workers' relative stability, in fact, is what had attracted Chavez to them as an organizing base, and it was the main reason for the willingness of those in the NFWA to strike; they could feel the pressure of rising expectations that precedes social movements.

Even so, vineyard workers were still living in poverty, at average family incomes of no more than $2000 to $2300 a year; there were thousands who still would not even consider the great financial risk of striking—especially not in this part of the season, when piece-rate payments for picking brought in the greater part of their income. Even the NFWA claimed no more than 1100 adherents. Hence, growers felt they could ignore the union demands; even if the strikers could somehow manage to hold out for an extended period, there would be plenty of other workers to take their places.

The growers had the usual trappings of the wealthy—large comfortable homes, luxury cars, private airplanes, sons and daughters in private colleges. But they were proud, hard-working men who usually managed and often worked in their own vineyards, packing and processing plants, cold storage facilities and distribution systems. They could not accept the idea that the hired hands should have a voice in the businesses they personally operated; that was strictly a family matter. Most of the growers had come to the Delano area from southern and eastern Europe in the late 1920s, saved frugally, bought parcels of cheap, parched land and laboriously brought sparse quantities of water up from far underground to grow their grapes. Their years of

hard work were rewarded in 1951 when subsidized federal water began pouring into the area through the Friant-Kern Canal; the irrigation water cost $700 an acre-foot to deliver, but the growers were
charged only $123 an acre-foot.

But though the growers now controlled a $175-million-a-year in-
dustry, they truly had come from rags to riches. John Giumarra Jr.
spoke proudly, for instance, of how his family had built the largest
of the vineyard operations, a 12,000-acre complex that grossed $5.5
million to $7.5 million annually:

Joe, my three other uncles and my father came over from Sicily—it was
right after the first war. It was bad, believe me. The Italian government
needed money—foreign credit and that sort of thing. Confiscated everything. Even my grandmother's wedding ring—really! They started a little
fruit stand in L.A. Sold what they grew up here—all through the Depression. Then . . . well, there's eleven Giumarra families around here now,
all of them on this farm. Over fifty people, and they all work here, every
day. Except the kids, of course. They're in school.

Strikers pictured the growers as devils. They weren't really evil,
but they were quaintly out of touch with what had been going on in
urban industrial areas beyond the vineyards since they had moved in
beside the Mexican-Americans. They seemed sincerely perplexed that
anyone would suggest farm workers needed—or wanted—anything
but what the *patron* granted them. The growers hadn't needed a union;
they had only needed a chance to work hard. Besides, the growers asserted, they were providing the best they could for their employees.
They might be running multimillion-dollar corporations now, but they
claimed to operate on the smallest of margins. Some of the growers
were heavily mortgaged as well, and a few were on the verge of bankruptcy.

What the growers' precise financial position was, or what they
thought or said, however, was really beside the point in this struggle.
What counted was that they had power. They owned all the land; they
were the economic pillars of the community. Their money kept
churches, schools and local businesses going; they helped finance the
campaigns of local politicians and law enforcement officials; their
operations were secured by financial institutions that resisted any
change that might upset their mutually profitable arrangements with
growers. The growers met regularly with the people who ran Delano,
over lunch, drinks or dinner at the Elks Club, in the *right* part of the
nondescript little town of 12,000, across the Southern Pacific tracks
from the run-down section where most of the Mexican-Americans
lived in small, crumbling houses. Naturally, the dominant Anglo com-

munity shared the growers' views, and backed them wholeheartedly. The Migrant Ministry might be working with Chavez, but Delano's Ministerial Association was quick to proclaim that it "does not encourage demonstration or interference in the farm labor situation." Local newspapers carried stories and editorials supporting the growers. Even the local CSO chapter sided with them; the merchants and labor contractors among its members made certain of that.

But the growers were not patient men, nor capable of subtle tactics. They were *damned* irritated at the gadfly pickets who marched outside their vineyards waving red and black flags, calling them names and shouting words that might encourage nonstriking workers to join the walkout. The growers would not sit idle, awaiting realization of their prediction that the strike would swiftly disappear. *They* were the masters, and they meant to prove it openly.

Red-faced with anger, growers in neatly pressed khaki trousers paced restlessly at the borders of the vineyards, kicking at the blackish dirt with sturdy boots as pickets circled before them. The pickets were indistinguishable in appearance from the workers behind the growers —dark, sinewy men in faded jeans and denim shirts, chubby women in loose blouses and slacks, faded red kerchiefs knotted around their necks or pulled about their faces protectively, floppy straw sombreros shading them from the blazing sun in which they worked amid swarms of gnats. They moved steadily through endless rows of eye-level vines heavy with grapes in dusty hues of red, green and blue—Thompsons, Ridieres, Carrignanes, Palominos and a dozen other varieties destined for the dinner table or winepress. The workers would stoop down, deftly unburden a vine with a quick snap of metal clippers, plop the grapes into a garishly labeled wooden box and move on to the next vine, feigning indifference or smiling weakly as pickets demanded that they, too, join *la huelga*. The words came at them in rapid Spanish and English, sometimes through battery-powered bullhorns or loudspeakers.

"Why do you work for so little money? A dollar and a quarter? We can get you a dollar-forty! Don't be a scab! Join your friends! Come! Come! Strike!"

"You—you with the stringy hair—come here and hear what I've got to say! *Si, usted!* You want to be a slave all your life? We're trying to help you people get decent wages. Come out here and listen to us! What has the grower ever done for you? Does he invite you to his house? Wipe that stupid look off your face and come out here!"

The stronger invective often was delivered by the women pickets whose presence helped keep the NFWA from taking violent action.

This is not to say that frustrated pickets didn't sometimes toss rocks as well as epithets. One even broke a grower's leg by sideswiping him with a truck. But the incidents of picket violence were relatively few. Not many of the NFWA's members had ever been in a strike before, but they generally heeded the NFWA's mimeographed sheet of picketing instructions, which began with an admonition that "this is a nonviolent strike."

Growers were under no such constraint. They provoked, angrily shoved and sometimes beat pickets who came close to the "no trespassing" signs. Growers climbed into shiny pickup trucks, shotguns on the seats beside them, and drove furiously along the property lines, daring pickets to cross, covering them with blinding clouds of dust, sometimes with sulphur spray supposedly meant for roadside vines. Truck radios were turned up full blast to drown out the pickets, or workers were moved far inside the vineyards. Growers got court orders to limit the number of pickets, even to prohibit them from shouting the words they tried to keep the nonstrikers from hearing. Then they called in armed private guards and masses of police and sheriff's deputies to enforce the orders and harass pickets.

The growers played right into Chavez' hands. The growers' control of the local power structure made it impossible for strikers to rely on local sources for what they *had to have* to keep the growers' prediction of quick failure from coming true. Financing, manpower, and pressure would have to come from outside the vineyard area. What better way to attract it than to be the nonviolent underdog in a struggle for modest demands against an opponent who insisted on acting like an all-powerful bully? This was the day of the student, civil rights and peace movements, of the War on Poverty, and strikers won active support from a remarkable variety of outsiders, ranging from political radicals to orthodox trade unionists, from self-conscious champions of the "working class" to middle-class housewives, from avowed atheists to clerics. The supporters saw the strike as a demand for equal opportunity, free of the ideological motivation that would have divided them, and part of their own battles against society's power structure.

The outsiders flocked to the vineyards from all over California with money, food and clothing, and new ideas, tactics, influence and technical skills the farm workers lacked. They soon transformed the economic struggle on the isolated back roads of Kern and Tulare counties into a worldwide cause—a civil rights movement with religious overtones as well as a strike.

Growers raised the familiar cry of "outside agitators," and cited the relatively small number of strikers as evidence that their workers really didn't want such help. But the outside agitation, like the strike, was now here to stay.

NFWA representatives and volunteers spent as much time rounding up support at university rallies, church affairs, political gatherings and union meetings in urban areas as they did in manning the picket lines. But activity in Delano was essential to attract the support, and they conducted it in a manner designed to draw maximum public attention.

AWOC conducted some fund-raising drives in Filipino communities outside Delano and engaged in urban demonstrations demanding recall of a Philippines' consul who had made a radio appeal for Filipinos to abandon the strike. But AWOC otherwise operated almost entirely within the strike area, where it relied largely on the orthodox methods of the AFL-CIO. Small groups of regularly assigned pickets were sent from the Filipino Community Hall in Delano to stand with signs in front of vineyards, packing sheds and cold storage plants.

The NFWA's operations were downright disorderly by comparison; but they were fashioned to fit a peculiar situation.

"It's like striking an industrial plant that has a thousand entrance gates and is forty square miles large," noted Terry Cannon, one of the bright young NFWA volunteers. "And if that isn't bad enough, you don't know each morning where the plant will be, or where the gates are, or whether it will be open or closed, or what wages will be offered that day."

Caravans of strikers and volunteers roved the back roads continually, driving anxiously along the black ribbons of pancake-flat asphalt that pointed to the horizon in all directions, hoping to discover just where growers had assigned work crews within the 38,000 acres of struck vineyards. Two priests even took to the air on one occasion, guiding a light plane low over the center of a sprawling vineyard while Chavez spoke through a loudspeaker to nonstrikers working below.

Some of the NFWA cars had two-way radios; but the growers and the police also had radios and airplanes, and it was a rare occurrence when pickets confronted nonstrikers without the intimidating presence of law officers and employers. Undaunted, strikers followed workers home to plead their cause, sometimes none too gently.

Yet the number of strikers remained in the hundreds, the number of workers in the thousands, partly because growers continued to replace strikers as quickly as they left their vineyards, and because many who left did not do so to picket but to work in nonstruck vineyards. There were enough pickets, however, to form the hard core of dedicated members that Chavez required for future success. The picket line became their training ground, where they would make an irrevocable commitment. They learned to speak up, to persuade, to devise strategy and to fight for what they wanted. "A picket line," said Chavez, "forces you to look at life as it is. It is a tremendous educational process to put your job on the line, to force the employer to deal with you . . . the best labor school we could ever have."

The NFWA's operations were centered in a converted grocery store near the city dump at the edge of Delano. The transmission towers of a Voice of America relay station looked down on the dilapidated gray stucco building from across a broad cotton field. The unpainted walls inside were covered with newspaper clippings, photos of pickets and slogans and other inspirational material. Clothing, sleeping bags, empty soft drink and beer bottles were strewn about; cigarette butts littered the floor. Flimsy plywood partitions formed tiny rooms crowded with scarred desks, squeaky mimeograph machines and young ministers and long-haired members of the Student Non-Violent Coordinating Committee, Congress of Racial Equality, Students for a Democratic Society and other activist groups of the 1960s. Newcomers were coming and going constantly. Their work often was self-serving, inefficient and disorganized, and the wild distortions and sometimes outright lies of the single-minded, naive, uninformed and inexperienced partisans among the volunteers could be maddening. But if not always well done, their work was absolutely essential—and frequently exhausting.

"The trouble with this strike," as a typical volunteer from the University of California explained, "is that you have to be up before the workers—and they're out there at five in the morning—then you have to spend the whole day picketing, trying to convince them to come out. . . ." She paused to dip a brush into a jar of poster paint and scrawl the word "HUELGA" across a giant white balloon that had been filled with helium; it would be held high over the vines to attract nonstrikers. "And then," she continued wearily, scrubbing at black paint smeared across her hands and face, "you have to stay up all night figuring what to try next."

Soft sounds of Spanish interspersed the volunteers' conversations as strikers wandered in. Some, evicted from grower housing, were trying to arrange for a place to stay—usually on the floor of someone's house. Others wanted loans from the NFWA's credit union, help finding work outside the strike area or someone to baby-sit while they picketed the next day. Some went out the rear door, across a bumpy dirt lot crowded with the well-worn cars of the young volunteers, and into a pink stucco building filled to the ceiling with canned food, eggs, sacks of beans, rice and flour, and second-hand clothing. They carried scrip, given for picketing or joining the strike, which they exchanged for the food, donated by supporters in Los Angeles and the San Francisco Bay Area.

Chavez presided over all from behind a desk with a bright red Formica top which his brother Richard had put together, wearing a red plaid shirt that had become almost a uniform for him, calmly answering a constantly jangling telephone and giving advice, direction and greetings to those who kept popping in and out of the tiny office. Chavez conceded matter-of-factly that he and those around him might indeed be described as "fanatics." Most of them worked day and night for no more than $5 a week, food and a floor to sleep on, and under NFWA orders "to be servants," as Chavez put it, "with their only objective to help farm workers have a union." Chavez felt that was the only way it could be done; that "the only ones who make things change are fanatics." He couldn't "ask people to sacrifice if I won't sacrifice myself," and neither could the volunteers. "If you don't live the same kind of life as the poor people you are trying to help," asked one volunteer, "why should they trust you?"

Many of the volunteers were attracted by the widespread public attention focused on Delano early in the strike by groups of urban clergymen. They made well-publicized visits to the picket lines with the avowed purpose, as one group declared, of reducing "the possibility of intimidation and violence from growers," and joined the NFWA and Mexican-American legislators in demanding investigation of alleged misconduct by local law enforcement officers.

As if to prove the allegations, the Kern County sheriff and his deputies tried to silence the pickets, on grounds that their words might prompt violence. They arrested a minister and held him in jail for twenty-four hours for reciting Jack London's celebrated "Definition of a Strikebreaker" * to a crew working behind a picket line, because

* "After God had finished the rattlesnake, the toad and the vampire, He had some awful substance left with which He made a strikebreaker. A strikebreaker is a two-legged animal with a corkscrew soul, a water-logged brain and combination backbone made of jelly and glue. Where others have hearts, he carries a tumor of rotten principles. When a strikebreaker comes down the street, men turn their backs and angels weep in Heaven and the devil shuts the gates of Hell to keep him out. No man has a right to scab as long as there is a pool of water to drown his carcass in, or a rope long enough to hang his body with. Judas Iscariot was a gentleman compared to the strikebreaker. For betraying his master, he had character enough to hang himself. A strikebreaker has not. Esau sold his birthright for a mess of pottage. Judas Iscariot sold his savior for thirty pieces of silver. Benedict Arnold sold his country for a promise of a commission in the British Army. The modern strikebreaker sells his birthright, his country, his wife, his children and his fellow men for an unfulfilled promise from his employer, trust or corporation. Esau was a traitor to himself; Judas

London's words were "threatening and vile," and then prohibited pickets from even using the word *huelga*. The NFWA got precisely the attention it sought when deputies arrested forty-four pickets, nineteen ministers and twelve women among them, for chanting *"Huelga"* in front of a vineyard during a "Day of Christian Concern," which was called to test the prohibition. The chief deputy stood before television cameras arguing that the pickets were "disturbing people who were trying to make a living," and thus were guilty of "unlawful assembly." A court later ordered release of the arrested pickets and eventually declared the sheriff's gag order unconstitutional—but not before TV crews had recorded a highly emotional scene of 350 strike supporters kneeling in prayer outside the county courthouse and rising to sing "We Shall Overcome."

Telling evidence that this would not be the usual quickly abandoned farm strike came on a cold December day two months later when Walter Reuther of the Auto Workers Union marched through Delano at the head of a cheering column of strikers, Chavez, Itliong and reporters from all over the country beside him. *"Viva Reuther!"* the marchers shouted *"Viva Reuther!"* The cheers seemed endless; and for good reason. Here was the leader of the country's most powerful industrial union pledging to support these obscure and penniless farm workers "until you've won this strike—as long as it takes!"

Reuther, the most persuasive and dramatic of labor's orators, told them emotionally that "this is not *your* strike; this is *our* strike! We will mobilize every weapon we have and fight back. . . . You are leading history, and we march here together, fight here together, and we will win here together! It may take time, but if we stick together we will eventually gain social and economic justice for the farm worker as we did for workers at Ford, General Motors and other big companies."

Reuther had flown to Delano after adjournment of the AFL-CIO's national convention in San Francisco at the urging of the Auto Workers' regional director, Paul Schrade, the brightest, surely, in the cadre of bright young activists who worked with Reuther. Schrade had pushed through a convention resolution urging "moral and financial" assistance for the strikers, over the indifference of AFL-CIO President Meany and the hostility of the Distillery Workers Union, whose members were threatened by NFWA plans to boycott the wines and liquors of Schenley Industries, which owned one of the struck vineyards.

Iscariot was a traitor to God; Benedict Arnold was a traitor to his country. A strikebreaker is a traitor to his God, his country, his wife, his family and his class."

Schrade tried unsuccessfully to convince Meany himself to come to Delano, but Reuther's presence was enough to accomplish Schrade's main purpose of "putting the strike on the national scene."

Reuther did more than provide publicity and inspiration. His pledge of support included a monthly contribution of $5000 from the Auto Workers and the AFL-CIO's Industrial Union Department, to be split between AWOC and the NFWA. AWOC already was getting more than that through the AFL-CIO's national office, but the NFWA was relying largely on contributions from individual supporters and barely meeting its monthly costs of $25,000. It was the first major union support offered the NFWA, but Chavez thought very hard before accepting it. At one point he came close to tears, torn between great need, genuine admiration for Reuther and fear that too much outside labor support would destroy the independence and special nature of the NFWA. The amounts of money Reuther promised didn't always come in regularly; but the Auto Workers became the strongest and most consistent supporter of the farm workers within organized labor, even after Reuther's death in 1970 and Schrade's subsequent defeat for reelection as regional director against opponents who charged he spent too much time with farm workers, too little with auto workers.

A group of growers met privately with Reuther on the evening of his visit to Delano. They were impressed by his show of support for the farm workers—but not impressed enough to honor Reuther's request for elections to determine if their workers did want the union representation demanded by strikers. The state Conciliation Service made a similar request. But growers stuck doggedly to the contention, as one put it, that their workers "have already voted against the union —with their feet, so to speak—by staying on the job and working during the so-called strike."

What growers didn't mention, however, was that an undetermined number of those who had "voted with their feet" had been recruited from Mexico and the Southwest to replace strikers. Busloads of them were driven across the picket lines under police escort. Many were Mexican nationals who carried permits, commonly called "green cards," which allowed them to live and work in this country without becoming citizens. They were supposed to live here permanently and were not supposed to replace strikers or any other local workers, but the law was enforced loosely by the understaffed federal agencies in charge of such matters, and legally determining residence status and what constituted "strikebreaking" were tricky matters in any case. The NFWA tried legal action, but growers held it off by arguing that their regular workers really hadn't struck, or that those who had struck had abandoned both their jobs and the picket lines. Growers also employed illegal Mexican aliens who carried no permits at all, although how many they hired wasn't clear. But there were, certainly, hundreds, perhaps thousands, of Mexicans in the vineyards who, as Chavez noted, "can afford to work for much less than workers who maintain residence in our country, because the standard of living where they live is much lower. . . . That's using the poor of Mexico against the poor of California."

This easy availability of outside strikebreakers and the continued reluctance of local workers to risk what little they had by walking off the job for an uncertain future meant that strike activities alone, however unorthodox, could not accomplish the NFWA's purposes. Another weapon was needed, and Chavez found it in the boycott. Cutting the sales of an employer's product could be every bit as effective as denying him an adequate work force, and the NFWA already had the urban following necessary to wage such a boycott. The law also could be used to advantage; the farm workers' exclusion from the federal labor laws that gave others the right to union elections on demand also freed farm workers from the restrictions against secondary boycotts that applied to workers covered by the law. Hence, the NFWA could ask shoppers not only to boycott particular products but also to boycott the stores that sold the products.

The boycott was to become the farm workers' indispensable weapon —their "last nonviolent alternative," as Chavez said. Organized labor had never made much use of the boycott; but, said Chavez, "Gandhi taught that the boycott is the most nearly perfect instrument of nonviolent change, allowing masses of people to participate actively in a cause. . . . Even if people cannot picket with us or contribute money or food, they can take part in our struggle by not buying certain products. It is such a simple sacrifice to make."

The NFWA chose two highly vulnerable targets to start its boycott campaign: Schenley Industries and the DiGiorgio Corporation. Both were huge conglomerates with annual sales ranging from $230 million to $500 million, but the vineyards they operated in the strike area were only a very small, low-profit part of their overall operations. Schenley was far more interested in its liquor sales, DiGiorgio in the sale of canned goods that the corporation processed. Their products were sold nationwide and had dozens of easily identified labels. Further, most of their nonfarm operations were unionized, and Schenley, a heavy advertiser in the labor press, was especially concerned that the firm not appear to be antiunion.

In early 1966, barely three months after the strike started, two dozen NFWA strikers and staff members were dispatched to thirteen major cities across the country. They lined up help from other unions simply by appearing at union offices, penniless and with no place to stay, and asking for aid. With union help, they recruited thousands of volunteers to pass out leaflets, picket stores and demonstrate. These tactics eventually forced Schenley and DiGiorgio to the bargaining table; and, as Chavez had hoped, it also taught some extremely valuable lessons to the farm workers who took part, and won the NFWA thousands of new supporters. They included several regional joint councils of the Teamsters—the country's largest single union—and the AFL-CIO's national executive council, which voted "full support" to the DiGiorgio boycott.

9

Miracle in Delano

Grower attempts to undermine the NFWA's new urban support were extremely ineffectual. They did most of their arguing in local farm areas, where they formed community groups to join them in red-baiting and other tactics of the political right, which only reinforced the views of the NFWA's liberal supporters. Growers denounced the strike for being a civil rights movement, attacked the strikers' clerical helpers as radical "apostles of discord" whose churches were in danger of losing financial support, and brought in the National Right to Work Committee to proclaim that the whole thing was an onslaught on "personal freedom." The John Birch Society concluded that it was a subversive plot hatched in Saul Alinsky's "School of Revolution."

Growers hoped to get at least as much from the California Senate's Committee on Un-American Activities; but though the committee dutifully found that the strike was supported by "known members of the Communist Party," and "new left and subversive organizations," it reported that the strikers themselves were unsubversively aiming at nothing more than that great American goal of "better wages and working conditions."

One of the more bizarre attempts to discredit the NFWA was disclosed six years later when Jerome Ducote, a private investigator active in right-wing causes, offered to sell the union files he admitted stealing from NFWA offices between 1966 and 1968. Ducote claimed growers hired him to uncover material that would link the NFWA to "subversives," and although he didn't find any such documents, he did come away with mailing lists, financial records and boycott plans that were important to the union. The NFWA notified the FBI immediately after Ducote offered to sell the files back, but he wasn't arrested until seventeen months later—nine years after the first burglaries. He was charged with grand theft, but though growers admitted giving him money for information and other help in fighting the NFWA, they denied his assertions that they had asked him to engage in burglaries.

Growers got plenty of encouragement from the agricultural establishment in opposing the NFWA. Buck up, the California Farm Bureau Federation told them, a picket line actually could be a blessing in disguise—"a means of sorting the good, loyal worker from the undesirable." The Farm Bureau advised that tighter supervision by growers would take care of most problems, but that growers might want to make a few concessions, since "the only deterrent to unions is worker satisfaction." The Bureau suggested this wouldn't take much more than supplying water and paper drinking cups on the job and, to really do it up right, "coffee and doughnuts." Growers could rid themselves of "misfits" who might still be dissatisfied by issuing identification cards that "reliable and responsible employees" could present when seeking work.

Mobilization of strike support continued at a rapid pace, with a strong assist from Senator Robert Kennedy and California's Roman Catholic bishops. They spoke up at hearings that the Senate's Subcommittee on Migratory Labor held in the vineyard region just three months after the boycott began. Nearly 1000 farm workers, waving colorful, hand-lettered placards, jammed into a sweltering high school auditorium for the hearing in Delano, while 300 others milled outside anxiously.

Except for James Vizzard and some other individual priests willing to brave the censure of their superiors, the church to which most of the strikers belonged had played only a small role in the strike. But pressures on the church hierarchy had become irresistible, and the farm workers broke into loud cheers at the testimony of Hugh Donohoe, the slight, white-haired Bishop of Stockton. He announced, with just a touch of brogue, that all seven of the state's Catholic bishops would support the proposal of Subcommittee Chairman Harrison Williams to extend the labor laws to farm workers; and, Bishop Donohoe added, they would support the strikers' demand for unionization. The bishops believed the strikers were merely "seeking a basic right," and were now convinced "that unless farm workers are given the chance to organize, they are going to become the wards of the state."

Kennedy took a similar position. "When you're talking about having meals to feed your children and money to buy clothes and continue an education," Kennedy told grower witnesses who insisted their workers didn't want to strike, "then you'll have to make the judgment of whether you're going to be able to go on strike or whether you're going to have to go to work." And if the growers were so certain their employees didn't want a union, why not "permit the people to vote and decide for themselves"?

Kennedy also turned attention to Kern County's curious law enforcement practices in an exchange with Sheriff Leroy Galyen, a rotund figure in a rumpled suit whose manner was as distinctly small-town lawman as Kennedy's was urbane Bostonian. Kennedy looked genuinely astonished as Galyen testified that he had arrested more than three dozen pickets for being *"potential* troublemakers."

"How can you arrest someone if they haven't violated the law?" Kennedy demanded.

"Well, I heard some of the people out in the fields were going to cut up the pickets. So I arrested the pickets . . . for unlawful assembly."

Kennedy suggested acidly that the sheriff "read the Constitution of the United States."

Kennedy's support was among the most important the strikers were ever to receive; it brought them into the highest circles of liberal wealth and political influence, and it buoyed their self-esteem immeasurably. Political motives played a part in Kennedy's support—there were political motives in *everything* Robert Kennedy did. But his support was deep and sincere; and it was unflagging until he was assassinated two years later while walking down a Los Angeles hotel corridor just a few feet ahead of Dolores Huerta and Paul Schrade, after delivering the speech in which he had singled out the farm workers for helping provide his small margin of victory in California's presidential primary. "Whenever we needed him, wherever we asked him to come," said Chavez, "we knew he would be there. He approached us with love; as people, not as subjects for study . . . as equals, not as objects of curiosity. . . . His were *hechos de amor.* Deeds of love."

The NFWA made its most dramatic bid for support immediately after adjournment of the Senate subcommittee hearings, when 100 farm workers and supporters set out from Delano on a 300-mile march to the state capitol in Sacramento. They were to arrive on Easter Sunday, twenty-five days later, to demand that Governor Brown and the state legislature grant farm workers "justice, freedom and respect" in the form of the legal rights that would make their struggle on the picket lines unnecessary. The marchers did not get what they wanted; the governor, fearful of alienating powerful agricultural interests, refused even to meet with them, much less call the special legislative session their demand required. But they gained valuable support as they tramped through the San Joaquin Valley, demonstrating the breadth and dedication of the coalition that had formed around the strike and bringing a sense of hope and solidarity to the farm workers who joined them en route.

The workers provided marchers with money, food and lodging, and participated in nightly Masses, rallies and meetings where they learned what had been happening in Delano, and how they might do the same thing in their own areas. It wasn't all inspirational talk; perhaps the most effective organizing was done through satirical skits, presented by the NFWA's theatrical group, El Teatro Campesino. They laid out the issues in broad simple terms and turned the weapon of ridicule against the growers, whom many workers had passively regarded as unassailable.

By day, they marched beside the flat, green fields of the valley, waving brilliant red banners and chanting, always chanting—dark-skinned farm workers; intense young students; union men and women from the cities; black civil rights workers; nuns in flowing habits; priests and ministers in somber black suits; children, squirming uncomfortably in the broiling sun. Among the marchers, tall and patriarch-like, was Chavez' father Librado, now eighty-two. They were led by men carrying the flags of Mexico and the United States, a wooden cross with the word *"Huelga"* burned into it, and, like those who led the peasant armies of Emiliano Zapata, an embroidered image of *La Virgen de Guadalupe*. It was patterned quite consciously after the Lenten *peregrinaciós* of Mexico, the pilgrimages that combine penance with protests by the poor.

The 52 marchers who covered the entire route from Delano were joined by more than 3000 supporters for the final five-mile leg of the journey, and 5000 more were waiting as they paraded boldly through tree-lined Capitol Park and onto the marble steps of the capitol. They were greeted by dozens of leading churchmen, AFL-CIO and Teamster officials, Democratic officeholders and candidates, and chief representatives of the state's Mexican-American and civil rights organizations. Governor Brown's decision to spend Easter Sunday with his family, at the home of singer Frank Sinatra in Palm Springs, angered but did not dismay the enthusiastic crowd. The protest rally was turned into a celebration of the NFWA's first victory, achieved just a week earlier when Schenley Industries agreed to negotiate a union contract.

Schenley had easily harvested its grapes despite the strike; but the boycott, said a Schenley vice president, raised "a threat of serious damage to our business on a nationwide scale." NFWA supporters were flooding the country with publicity depicting Schenley as a corporate giant oppressing a tiny band of poor farm workers, Teamsters were refusing to distribute Schenley's liquors in northern California, and there was a rumor that bartenders in Los Angeles were about to stop pouring Schenley. The initial reaction of Schenley's board chairman, Lewis Rosensteil, was to order his West Coast representative, Sidney Korshak, to sell the firm's vineyard. But Korshak convinced Rosensteil there was a better way to salvage Schenley's reputation.

Chavez was summoned from the march, a recognition agreement was reached quickly with the help of AFL-CIO officials and, shortly afterward, Chavez signed one of the few contracts ever negotiated by a farm union outside Hawaii. Schenley, which had already joined other growers to raise base pay to $1.40 an hour in hopes of easing union pressure, agreed to raise pay another 35 cents, and to grant rights that were unheard of among most farm workers. They included a union shop, which required all Schenley field workers to join the NFWA, and requirements that Schenley go first to the union when seeking new workers and consult with the union before changing any work procedures or continuing operations the workers claimed to be hazardous.

DiGiorgio tried to escape the NFWA's growing pressure by offering to hold a union representation election, but under conditions that would give the corporation the maximum advantage. The NFWA would have to call off its strike and boycott against DiGiorgio immediately, allow the ballot to include a grower-controlled employee association that had been formed since the strike began, and agree that if the NFWA did win the election it would not resume the strike, even if subsequent contract negotiations broke down. Chavez rejected the offer; but however devious the proposal, it was a major concession, and a sign that stepped-up boycott pressure might result in a legitimate offer.

The mere threat that the boycott might be extended to other firms brought the NFWA a rapid series of victories at a half-dozen of the state's major wineries, including two—Christian Brothers and Novitiate—that were operated by Catholic orders. The wineries held elections or checked the union membership cards of their employees to determine if they wanted NFWA representation, and then negotiated contracts similar to the Schenley agreement with a minimum of fuss.

DiGiorgio wouldn't fall so easily and, as lettuce grower Bud Antle had done in the Salinas Valley five years earlier, would use the Teamsters Union against the organizers. The NFWA tried for two months to reach an agreement with DiGiorgio on election procedures: then, in the midst of the negotiations, DiGiorgio abruptly announced that the corporation would hold an election on its own, under rules the NFWA negotiators had opposed. Striking NFWA members would not be allowed to vote, and though AWOC was not demanding representation rights at DiGiorgio, AWOC would be on the ballot along with the NFWA and the Teamsters. That would split the vote badly and possibly swing the election to the Teamsters, which had begun organizing DiGiorgio field workers with the corporation's active support. The NFWA applied heavy pressure through the AFL-CIO and supporters in the Catholic hierarchy to get regional Teamster leaders to order the organizers to withdraw, but the organizers convinced them to reverse the order.

The Teamsters Union represented DiGiorgio cannery workers and was conducting an organizing drive in citrus groves to the north in conjunction with AWOC's Al Green; that, the union asserted, explained its presence in DiGiorgio's vineyards. But if the Teamsters weren't there on the direct invitation of DiGiorgio, they certainly were there with the corporation's blessing. DiGiorgio supervisors and foremen escorted Teamster organizers; helped pass out Teamster petitions, dues authorization forms and literature that attacked the NFWA as a collection of "beatniks, out-of-town agitators and do-gooders"; sent pro-Teamster letters to employees and, on several occasions, fired or laid off NFWA sympathizers.

Given these circumstances, the NFWA didn't even try to win the union representation election that DiGiorgio had set up. It decided, rather, to discredit the election by documenting DiGiorgio's pro-Teamster activities, getting a court order that removed AWOC and the NFWA from the ballot and urging DiGiorgio employees to boycott the voting.

NFWA representatives talked with workers at their homes, circulated among them at lunch breaks while Teamsters wooed them with free beer and soft drinks, and greeted them on election day with a line of 300 pickets shouting, "Don't vote!" As anticipated, the Teamsters got most of the votes cast—201 of 385. But 347 DiGiorgio employees didn't vote—almost half of those eligible. That and charges of unfair electioneering made against DiGiorgio and the Teamsters by the NFWA, AFL-CIO and a group of clergymen was enough for the NFWA to successfully demand another election.

The NFWA took its demands to Governor Brown, who was in a tough reelection campaign against Republican Ronald Reagan. Brown still was fearful of alienating conservative grower interests; but he needed the liberals within his party, and extensive lobbying by the

NFWA and its allies had won the support of several liberal Democratic organizations for a new election at DiGiorgio.

Brown agreed to an investigation by Ronald Haughton, one of the country's most respected arbitrators. Haughton, co-director of labor studies at the University of Michigan and Wayne State University in Detroit, pointedly declined to make any charges of his own, but recommended that a new election be held in order to settle the dispute "fair and equitably." It took Haughton almost two months to set up the election because of a dispute with the Teamsters over ground rules. He got the NFWA to suspend its strike and boycott as a precondition, and DiGiorgio to agree that those who had struck could vote, even if not currently employed at DiGiorgio. It was also agreed that the election winner would not strike to enforce unresolved contract demands, but submit them to Haughton and another arbitrator for decision after forty-five days. DiGiorgio nevertheless refused to agree to an election because the Teamsters would not accept the preconditions. Haughton recommended that the election be held anyway, and the NFWA and its allies staged a series of demonstrations at DiGiorgio's San Francisco headquarters to demand that Haughton's recommendation be followed.

But DiGiorgio wouldn't budge, and the other grape growers meanwhile arranged a hearing of the state senate's Fact-Finding Committee on Agriculture to try to discredit the NFWA with another session of red-baiting and employer testimony that the vineyard workers really didn't want to be unionized. The committee had a list of 5000 "outsiders" who had been in Delano, thanks to the diligence of the Kern County Sheriff's Department in taking down the license numbers of every car seen near the picket lines or NFWA headquarters. One of those outsiders, the committee reported darkly, was Mickey Lima, the northern California chairman of the Communist Party. Lima was subpoenaed, but testified that, although his car had been in Delano, he had never been there; it was his daughter who had driven in the car to the strike area.

Undaunted, the committee summoned Saul Alinsky, whom grower witnesses had portrayed as the clandestine guiding hand behind the NFWA. The vineyard strike, declared one witness, was "an Alinsky-inspired attempt to sow distrust, racial and religious discord and economic disaster . . . attempted revolution." Alinsky, peering through thick glasses, cheek on one hand, a cigarette in the other, calmly informed the committee that "I am not now and never have been a member of the John Birch Society, the Ku Klux Klan, the Minute Men, the DiGiorgio Corporation or the Communist Party."

Besides, Alinsky hadn't contacted Chavez or anyone else in the NFWA since they began attempting to organize farm workers—"not by spiritual séance or in any other way."

DiGiorgio finally had to agree to the election after the Teamsters withdrew and thus removed the corporation's excuse for further delay. Heavy public pressure from Catholic leaders and others had made it clear an election would inevitably be held, with or without Teamster agreement on the preconditions; and the precondition allowing NFWA strikers to vote faced the Teamsters with almost certain defeat. For the NFWA had rounded up hundreds of DiGiorgio strikers scattered throughout the Southwest, paying their transportation back and in some cases finding them local jobs or financially supporting them. To add to the heavy odds, the NFWA had merged with AWOC to form a single organization, the United Farm Workers Organizing Committee, which would present a united front against the Teamsters.

The merger had been coming since 1965, when AFL-CIO President George Meany appointed Bill Kircher, an old opponent of Walter Reuther within the Auto Workers Union, as the AFL-CIO's national director of organization with the primary assignment of organizing farm workers. Kircher, strapping, outspoken and pragmatic, soon was convinced that the NFWA's way was the only way; that the NFWA was going to organize farm workers with or without the AFL-CIO's help. He got ready agreement from Meany, who was moved as well by the AFL-CIO's rivalry with the independent Teamsters Union. Suddenly, Meany was saying things like "the only effective farm workers union will be one built by the farm workers themselves," and Kircher was offering Chavez the strength and protection of the AFL-CIO, and openly defying the wishes of some AWOC leaders by taking a prominent part in the march to the state capitol and other NFWA activities the AWOC leaders scorned as "civil rights demonstrations."

It took Kircher five months to convince Chavez; the NFWA wanted the use of the AFL-CIO's extensive resources, but wanted independence even more. Chavez was finally swayed by Kircher's offer of a monthly organizing budget of $10,000, on-the-scene help from Kircher and other AFL-CIO leaders and freedom to continue operating in the NFWA manner, albeit without some of those volunteers who greeted AFL-CIO affiliation with charges of "sellout."

Kircher immediately closed AWOC's office in Stockton and shunted aside Al Green and others who objected to the NFWA's methods. Operations were moved to Delano, where the merged organization, known as UFWOC, was run by an executive board consisting of four former NFWA officers headed by Chavez, and three of AWOC's Filipino leaders headed by Larry Itliong. Nearly fifty AFL-CIO organizers were assigned to work on the DiGiorgio election campaign with Fred Ross, whom Chavez had lured from semiretirement to become UFWOC's director of organization.

The election was UFWOC's first victory. Strikers came from as far away as Texas and Mexico to mark ballots that asked simply if they wanted "to be represented by UFWOC." More than 1300 of the 2000 eligible voters went to the polls; 813 said "yes," 530 "no."

The victory against one of the country's most prominent foes of farm unionization inspired organizing activities and strikes throughout California and nine other states, most notably in Texas, where Chavez led a march on the state capitol. But UFWOC had to concentrate on defeating the rest of the Delano growers, and lacking the local resources, leadership and advance work of the farm workers in California, most of the outside movements died quickly under the heavy pressure of powerful growers and their allies in law enforcement and political office.

The contract eventually won from DiGiorgio, in part through arbitration, went beyond even the pioneering Schenley agreement. It set up an employer-financed health and welfare fund, for instance, based layoffs and promotions on seniority, and granted holiday pay, vacations and unemployment benefits. But DiGiorgio was soon to dispose of its farm properties, in accord with an order from the Bureau of Reclamation. The Bureau had responded to pressure from land reform groups by ruling that a provision of the reclamation laws, largely unenforced until then, required growers getting federally subsidized water to sell any holdings in excess of 160 acres. UFWOC argued for a contract clause that would have bound buyers of DiGiorgio's 47,000 acres of excess land to honor the contract and the union recognition it conferred. But the arbitrators ruled in favor of DiGiorgio's argument that the land could not be sold under those circumstances, since the potential buyers were Delano grape growers who were still opposing the union. By the time the last of thirty-one parcels of land was sold in early 1969, less than two years after the DiGiorgio contract was signed, UFWOC's victory had disappeared, and with it the precedent that the contract might have set. For none of the buyers would recognize UFWOC.

Nor did the DiGiorgio settlement end UFWOC's problems with the Teamsters Union. A short time later, while UFWOC was trying to negotiate a settlement with another major Delano grower, Perelli-Minetti, the firm announced it would sign a contract with the Teamsters. Perelli-Minetti suddenly discovered its employees wanted to be

represented by the Teamsters; for good reason: the Teamsters had recruited many of those employees and brought them to work across
UFWOC picket lines, sometimes after violent confrontations. UFWOC
immediately called a boycott against the bulk and bottled wines and
brandies that were widely distributed by Perelli-Minetti, and again
turned church pressure on the Teamsters. Within a few months, an
interfaith committee of California clergymen arranged a peace treaty
between the AFL-CIO and the Teamsters. The Teamsters promised
to stay within their customary jurisdiction in canneries and processing
plants and leave field workers to UFWOC. The Teamsters abandoned
their contract with Perelli-Minetti, aptly described as a "sweetheart
agreement" that granted a pay raise but little else to workers, and
UFWOC was to negotiate a contract with the firm on its own terms.
The Teamsters also dropped a challenge they had raised to UFWOC's
recognition by Gallo, the world's largest winery.

The Despite the unprecedented victories, UFWOC's concrete gains were
slight: a dozen contracts covering only about 5000 of California's
250,000 farm workers, most of them employed by growers of wine
grapes, whose operations were highly mechanized and required comparatively few workers. UFWOC's pressures had forced an increase
of 25 cents an hour in the base pay of most other vineyard workers,
but otherwise the union had barely touched the more numerous growers of table grapes; and now was the time to do it. UFWOC started
with the biggest, the giant Giumarra Corporation. "If we can crack
Giumarra," declared Dolores Huerta, "we can crack them all."

UFWOC reiterated its demand for a union election among Giumarra's 3000 workers, concentrated most of its pickets on the corporation's vast holdings and geared up its boycott machinery to try
to halt the sale of Giumarra grapes. But Giumarra easily recruited replacements for employees who joined the picket lines, got a court
order that neutralized the pickets by forcing them to stand 50 feet
apart, and tried to escape the boycott by shipping grapes under 100
different labels supplied by other growers in California and Arizona.
UFWOC had little choice but to declare a boycott against all grapes.
"It was the only way we could do it," Chavez recalled. "We had to
take on the whole industry. The grape itself had to become a label."

The grape became, certainly, one of the best-known symbols in the
country as the target of what developed into the most extensive and
most successful boycott in U.S. history. It began in January of 1968,
when Huerta and sixty UFWOC members set out in an old bus for a
3000-mile trip to New York City, the largest single market for western grapes. Some of the farm workers got out along the way to work

with volunteers on setting up boycott committees in more than thirty other cities. Eventually, 200 strikers and their families were working with 500 full-time volunteers on committees in more than 400 communities across the United States and Canada.

Strikers had to leave their homes, and sometimes their families, to live for extended periods in the totally unfamiliar urban surroundings, and were paid only $5 a week and minimal expenses. But their presence was essential if the farm workers were to continue building their own union, and it dramatized their cause in a way that outsiders working alone could never have done.

The most dramatic act was performed by Chavez himself, a month after the farm workers began the difficult task of seeking help in the cities. Chavez provided them and their potential supporters an extreme example of sacrifice by undertaking a twenty-five-day fast which he dedicated to reaffirming the principles of nonviolence. Chavez wanted to focus maximum attention on the farm workers' effort, but he was also sincerely concerned that the strikers' frustrations were turning them toward violence. There had been no serious violence in the strike yet, despite a spate of minor attacks and extreme provocations for which union and grower forces blamed each other; but there was danger that Chavez, emerging as the Martin Luther King of the newly aroused Mexican-Americans, might be supplanted by men from the Southwest who were preaching a "brown power" version of the call to arms being raised in riot-torn ghettos by black militants. "Some of our people accused us of cowardice," Chavez said. "They told me: 'If you go out and kill a couple of growers and blow up some cold storage plants and trains, the growers will come to terms. This is the history of labor; this is how things are done.'"

Chavez now feared that "someone would hurt someone" if picketing continued at the struck vineyards, and was well aware, too, that victory would come from urban boycott activities rather than from the picketing. He called off the pickets, sent some strikers back to work to ease the strain on UFWOC finances, and retired to a storeroom at UFWOC headquarters to fast, pray and read the Bible and the writings of Gandhi. Chavez announced the fast and its purpose six days after it began. "No union movement," he declared, "is worth the death of one farm worker or his child or one grower and his child. . . . Social justice for the dignity of man cannot be won at the price of human life."

The storeroom became almost a religious shrine. Tents were erected outside to shelter UFWOC members and supporters who came in pilgrimage from all over the state. They celebrated daily Masses conducted by a young Franciscan priest who wore vestments fashioned of burlap and the red and black banners of UFWOC and offered "union-made wine" to communicants, held prayer vigils and stood in line for hours to talk with Chavez as he lay on a cot in the small, white-walled storeroom. Some refused to accept his sacrifice and tried to force food on him; but all were sent away with the same message: "Go home and organize!"

Giumarra inadvertently helped publicize the fast and generate more support for the boycott by insisting that UFWOC be held in contempt of court for previous violations of orders against mass picketing. Chavez tottered into court weakly on the arms of two aides, his path lined by 1000 farm workers kneeling in silent prayer, to get the judge to postpone the hearing in deference to his condition. It was not a scene that would win growers much sympathy from the public which was being asked to bypass their grapes, and Giumarra quietly dropped the contempt charge for fear of being trapped into such a situation again.

Chavez broke the fast before 4000 supporters at an ecumenical mass in Delano's city park. Robert Kennedy was at his side as he slumped in a chair and nibbled feebly at a tiny bit of bread handed him by a priest. Senator Kennedy took a portion from the same home-baked loaf, then hailed Chavez as "one of the heroic figures of our time," endorsed UFWOC's legislative goals, and congratulated those who were "locked with Cesar in the struggle for justice for the farm workers and for justice for Spanish-speaking Americans." Chavez reminded his followers, in a message read by an aide, that "we have our bodies and spirits and the justice of our cause as our weapons." He was convinced, Chavez said later, that the fast had turned his followers from the violent path that militants everywhere else were trodding and had made UFWOC's nonviolent position clear to the public, "ourselves and our adversaries."

The ordeal sent Chavez to a hospital, where he lay immobilized for three weeks with severe back pains attributed to a lack of calcium in his diet, and for much of the next eight months he directed the union from a hospital bed at home. Chavez became a near-fanatic vegetarian who praised the virtues of carrot and celery juice to just about anyone within hearing; but the pain did not subside until Dr. Janet Travell, a physician who had treated John F. Kennedy, correctly diagnosed that Chavez was suffering from the same back problems as the late President. His spine was twisted out of alignment because one leg was shorter than the other. Dr. Travell, who treated Chavez at the request of Senator Edward Kennedy, had Chavez perform special exercises, put a lift in one shoe and, like President Kennedy, sit in a rocking chair when working at his desk.

The fast focused increased attention on the boycott, and the UFWOC members who had been sent to the cities found thousands of allies, in barrios, on college campuses and in churches, synagogues, and union halls, to give them food, money, lodging and other support. Supporters contributed $20,000 a month to supplement the $10,000 UFWOC was getting directly from the AFL-CIO, made untold thousands of posters, signs and bumper strips demanding that shoppers "boycott California grapes," and engaged in an astounding variety of well-publicized activities. Students at Holy Angels School in Sacramento held a cupcake sale that raised $5 for the cause; Ethel Kennedy held a glittering cocktail party in New York that raised $20,000; supporters dumped grapes into Boston Harbor in a latter-day version of the Boston Tea Party; prominent entertainers held benefit concerts; labor, political and religious leaders spoke out at news conferences, before legislative committees and in newspaper advertisements, arranged rallies and church services in behalf of the farm workers, and joined the picket lines that were at the heart of the boycott.

Boycott committees kept in close contact with each other, and it was rare for a shipment of grapes to enter a city without being greeted by pickets who had been dispatched from commune-like "boycott houses," along with supporters who were on call for such occasions. They demonstrated at produce terminals, then followed the grapes to supermarkets—picketing, singing, chanting, leafletting customers, confronting store managers with their demand for removal of the grapes. Other grape shipments were followed to the waterfront, where pickets urged sympathetic longshoremen not to load them onto ships that were to carry them to Europe and the Far East.

Entire supermarket chains quit stocking grapes; student supporters had grapes stricken from the menus of cafeterias and university dining halls; church leaders kept them from their schools and hospitals and urged their millions of followers to cease buying them; the union-oriented mayors of three dozen industrial cities, including New York, proclaimed support for the boycott and in some cases ordered municipal agencies to stop buying grapes. Legal action forced longshoremen to load the overseas shipments, but there also were boycott committees in major cities abroad, backed by the World Council of Churches and major European unions.

In New York, where growers normally sold about 20 percent of their crop, sales plummeted 90 percent during the summer of 1968 and wholesale prices dropped by as much as one-third. Shippers were forced to put tons of grapes into cold storage or ship them to other areas, creating a surplus that helped drive prices down and cut sales nationally by 12 percent. Overall sales returned the growers about $2.5 million less than they had anticipated for the summer, and the antiboycott campaign, importation of workers to replace strikers and other new expenses were steadily increasing their costs.

Growers could have stopped it all by simply agreeing to union representation elections; but they still were unwilling to give up *any* of their unilateral authority in labor relations. The growers got strong backing from the Farm Bureau Federation, whose statewide president called the boycott "the worst crisis that California agriculture has ever faced," and from others in the agricultural establishment who feared that unionization in California's vineyards would lead to unionization on farms throughout the country. Growers expanded their markets to the South and elsewhere outside liberal eastern and midwestern cities and frightened off some boycott supporters with damage suits alleging violations of the law against secondary boycotts by industrial unions. Then they joined with their anxious allies to get help from newspapers, chambers of commerce and other business groups, and from conservative figures in government and politics who depended on their support.

The grower interests spent more than $2 million on an advertising and public relations campaign directed by Whitaker & Baxter, the firm that had previously waged the major campaigns against Medicare and reapportionment of rural-dominated legislatures. Bumper strips urged people to "Eat California Grapes, the Forbidden Fruit," and newspaper ads said they could "feel better in all respects" by "buying and enjoying fresh California grapes." Other ads, and editorials and columns, charged that UFWOC was undermining "consumer rights" and violating its own precept of nonviolence chiefly to extract dues from well-paid workers whom it did not actually represent.

The John Birch Society and National Right to Work Committee formed so-called consumer groups to spread the message and dire warnings that UFWOC sought "control of America's food supply." Giumarra and thirteen other growers secretly set up and financed an "Agricultural Workers Freedom to Work Association." The association had very few members, but it did have an "executive secretary" who was sent on speaking tours to claim he represented a large body of farm workers who opposed unionization, and to win praise from conservative legislators and columnists for being "a true farm worker."

Growers got strong support from California's new governor, Republican Ronald Reagan, who announced at the height of the boycott that he had "probably eaten more grapes during the past year than ever." Reagan resisted all efforts to grant union bargaining rights to farm workers; appointed growers to run the state's Farm Placement Service; joined the state Board of Agriculture in waging an antiboycott campaign, and provided growers with convict help and welfare recipients, until blocked by a state Supreme Court ruling. It held, in significant contrast to the attitudes of Reagan and governors before him, that the "interests of the growers are private, not public."

Richard Nixon proved to be at least as firm a grower ally during and after his successful presidential race in 1968. He gleefully plopped grapes into his mouth during campaign rallies and declared, in one of his more misleading public statements, that the boycott was illegal and unnecessary. Nixon said that was because "we have laws on our books to protect workers who wish to organize . . . a National Labor Relations Board to impartially supervise the election of collective bargaining agents and to safeguard the rights of organizers." Nixon knew farm workers were excluded from these laws; he, of course, had been a member of the congressional subcommittee that had recommended their continued exclusion after hearings during the DiGiorgio strike in 1949. But Nixon was not one to let down his supporters or miss an opportunity to condemn his Democratic opponent, Hubert Humphrey, for supporting "lawbreaking" by endorsing the boycott as the only way for farm workers to win bargaining rights.

As President, however, Nixon didn't overlook the farm workers' exclusion from the National Labor Relations Act. He had said during the campaign that "the law must be applied equally to all"; and once elected he moved to apply it to farm workers—but only those parts of it that prohibited secondary boycotts and allowed the President to block serious strikes for eighty-day "cooling-off periods."

Nixon's efforts were part of a legal campaign that centered on a "Consumer Food Protection Act" introduced by another major grower ally, Senator George Murphy. The measure, described by Democratic Congressman Phillip Burton of San Francisco as "one of the worst union-busting bills of the twentieth century," would have outlawed the boycott, made it illegal to strike at any time a grower could be hurt and put farm labor relations under a presidential board. But though the legislation failed, so did bills by liberal Democrats to extend the NLRA in its entirety to farm workers.

Supermarket chains began resisting the boycott strongly, now that heavy pressure was being exerted by their natural allies in government and business. Retailers also set up "consumer rights committees," and placed ads that proclaimed their "neutrality" and support for free enterprise. If a customer didn't want to buy grapes, that was the customer's concern, but food stores had a moral obligation to make grapes available. "No one has the right to tell our customers that they cannot buy a product because one group wants to put bargaining pressure on another," declared a typical ad. "Our customers should have the 'freedom of choice.' "

This did not appreciably increase domestic grape sales, however. Growers needed more substantial help; and they got it from the Department of Defense. The Department also professed "neutrality," but felt it a patriotic duty to take advantage of the availability of large quantities of grapes at lowered prices. Department grape purchases shot up from 6.9 million pounds in the 1967–68 fiscal year to 11 million pounds in 1968–69, partly because of an increase of 350 percent in shipments to U.S. troops in Vietnam. The Vietnam shipments jumped from 500,000 to 2.5 million pounds over the year—enough grapes to provide eight pounds to each and every serviceman.

Department representatives were summoned before the Senate Subcommittee on Migratory Labor to explain what members felt to be a deliberate undercutting of the boycott. The Department spokesmen cited increased "troop acceptance" of grapes, alleged shortages of other fresh fruit, the superior "caloric value" of grapes and a need for menu planners to follow the dictates of "objective and systematic management" without regard to such external matters as labor disputes. Democratic Senator Alan Cranston of California asked angrily whether the Department officer in charge of food procurement, Dale Babione, had ever seen an order from Defense Secretary Melvin Laird that called for the Department to show "a social consciousness . . . in evaluating the domestic impact of all its actions." Babione said he hadn't heard of the order, and believed, in any case, that the Department was obliged to continue its current rate of grape purchases, whatever the domestic consequences. The Department maintained that position, despite the insistence of Cranston and others in Congress that neutrality dictated cutting back purchases to preboycott levels.

But though the Defense Department did a great deal to shore up growers who were weakening under boycott pressures, it also gave UFWOC another attention-grabbing issue. The union waged a major campaign against the government purchases, in part through a hyperactive legal department. Previous farm union organizers had not even tried to match the growers' heavy and often decisive use of court action against them; but growers and their supporters were hit with a steady barrage of lawsuits by young attorneys who worked with UFWOC all over California, many as volunteers, none for anything but a bare minimum salary.

Grower suits to limit or halt picketing were met with suits charging growers with assault and harassment of pickets, illegal use of alien workers and violations of laws requiring safe and sanitary working conditions and guaranteeing freedom of assembly and association. Damage suits charging boycotters with restraint of trade were met with countersuits charging growers with violating antitrust laws by conspiring to block union contract negotiations, dividing up the grape market among themselves, maintaining artificially high prices and low wages, illegally using federally subsidized water and so forth.

Few of the lawsuits came to a decision, but they exposed grower tactics and provided UFWOC members and supporters a continuous flow of issues to keep them active, militant and highly visible.

UFWOC increased its pressures considerably by exposing the growers' heavy use of poisonous pesticides. The union's concern helped prompt a survey by the California Department of Public Health indicating that at least 15 of every 100 farm workers suffered from pesticide poisoning, and that the rate would grow now that the organic phosphates causing "serious disabling illnesses" and deaths were being widely substituted for DDT.

Grape pickers commonly exhibited the flu-like symptoms of poisoning by the chemicals that were applied to vineyards according to standards determined almost solely by the pesticide manufacturers, and when an increasing number began coming to UFWOC clinics for treatment, the union went to Kern County's agricultural commissioner to determine which chemicals had caused the illness and how they had been applied. But the commissioner refused to disclose the data. He said the records were "trade secrets" entrusted to him by the firms that applied the pesticides and he was not about to give UFWOC ammunition for "phony lawsuits" against growers and the companies. The union immediately filed suit in the county's superior court; but though the court acknowledged that many pesticides could cause serious illness and death, it also refused public access to the records, on grounds that UFWOC was merely seeking publicity to use in the boycott.

The court's refusal was enough to give UFWOC plenty of publicity anyway. The union got even more when boycotters discovered a batch of grapes in a Washington, D.C., supermarket that supposedly carried a heavy residue of Aldrin, a pesticide that has since been banned because of signs that it might produce cancer. The boycotters presented the Senate's Subcommittee on Migratory Labor a laboratory analysis showing the grapes carried eighteen times the maximum residue allowed by the Federal Drug Administration. Senator Murphy and other grower supporters challenged the test results as false; but neither they nor the boycotters could conclusively prove their conflicting claims because of the extreme difficulty of accurately testing for Aldrin. But true or not, UFWOC's claim gave some shoppers still another reason to avoid grapes. It also aided the union in its drive to help ban DDT and other dangerous pesticides and force growers to agree to contract provisions giving workers a strong voice in use of the chemicals whose dangers previously had been regarded indifferently by workers and growers alike.

Chavez weakened UFWOC's growing support by changing his stand on extension of the NLRA to farm workers. UFWOC and its political allies had argued for several years that farm workers merely sought equal rights—that they wanted no more than industrial workers were granted under the act. But though this meant farm workers would be covered by the original provisions of the act, which granted the legal right to union recognition, it meant they also would be covered by later amendments that prohibited secondary boycotts. The boycott had become UFWOC's only effective weapon, and by early 1969, Chavez saw that the union could not give it up. Getting a grower to recognize the union was one matter, but getting him to agree to a contract would take heavy pressure, which UFWOC could mount only through a boycott.

Hence Chavez argued that only the original provisions of the NLRA should be extended to farm workers. The NLRA had been amended in 1947 only *after* industrial unions had used the freer provisions of the original act to firmly establish themselves over a twelve-year period. The act had been intended for just that purpose and, Chavez reasoned, "We, too, need our decent period of time to grow strong under the life-giving sun of a public policy which affirmatively favors the growth of farm unionism . . . what has proved beneficial to the nation in the past when unions were weak and industry strong." Chavez argued as well for a special provision that the fledgling industrial unions had not needed. The provision would have made it illegal "for a grower to employ anyone during a strike or lockout who has not actually established a permanent residence in the United States."

Chavez' logic was irrefutable. His argument, however, was raised at a time when the AFL-CIO and other UFWOC allies were pressing hard for passage of legislation to extend the NLRA to farm workers in its current form. Chavez was still arguing for equal rights, yet many of his supporters failed to grasp the difference between what industrial unions had been granted and what they now had under the act. AFL-CIO leaders knew the difference; but they were angered that Chavez had not consulted them before changing his position and felt they couldn't sell the idea of what seemed to be special treatment to Congress or to their own members—especially not to those who worked in the retail trades that could be hurt by a secondary boycott. As a result, the AFL-CIO continued to lobby for simply extending the NLRA to farm workers in its entirety and ignored Chavez' call for special legislation. With union forces taking conflicting approaches, however, the odds for passage of any farm labor legislation became prohibitive.

As if to try to prove Chavez' contention that UFWOC would be better off without NLRA coverage, the union moved ahead with an extensive secondary boycott against Safeway Stores, the West's largest food chain. Growers relied heavily on Safeway—Giumarra marketed fully one-fifth of its grapes through the chain, for instance—and if UFWOC could cut Safeway's patronage to the point that the chain quit stocking grapes, or at least reduce its grape sales substantially, the growers would be under great pressure to bargain with the union.

Chants of "Boycott Safeway! Boycott Safeway!" rang out in front of supermarkets and at rallies and demonstrations in 100 cities as the boycott was launched at the start of the 1969 grape harvest. On the same day, a group of UFWOC members began a 100-mile march to the Mexican border to mark an extension of the vineyard strike to the Coachella Valley and to try to convince Mexican nationals not to act as strikebreakers. The activities were coordinated to put maximum pressure on the highly vulnerable Coachella Valley growers who depended on getting their crop to market before arrival of the later-maturing grapes grown elsewhere.

Safeway's board of directors, which included directors of major agricultural corporations, banks and others closely associated with farming, held firm against the demand to clear grapes from the chain's markets. But the board did make the significant concession of endorsing NLRA coverage for farm workers. As intended, that helped ease the direct pressure on Safeway.

Growers had far less success in their attempts to counter the boycott. Early-season sales of Coachella Valley grapes dropped 15 percent below the previous year and grapes that had sold for as high as $7 a box were selling for as low as $3. Tons of fresh grapes were put into cold storage, sold at even lower prices to wine makers and food processors, or just left in the vineyards.

The break finally came midway through the harvest. A spokesman for ten growers who produced one-third of the Coachella Valley's grapes—15 percent of the state's entire crop—suddenly announced, "We are ready to negotiate tomorrow." The message was sent to the federal Mediation and Conciliation Service by Lionel Steinberg, a prominent Democrat who served on the state Board of Agriculture and operated three of the valley's largest vineyards. Although Steinberg was one of the few political liberals among growers, it was not liberalism that moved him. He was as conservative as his fellow growers in labor matters; but, he declared, "it is costing us more to produce and sell our grapes than we are getting paid for them and the boycott is the major factor in this ridiculous situation. . . . We are losing maybe 20 percent of our market." The boycott is "illegal and immoral," Steinberg added, "but it also is a fact and we must recognize it and try to deal with it in a manner fair to both sides."

Strictly speaking, the Mediation and Conciliation Service had no jurisdiction in farm labor disputes, and was directed by a Nixon appointee. "As a public service," however, three government mediators were dispatched to Los Angeles to oversee contract negotiations between representatives of UFWOC and the ten growers. For more than three weeks the mediators moved between two rooms where union and grower negotiators separately drafted demands and offers. They sometimes went at it fourteen hours a day, but could hardly get the parties together in a single room, much less get them to agree on contract terms.

UFWOC negotiators were extremely cautious. An agreement with these few growers would be a major breakthrough, but it also would weaken the boycott against hundreds of other growers because shoppers would have difficulty distinguishing between nonunion grapes and those from vineyards under union contract. The union wanted contracts with the entire table grape industry, and purposely sought to prolong the negotiations in hopes of forcing other anxious growers to the bargaining table through an intensified boycott.

UFWOC demanded nothing less than the contract terms agreed to previously by wine grape growers. But that was asking too much of the Coachella Valley growers; despite their economic distress, they could not yet conceive of granting UFWOC such rights as virtual control over hiring and, especially, the right to veto use of some pesticides and help determine how others were to be applied to their vineyards.

Heavy pressure was put on to keep the ten growers from weakening. Alan Grant, head of the state Farm Bureau and now chairman as well of the Board of Agriculture, rushed to the Coachella Valley to hold a news conference. He assured the growers that the boycott would soon be over because of new efforts to pass bills outlawing boycotts by farm workers. Senator Murphy, who was carrying the major bill, demanded an investigation of possible "collusion" between UFWOC and the ten growers, and the California Grape and Tree Fruit League tried to discredit them further by issuing an imaginative report claiming the boycott actually had been a "total failure." Stronger, wealthier Delano growers who had been close personal friends deliberately snubbed the ten, and though one of the most influential of the Delano growers joined the negotiations, there were suspicions he was merely spying. On the very day he joined the talks, eighty-one of the other growers filed a $75 million damage suit against UFWOC, which sought to outlaw the boycott as a violation of the Sherman Anti-trust Act. That was the last straw. Within hours, mediators concluded that neither side would ever budge on even the most minor contract issues and so called off the "hopelessly deadlocked" negotiations.

Steinberg tried to settle on his own, but he did not offer UFWOC nearly enough to make it worthwhile to sign with just one table grape grower, however prominent. The other nine growers asked President Nixon to appoint a fact-finding committee to recommend a settlement, but UFWOC would not subject itself to such pressure from Nixon appointees.

Steinberg estimated that Coachella Valley growers lost $3 million during the 1969 harvest. But the standoff continued until just before the start of the next year's harvest, when the unrelenting force of the boycott and the mediation efforts of a committee from the National Conference of Catholic Bishops brought Steinberg back to the negotiating table in a mood to bargain. UFWOC also was ready to settle, since other growers had told the bishops' committee privately that if Steinberg could reach an agreement they would follow him rather than face another losing year. First came another Coachella Valley grower, K. K. Larson, who insisted that UFWOC submit to an election. Larson had been on a grower "truth squad" that toured the country declaring that vineyard workers did not want UFWOC representation; but he quickly agreed to a contract after his employees voted 152–2 for UFWOC.

Agreements were reached rapidly with most of the other Coachella Valley growers, and with three of the most influential growers in the major vineyard areas to the north. They included Hollis Roberts, who grew eighteen fruit and nut crops on 46,000 acres of corporate holdings spread across five San Joaquin Valley counties, and two Delano growers, Anthony Bianco and Bruno Dispoto, who had been among UFWOC's most outspoken opponents. Roberts had been forced to virtually abandon grape growing, Bianco declared bankruptcy and, like many of the other growers, Dispoto was feeling the pinch of banks and other creditors. Dispoto didn't believe the creditors "were much in favor of continuing to finance growers who were doing nothing about the union. . . . Sometimes you have to make decisions that you are not too happy about, but if that decision will keep your business alive, you make it."

By mid-July of 1970, the rest of the Delano growers were calling for peace. Their harvest would start soon and they, too, wanted agreements before their grapes got to the supermarkets where many shoppers were now demanding "union grapes." There were twenty-six growers, men who produced half of California's entire grape crop and employed 8000 workers. They now were convinced, said John Giumarra Jr., "that unionism has finally come to this industry and there's no sense pretending it will go away. The thing to do is to come to the best possible terms."

The growers tried to disarm UFWOC at the last minute by having Governor Reagan offer to hold state-supervised union elections and then by announcing they would negotiate only if the boycott was called off. But UFWOC would neither agree to elections whose rules would be designed to defeat the union, nor give up the only weapon it could use in negotiations.

Within a week Giumarra and other growers were meeting secretly with Chavez and other UFWOC and AFL-CIO representatives, a committee of farm workers who insisted on being involved in every detail, and members of the bishops' committee who had spent the past two months persuading growers to agree to the peace talks. A contract agreement was reached after two weeks, on terms similar to those accepted previously by other growers. Base pay, currently $1.65 an hour, was to be raised immediately to $1.80, go up to $1.95 in 1971 and to $2.05 in 1972. Another 12 cents an hour would finance the first health and welfare benefits ever granted these workers, and there would be a 5-cent increase in the piece-rate bonus of 15 cents for each of the three to four boxes of grapes the average worker picked hourly.

It was not the economic provisions that marked the contract as a victory for the farm workers, however. They had not struggled five years merely for pay raises and fringe benefits, as important as those were to their well-being; nor had growers absorbed millions of dollars in losses for purely economic reasons. The growers had been fighting to maintain complete control over the working lives of their employees, but now they were agreeing to get their workers from a union hiring hall, to set up joint worker-grower committees to regulate pesticides and to create machinery through which employees could effectively press grievances against them. An auto worker or steel worker would consider all this routine. But it was downright revolutionary in an industry that had languished for a century in the dark ages of labor relations.

The Delano growers, on that hot July day when they signed the contracts in UFWOC's crowded hiring hall, put a stamp of permanence on the movement that had brought agriculture into the twentieth century. The farm workers who led the way had "lost all their worldly possessions," as Cesar Chavez told the joyous crowd, "but in struggling for justice, they found themselves."

"What's happened here is a miracle," added Dolores Huerta. "But it didn't come about by magic."

10

The Teamster Alternative

The "miracle" in Delano signaled the inevitable. California's farm workers were going to be organized, and the next target would be those in the nearby Salinas and Santa Maria valleys, which produced 70 percent of the nation's iceberg lettuce, and much of its strawberries and broccoli, cauliflower, tomatoes, carrots, artichokes, celery, garlic and other vegetables. It was called "America's Salad Bowl," a flat, fertile place where morning fog hung heavy over land carpeted green for 100 miles.

Men and women hovered over the land, gripping hoes so short the handles scarcely protruded above their fast-moving hands as they stooped and cut, stooped and cut. Most worked under the supervision of men with the broad accents of Texas, Oklahoma and Arkansas who had wielded hoes for small independent growers before giant corporations bought up the land and hired them to manage their new holdings. These men had been among the Dust Bowl Refugees of the 1930s whose own violently opposed demands for better working lives helped inspire the national concern that eventually led to the "miracle." Many had been lured into urban employment when the Great Depression lifted, of course, but those who remained as managers joined the corporations to oppose the demands of the Mexican-Americans who had replaced them at the bottom of the economic totem pole.

"It's damn hard to eat this stuff," declared one of the corporate managers from the height of his 1970 standing in the middle class. "People who aren't even citizens are telling you what to do. That's what it amounts to. . . . You don't have any control anymore. . . ."

What the vegetable growers had been "told" was to agree to union recognition elections in which UFWOC seemed a certain winner. Chavez made the demand a month before the vineyard settlement was announced, confronting growers with the prospect of signing UFWOC contracts or facing a boycott like that which had been so costly for grape growers. There was, however, an alternative that the growers had overlooked until the inevitability of unionization arrived with Chavez' demand. They might arrange to bypass elections and sign with another union that would demand less than the aggressive, unorthodox UFWOC and at the same time ease the sting of a boycott by enabling the growers to point out that their workers *were* unionized.

The growers found their alternative in the Teamsters, the union that one grower, Bud Antle, had used to fend off the Agricultural Workers Organizing Committee a decade earlier. Antle had not bothered with an election, of course, but the Teamsters had since shied away from this procedure. In 1967, for instance, the union rebuffed two dozen major growers who called representatives of the Western Conference of Teamsters to a secret meeting in Los Angeles, where they also offered recognition without elections as a way to slow UFWOC's drive.

Circumstances had changed, however. Field workers were now threatening strikes and boycotts that could endanger the flow of produce handled by truck drivers, cannery workers and other Teamster members, and Teamster officials were eager for representation rights that would enable them to control the field workers. UFWOC and its influential supporters undoubtedly would protest any Teamster move as a violation of the jurisdictional agreement the union had made with UFWOC in Delano in 1967, and demand elections to prove that the Teamsters didn't actually represent the field workers.

That prospect alarmed the director of the Teamsters' Western Conference, Einar Mohn, who was unusual among Teamster leaders in his sensitivity to liberal public opinion. But it did not overly concern many of those who represented the Western Conference in the Salinas and Santa Maria valleys, including a ruthless young official, Bill Grami, who saw the signing of field worker contracts as a way to rise in the Teamster hierarchy. The potential was immense: more than 30,000 workers in the two valleys alone. That would bring a lot of new money into the dues and pension funds used by Teamster leaders to gain power and influence.

Some of the vegetable growers approached Grami in July, during negotiations on new contracts for truck drivers. They agreed the Teamsters should be called in to represent field workers, and came up with a rationale for it after the truckers called a strike. The drivers declared they would not return to work until contracts were also granted to field workers; they wanted protection from field strikes, and Grami claimed that he had received many "informal requests" from field workers for Teamster representation.

The deal was made when the growers met to ratify the new truckers contract, which their negotiators worked out after a week-long strike. Cal Watkins, who helped manage Inter Harvest, the largest and newest of the corporate lettuce growers, recalled that the growers agreed as a body to approach Grami and other Teamster representatives and, not surprisingly, found them "interested and receptive." The Teamsters "announced that any firm interested in recognizing the Western Conference of Teamsters" could do so. "The union did not at that time claim to represent any agricultural workers," Watkins added, but said it "would take the responsibility for signing up the workers."

Virtually all of the 170 growers in the area soon announced that they had signed Teamster agreements. The announcement came just one day before Chavez was to announce the vineyard settlement and the start of a new organizing drive in the vegetable fields. The growers and the Teamsters hadn't even agreed on specific contract terms; they were in so great a rush to head off UFWOC that they merely signed agreements that promised the terms on pay and working conditions would be filled in later. They did agree, however, that the terms would not be decided in consultation with those who would work under them; terms were left solely to Anglo Teamster and grower representatives, whose many common interests included that of keeping decision making from the Mexican-American field workers. The workers would not even be allowed to ratify the contracts. But they would be required to join the Teamsters and have dues of $1.25 a week deducted from their paychecks; if they didn't join, they'd be fired.

Most workers did get basic pay raises of 10 to 50 cents an hour in return for forced membership in the Teamsters, some minimal health and welfare benefits and even, in a few cases, unemployment insurance coverage. But instead of the strict protections against pesticide use in UFWOC's grape contracts, they merely got an employer promise to follow government regulations in such matters; instead of being allowed to press grievances and discuss work rules and other on-the-job concerns with employers through their own elected committees, they got only the right to talk individually with appointed Teamster representatives. Nor would there be any union hiring hall. Growers could continue getting workers however they pleased, and from whatever source, including parasitical labor contractors, just as long as they deducted Teamster dues from the workers' paychecks.

Teamster recognition obviously was a small price for growers to pay in exchange for maintaining their ability to make decisions on pay and working conditions in isolation from the direct collective demands of their employees. Since the Teamsters' main interest lay elsewhere, in transportation and food processing, growers also could expect that even the minimal terms of the contracts would not be strongly enforced and that strikes and boycotts were hardly a possibility. But on the chance they might still feel insecure, the contracts were written to stand for five years.

Chavez was outraged at the "Pearl Harbor type of sneak attack . . . an act of treason against the legitimate aspirations of farm workers." He declared "all-out war . . . war between the Chicanos and Filipinos together against the Teamsters and the bosses . . . the AFL-CIO against the Teamsters," and marched into Salinas with several hundred farm workers and an AFL-CIO contingent headed by Organizing Director Bill Kircher. Pickets went immediately to a farm where 250 workers had been fired for not joining the Teamsters, hundreds of workers struck at other farms and UFWOC began preparing for legal action and a nationwide lettuce boycott. Growers got a court order against what was ruled an illegal jurisdictional dispute, but the pickets kept marching nevertheless and Chavez began "a penitential fast against injustice."

It took less than two weeks of this to convince Einar Mohn and other high Teamster officials that peace had to be restored. Mohn also was under heavy pressure from the Auto Workers Union, a close ally of UFWOC that he had just helped to bring into a national "Alliance for Labor Action" with the Teamsters. Mohn prevailed on national Teamster leaders to order Grami to arrange a treaty with UFWOC through the bishops' committee that had been instrumental in the vineyard settlement. The treaty was almost a verbatim reiteration of the treaty signed in 1967 by the two unions. In reallocating jurisdiction over field workers to UFWOC, Grami also agreed that the growers who had recently signed Teamster contracts could switch to UFWOC.

But there was a catch. Growers who had signed Teamster contracts would not agree to give them up, and Grami claimed the treaty bound both unions to honor the growers' wishes.

"If we could get the Teamster contract from Chavez," said Herb Fleming, president of the vegetable growers' association, "then maybe in the long run Chavez would have to shape up and act like a businessman and it would work out. But as of now, we growers here are ready to fight to protect our workers from intimidation and our rights as farmers. We have the proper and legal contracts with the Teamsters Union; the Teamsters have assured us they will honor these contracts and we intend to do the same."

UFWOC and the bishops' committee tried for nearly two weeks to get the Teamsters and growers to relent. But they remained firm, helped by a state administration that would not answer Chavez' calls for union elections, and UFWOC members finally voted to strike.

It was, at the start, the largest and most effective farm strike since the mid-1930s. More than 5000 workers left their jobs at nearly 150 farms, and produce shipments were cut from 200 railroad carloads a day to 75 or less. Unable to stockpile or delay the harvest of their highly perishable vegetables, growers were losing an average of $500,000 a day. Unlike the vineyard strike, this dispute was violent, with beatings suffered by UFWOC and Teamster partisans alike. In the most serious incident, UFWOC's chief attorney, Jerry Cohen, was sent to the hospital with a brain concussion after two grower aides kicked and beat him unconscious outside a struck farm. Some of the turmoil was caused by officials of a Teamster cannery workers local who were charged with using $25,000 in union funds to hire some of the local's members to "guard" fields from UFWOC organizers. The officials later were removed from office for acting without Teamster authorization and one of them was convicted in federal court for using physical threats to get several growers to pay him $12,000 for "expenses."

Hundreds of UFWOC members and supporters lined the roads in front of the struck farms that sprawled out before them around Salinas, in the heart of the vegetable-growing region, glaring defiantly at sheriff's deputies and private guards and chanting endlessly. Boisterously determined, they shuttled constantly between the picket lines and a ramshackle building in Salinas that had become a new headquarters for Chavez and UFWOC's entire staff. When they weren't picketing, they were holding noisy outdoor rallies.

In Salinas, alone in a quiet, sterile motel suite strikingly like those that once housed the men who directed the battles of grape growers, Bill Grami directed two dozen Teamster organizers by telephone. UFWOC had "flagrantly violated" the peace treaty by striking, Grami reasoned, so he was free to begin organizing field workers again. Grami was especially angered that UFWOC had included the huge, financially shaky Bud Antle operation among its strike targets; the treaty had exempted Antle from UFWOC activities on grounds that his Teamster contract was signed long before the current dispute. The Teamsters had an investment to protect; Antle still owed half of a $1 million loan he had gotten from the union's Central States Pension Fund in 1963.

The growers went to court again, to get more than thirty restraining orders against picketing, and the Monterey County Board of Supervisors in Salinas adopted an antinoise ordinance that barred UFWOC from using any "voice-amplifying equipment." There were dozens of arrests, but pickets ignored these orders, too. Within a week, Inter Harvest was calling for contract negotiations with Chavez. Inter Harvest, which grew almost one-fourth of all Salinas Valley lettuce, was extremely worried over UFWOC's threat to call a boycott against the products of all firms that, like Inter Harvest, were owned by United Brands. That would mean, among other things, Chiquita Bananas sold through United Fruit, snacks peddled at A & W Root Beer stands and ice cream cones sold at Baskin-Robbins.

Despite the contract terms requiring Teamster membership, Inter Harvest manager Cal Watkins said Teamster organizers had been able to sign up only 108 of the firm's 1000 workers. He said, "The Teamsters had our contract, but UFWOC had our workers," and a poll by the bishops' committee backed him up. Other grower spokesmen nevertheless scoffed at Watkins' explanation as a face-saving way to escape a boycott, and counterpickets shut down the firm's operations after it signed a UFWOC contract. The pickets—Teamsters and grower allies who carried American flags and signs proclaming them to be "Citizens Against United" and the "Citizens Committee for Agriculture"—kept produce haulers off the job for a week, but finally obeyed a court order to cease picketing. Other growers also filed, but then dropped, a suit charging Inter Harvest with violating an agreement that no grower was to abandon a Teamster contract unless all other growers also abandoned their contracts.

Inter Harvest was followed by two firms, including one, Fresh Pict, which also feared national boycotts against products sold by affiliated companies, since it was owned by Purex.* But the other growers finally got a court order that the strikers did obey, if only because UFWOC was running short of the strike benefits of $5 a week and

---

* Shortly afterward, William R. Tincher, chairman of Purex's board of directors, complained in a trade publication that "Purex has been called communistic because we signed with Mr. Chavez." Tincher assured his readers that Purex acted only on the demands of retailers who wanted to avoid a boycott. "Purex," he insisted, "is not communistic. We pride ourselves on our contribution to the capitalistic life in America."

bare expenses it had been paying, and the growers had had time to round up replacements for the strikers.

The new court order was issued after the California Supreme Court set aside the earlier orders because the Monterey County Superior Court had heard only from grower attorneys before acting. This time, Superior Court Judge Anthony Brazil called in lawyers from both UFWOC and the growers before reiterating that growers were the victims of a strike by workers who illegally demanded that they tear up valid Teamster contracts. A judge in the Santa Maria Valley had upheld UFWOC's contention that the contracts were invalid because the workers had not voted for Teamster representation. But Judge Brazil waived that argument aside and ruled there could be only one informational picket at twenty-two of the Salinas Valley farms making up the strikers' prime targets, none at the eight others. Nor would UFWOC be allowed to call a boycott against any of the 170 growers who held Teamster contracts.

Most strikers were back on the job within a month after the strike began, crop shipments rose to at least two-thirds of normal, and UFWOC decided to do what it had done with great success in the vineyards. UFWOC called a boycott, despite the court ruling.

Officially, the strike continued, but the major effort was at food markets in sixty-four cities across the country, where UFWOC members and supporters urged shoppers to bypass lettuce from the struck growers. It was more difficult than the grape boycott, however. Lettuce was a staple vegetable, not a luxury fruit, and, as one boycott leader noted, "you can eat it in a sandwich or a salad and you don't think about it." Growers also were able to wage a strong counter-campaign on the theme that all lettuce was now "grown, harvested and shipped by union workers."

Bud Antle decided to stop it nevertheless; and it wasn't just his lettuce he wanted to protect. Antle's continuing financial problems had led him to sell 17,000 of his 43,000 acres to the Dow Chemical Corporation, which supplied him lettuce wrapping, boxes and pesticides, and UFWOC was threatening to boycott that firm's many products as well.

Antle sought his own injunction from another Superior Court Judge, Gordon Campbell, claiming that UFWOC's actions against his firm violated the state's Jurisdictional Strike Act *and* UFWOC's treaty with the Teamsters. It was true, said Antle, that his employees had not voted on any of the eight contracts he had signed with the Teamsters since 1961; but, he said, "my workers kept showing up for work—that was all the ratification I needed." Judge Campbell agreed, and ordered UFWOC not only to cease its strike and boycott but also to counteract what it had already done by urging the public to *buy* Antle's lettuce.

UFWOC immediately stepped up the strike and boycott, and drew exactly the response it wanted. Antle urged Judge Campbell to merely fine UFWOC for defying the court order, but the judge insisted on having Chavez arrested. UFWOC couldn't have asked for a better opportunity to win support for the boycott. Chavez was accompanied to jail by more than 2000 UFWOC members and supporters, including Ethel Kennedy and Coretta King. They cheered Chavez' parting advice to "boycott the hell out of them!" and then began a series of prayer vigils and other highly publicized demonstrations. After three weeks, with Christmas just two days away, Judge Campbell decided it would be wiser to release Chavez pending the outcome of a UFWOC appeal.

The boycott continued at an intensified pace throughout the early months of 1971, bringing heavy pressure on national AFL-CIO and Teamster leaders to end the interunion squabbling that was hurting members of both organizations. The bishops' committee was again called in, this time to work out a stricter version of the previous UFWOC-Teamster pact. It would be in effect for three years and any unresolved disputes would be subject to "the final arbitration" of no less than AFL-CIO President George Meany and Teamster President Frank Fitzsimmons. The Teamsters would allow an outside arbitrator to settle the dispute over the Antle contract and would not service any of the union's other field worker contracts. Dues money collected under the contracts would go into escrow while Teamster representatives tried to persuade growers to sign UFWOC contracts. UFWOC would meanwhile call a moratorium on the boycott that was hurting Teamster truck drivers, warehousemen and field workers as well as growers.

It didn't work. Only one grower switched contracts. The others announced through their association that "growers with Teamster contracts are going to insist the Teamsters honor them," and the head of the Teamster local in Salinas declared that "nobody has any right to arbitrate away our contract" with Antle. The growers' association did hold a series of negotiating sessions with UFWOC officials, but they only served to continue the boycott moratorium for another six months, until after the 1971 lettuce crop had been harvested and largely marketed. UFWOC resumed the boycott after the negotiations broke off in November of 1971, but by then the union was preoccupied with an array of other activities.

Running the new union was proving to be almost as difficult as establishing it had been. UFWOC's inexperienced members were ill prepared to administer dozens of contracts, operate hiring halls, deal directly with growers and supervisors who still intimidated or antagonized them, and convince new members that paying dues and joining in boycott demonstrations were essential requirements of membership.

Serious friction developed over UFWOC's inability to administer the union in an efficient, even-handed way that would satisfy growers and workers who knew very little about collective bargaining and who often would not accept the discipline of regularized labor-management relations. The greatest conflict was over the hiring hall, the most important device for granting the union authority promised by the contracts. The hiring hall was designed to provide equal job opportunities, but growers were more concerned with getting crops picked as fast as possible. They protested when dispatchers sent older workers whose seniority gave them a priority the growers had not previously honored, rather than the fast young workers requested by the growers.

There were protests as well from young workers who were bypassed, and from others who also demanded to know why they couldn't work wherever they pleased, regardless of seniority and other union rules. UFWOC's inexperienced dispatchers frequently gave in to the demands, or dispatched friends and relatives in place of members with greater seniority. Determining seniority was very difficult, in any case, because of heavy worker turnover.

On the farms, some UFWOC ranch committees either made hostile, unreasonable demands on growers to try to make up for past injustices or reverted to previous practices by passively allowing growers to ignore contract provisions.

Negotiating the contracts themselves proved to be a trial for growers and their representatives because of UFWOC's inexperience and insistence on full membership participation. Robert F. Spaulding, one of the West's leading management attorneys, described the contract bargaining sessions he helped growers conduct as "unique and sometimes unbelievable." He said:

The union's committee consists of up to sixty members, mostly right off the fields and the negotiations with management often are turned into noisy union meetings conducted mostly in Spanish. They argue with each other, and when we suggest cutting down the size of the committee to get some work done, we are denounced as members of the exploiting class. . . . The union representatives demand "continuous bargaining sessions," and when we ask about meals, sleep, or at least rest, they say apparently we don't understand the English language—that "continuous" means without stopping, and that is what they mean, too.

Training programs were begun under Fred Ross and meetings were held regularly in workers' homes and elsewhere, but it was a slow educational process. UFWOC also was busy setting up a medical plan called for in its new contracts—the first medical plan the farm workers had ever had. Farm workers commonly saw doctors only when seriously ill—if then. But employer contributions of 10 cents an hour and private donations enabled UFWOC to provide a mobile clinic that toured farm regions and to set up permanent clinics that members and their families could visit regularly for examination and treatment by volunteer physicians, nurses and UFWOC members who were trained as medical aides. The benefits were modest, but paid at least part of the costs of testing, hospitalization and medicine for those needing care outside the clinics.

AFL-CIO leaders still worried that UFWOC would ultimately fail. But they finally agreed to grant Chavez a charter that formally recognized the Organizing Committee as a union. UFWOC became a full-fledged affiliate of the AFL-CIO—the United Farm Workers of America, popularly known as the UFW. That gave the organization official standing, a role in AFL-CIO decisions and operations and at least the appearance of stability. There was a price, however. The AFL-CIO discontinued its $10,000-a-month subsidy; organizing committees were eligible for such assistance; affiliated unions were expected to finance their own operations.

As if the struggle in California wasn't enough, the UFW moved to secure a base in Florida, where grower strengths and farm worker weaknesses were even more pronounced. Most of Florida's farm workers were poor, disorganized workers imported from the islands of the British West Indies, and other black migrants who were hauled up and down the Atlantic Coast by labor contractors. They took whatever seasonal work they could find, under whatever conditions the contractors and growers found profitable to themselves, and lived in squalid, prison-like camps isolated behind high fences in the heart of large orange groves and sugarcane fields. Union organizers had tried to penetrate the plantation-like system, but never with any success. "If the supervisor sees us talking to a white man," as one cane cutter explained, "we get sent home sure. We say we want more money in the cane—we get sent home. Anything we do the supervisor don't like—we get sent home."

The UFW moved in on the heels of an NBC television documentary,

Migrant, which had finally given the public a glimpse of what was going on in the isolated fields of Florida. The documentary shed a particularly harsh light on the treatment of workers by Minute Maid, a Coca-Cola subsidiary with 30,000 acres of orange groves spread across 120 miles of south-central Florida. Openly embarrassed, Coca-Cola officials quickly improved conditions, at the same time that Chavez sent his cousin Manuel to talk with Florida's migrants about organization. Manuel had little success among the demoralized and distrustful workers elsewhere in the state, but Minute Maid's employees decided their improved conditions should include unionization. Coca-Cola officials agreed without much protest; they were mindful of the UFW's readiness to boycott their highly vulnerable products, and concerned with improving the firm's image after the damaging TV documentary.

The UFW's contract with Minute Maid immediately raised the base pay of almost 1000 workers by 45 cents an hour, gave them pay for time spent traveling to work between different parts of the firm's vast holdings, the first paid holidays and vacations in their lives, and the other rights and benefits granted UFW members under contracts in California. Coca-Cola also agreed to regularize employment by guaranteeing workers fifty hours of pay per week during peak seasons, even if that much work was not available, and to help workers find adequate housing off the company's property. It gave Minute Maid's workers job security and adequate housing for the first time and gave the firm an unusually stable work force.

Only one other Florida grower signed with the UFW, but the union had established a foothold. One of the UFW's few black leaders, a former DiGiorgio striker named Mack Lyons, was sent to Florida to begin the difficult task of building the same type of grass roots organization that had led to the union's California victories. Despite its continued preoccupation with California, the UFW was in Florida to stay.

Part of the union's organizing difficulties in Florida stemmed from a feeling among the black workers there, as among workers and the public generally, that the UFW was "a Mexican union." That feeling turned to resentment among some Filipino members of the union, to the point that their leader, Larry Itliong, resigned in 1971.

Itliong complained that the outnumbered Filipinos "were getting the short end of the stick" from the Anglo lawyers, clergymen and other activists who served as Chavez' chief advisers in devising tactics based largely on their experience and broad social goals, and on the cultural and religious background of the Mexican-Americans who dominated the union. Itliong had "the greatest admiration" for Chavez, but protested that Chavez had been "swayed by the grandiose thinking of a brain trust of intellectuals. . . . Nonfarm workers seem to have more influence on what has to be done than some farm workers. I couldn't get through to him." Although he was no Al Green, Itliong preferred the more orthodox tactics of the AFL-CIO group he had led into merger with Chavez' association. Itliong was unhappy, too, with his lesser role in the merged organization, the standard $5-a-week salary for all officers, and the reluctance of others on the union's executive board to continue allotting him $550 a month in expenses to help support his wife and seven children.

The head of the vegetable growers' association greeted Itliong's resignation as a split between those supporting "responsible unionism and those who view the union as a social cause and ignore contractual responsibilities." But Itliong did not throw in with the "responsible unionism" of the Teamsters. He quickly cooled his public anger and joined a project to develop low-cost housing for the UFW's retired Filipino members. Itliong did not urge other Filipinos to quit the union, and relatively few did, but they remained in a distinctly secondary role.

Itliong's action was not unique among those caught up in the hectic, often improvised activities that went on around the clock in UFW headquarters, although Itliong was one of the few to proclaim his unhappiness publicly. Others left quietly over similar complaints or because of exhaustion and anger over Chavez' insistence on overseeing even the smallest details of administration, down to the cost of long-distance telephone calls.

The problem was intensified when Chavez moved his headquarters from Delano to a former tuberculosis sanitorium isolated high in the pine-studded Tehachapi Mountain foothills fifty miles to the southeast. The UFW's main medical clinic, hiring hall, credit union and other service facilities were kept in Delano, but the administrative and tactical decisions were made at the new headquarters. Chavez and his staff lived and worked at close quarters in old wooden-frame hospital buildings and cottages tucked into one corner of a 280-acre plot. They called their little commune Nuestra Senora de la Paz (Our Lady of Peace), or simply, La Paz.

The move had been made in part to ease the demands on Chavez' time by farm workers and others who constantly dropped by for visits in Delano and to break members and growers of the habit of coming to him with grievances best left for them to work out through the union committees at particular farms. Yet Chavez still insisted on being completely involved in all staff decisions and on setting a killing pace. He rose before dawn, mixed a mug of hot lemonade and honey that would sustain him until he paused briefly for a lunch of raw fruit and vegetables, and then set to work in a small white-walled office. Chavez pored over every scrap of correspondence, bills and all the other minute details of operating the rapidly growing union. Everyone else at La Paz was also expected to devote full time to building the union—there was little else to do, in any case—and there were some who rebelled. But though there was such a heavy staff turnover that the union had trouble making its payments to the state's unemployment insurance fund, the UFW never lacked a dedicated core of members and volunteers to administer the union.

The new headquarters compound was closely guarded, for, as Chavez noted, "the moment you start changing things, you have to worry about security." Despite his personal distaste for security procedures, Chavez had not been left unguarded since the assassination of Robert Kennedy. He lived behind a high chain-link fence and traveled in the constant company of a bodyguard and two German shepherd dogs, Boycott and Huelga.

The most serious threat was relayed to the union by federal agents, who had been told by an informant that he and two other men were offered $30,000 to kill Chavez and destroy UFW records. The informant never said who allegedly offered the money, but did name the two men who supposedly took the job. One was arrested shortly afterward for an unrelated murder and the other for attempting to sell narcotics to one of the undercover agents who was investigating the alleged plot to kill Chavez. The agents paid the informant $500 for his information and offered him $10,000 more if he could substantiate it. Additionally, the UFW offered $10,000 for solid evidence and the Kern County Sheriff's Department conducted an investigation of its own after the federal agents concluded there was no proof of a plot. Nothing came of it, but the UFW wasn't taking any chances; Chavez was to remain under close guard.

Throughout the period, the UFW also remained active in the vineyards. Despite the contract signings in Delano, there were hundreds of small independent grape growers in northern and central California who remained nonunion; the UFW tried to sign them by striking the packinghouses that prepared their crops for shipment, and by waging a new boycott against Safeway Stores, the largest buyer of their fresh grapes, and against the major wineries that bought their wine grapes. But this confused the public, angered AFL-CIO leaders who had members in packinghouses, stores and wineries, and prompted a heavy counteroffensive by growers who already had the union under heavy attack in the lettuce fields.

The year—1972—was an election year and the growers had an ally in the White House, Richard Nixon, who was eager to line up the support of agricultural interests for his reelection campaign. Nixon had just appointed a conservative Republican, Peter Nash, as general counsel of the National Labor Relations Board, and Nash was only too happy to cooperate with growers who filed complaints charging the UFW with violating the law against secondary boycotts. Farm workers were not covered by the law, of course, and the NLRB had ruled repeatedly that it had no jurisdiction in farm labor matters. But the nature of the UFW's latest campaign gave Nash a pretext for acting anyway. By striking packinghouses and boycotting wines, Nash argued, the UFW actually was attempting to organize the non-agricultural workers who were employed in wineries and packing-houses. Further, the UFW was waging its boycotts in conjunction with AFL-CIO unions, which were covered by the law, and using non-agricultural workers on its boycott picket lines.

It was very flimsy legal reasoning, but from the Nixon Administration's viewpoint it was sound political argument. So Nash sought an injunction to ban all UFW boycotts until the NLRB could thoroughly investigate the grower complaints and issue a ruling. That probably would have taken a year and, fortunately for the UFW, the courts did not act immediately.

The UFW quickly made the Administration's move into a major political issue. The union's Democratic supporters raised loud protests, the UFW held demonstrations at Republican Party offices and campaign headquarters in major cities, and more than a million letters of protest were sent to GOP National Chairman Robert Dole.

Neither Nixon nor the Republican Party wanted that much election-year heat, and so a truce was arranged with the UFW, which was now anxious to shift its major efforts to lettuce. Nash dropped the court action in exchange for a UFW pledge to drop the wine boycott and promise not to organize nonagricultural workers or involve them directly in any future actions against wineries.

Intensification of the lettuce boycott spurred growers to launch an even stronger attack. Since they couldn't destroy the UFW under current law, they sought to enact new laws. A coalition of Republicans, large corporate growers and shippers, "right-to-work" committees and other conservative groups joined with the American Farm Bureau Federation in a drive to enact an Administration bill that would have made it virtually impossible for the UFW to organize. The bill would have set up farm union elections, but restricted voting to year-round workers, who would be almost certain to back their employers. The bill also would have banned all picketing at retail establishments and put other severe limits on boycott activities, and have made it impossible to conduct effective strikes.

Farm Bureau spokesmen urged growers to hold fast, pending congressional action. For if the bill passed, they were told by Alan Grant, the Bureau president in California, "no large part of agriculture need be unionized, now or in the future." Grant advised growers to stall for time by hiring replacements for strikers who demanded union recognition or by holding recognition elections and dragging out the subsequent contract negotiations with the election winners. The National Labor Relations Act prohibits such tactics, but in this instance the Farm Bureau readily acknowledged that the act really did not apply to agriculture.

The Farm Bureau and its allies didn't get very far in Congress, however. Their bill was carried by California's inept Senator Murphy against the strong opposition of the UFW's liberal Democratic supporters. So the grower coalition turned to the state legislatures, where agricultural interests had much more influence. A national campaign was started under the Farm Bureau's name to enact state laws that would be as restrictive as the proposed federal law—in some states even more restrictive. The bills passed with relative ease in Kansas, Idaho, Oregon, and Arizona; but then the UFW mounted a strong counteroffensive.

Demonstrations were held at Farm Bureau offices in thirty-four states, the governor of Oregon was pressured into vetoing the bill there, and the UFW shifted its entire staff to Arizona to fight the new law in that state.

The UFW couldn't realistically expect to repeal the law in Arizona, a conservative "right-to-work" state with a weak labor movement; but it could wage a strong enough campaign to greatly worry legislators in dozens of other states who were now being lobbied as heavily by UFW supporters as by the Farm Bureau lobbyists who sought the new state laws. The lettuce boycott also added to UFW pressures in Arizona, since about 20 percent of the country's lettuce was grown there, and mainly by the same growers who owned the Salinas Valley's lettuce fields.

The UFW moved into Arizona before the law went into effect, singling out Arizona lettuce in its boycott activities, striking melon growers whose crops would rot if not harvested quickly and starting a drive to recall Republican Governor Jack Williams for signing the Farm

Bureau bill into law. It was a large undertaking for Arizona's poverty-stricken farm workers; they averaged $14 to $15 a day on those days when they could find work, which was irregularly for at least half of them, and their children commonly worked alongside them in 100-degree heat. So Chavez once more provided an extreme example of sacrifice, at the same time dramatically calling the attention of outsiders to the union's cause. As he had done during the vineyard strike in 1968, Chavez undertook a fast.

The UFW set up headquarters in Phoenix, in a battered white stucco building that served as a community hall for the city's barrio. Chavez rested in a curtained alcove furnished with a cot and rocking chair while farm workers and supporters milled about with petitions calling for an election to recall the governor and stopped for words of encouragement or to take part in nightly Masses and rallies. Chavez had to be moved to a hospital for fear the fast was weakening his heart, but he continued fasting. Chavez finally broke the fast, after twenty-four days, before more than 5000 supporters at a memorial Mass for Robert Kennedy in the incongruous setting of a modern Phoenix hotel.

Chavez returned to the hospital to recuperate, but the UFW and its supporters continued gathering signatures on recall petitions and registering people to vote so they also would be eligible to sign. By November, four and a half months after they started, they had gathered 175,000 signatures—fully 40 percent of the number voting in Arizona's most recent gubernatorial election—and, in doing so, had registered nearly 100,000 new voters, including thousands of Mexican-American farm workers and other minority group members. The UFW needed only 108,000 signatures for a recall election, but state officials declared thousands of the signatures invalid because the signers, while registered to vote at the time they had signed the petitions, had later been purged for not voting in the state's last election. The recall election was blocked by these and other actions, including claims by state officials that petition signers had been "intimidated"; but the UFW accomplished its main purpose. The union had organized its Arizona supporters into a large political bloc that would have a noticeable effect on the future actions of politicians in Arizona and other farm states, and it had won new support for the lettuce boycott.

11

Death in the Fields

The UFW had to shift its major forces back to California in the midst of the Arizona campaign to fight a threat to the union's very survival. It was posed by a 7000-word initiative that grower forces put before California voters after the state legislature rejected their model law. The initiative, known as Proposition 22, was the most restrictive of the anti-UFW laws the Farm Bureau had proposed around the country. It would not only have made it virtually impossible for a farm union to win recognition elections and wage effective strikes and boycotts; it also would have prohibited a union that might win an election from bargaining on work rules, allowed unionized growers to hire nonunion workers and, among other matters, subjected union adherents to a $5000 fine, or one year in jail, for violations, while providing only administrative sanctions against growers who violated the law.

Grower groups spent $224,000 to qualify Proposition 22 for the ballot, most of it in payments to professional petition circulators who gathered 388,000 signatures. In doing so, they perpetrated what California's Secretary of State, Edmund G. Brown Jr., called "the worst case of election fraud" in state history. Brown, son of the former governor, based his charge on affidavits from petition signers and reports from district attorneys indicating that at least 15 percent of the signatures were forgeries or fraudulently obtained.

Handwriting experts verified widespread use of forged signatures in four counties. The district attorney in Kern County reported that at least 1000 of the 7300 signatures obtained there were forged, and the district attorney in Los Angeles found some petitions with 100 or more signatures written by one or two people.

In other cases, the Secretary of State's official summary of the complex proposition at the top of the petitions was covered with a card describing the measure as one aimed simply at peacefully settling labor

disputes and thus preventing inflated food prices. Some petition signers said they were told the measure actually was designed to help
farm workers and was supported by Chavez and the UFW.

More than a dozen people eventually were arrested for filing fraudulent petitions. But the state Supreme Court rejected requests by
Brown and the UFW to remove Proposition 22 from the ballot; the
court did not want to exercise "undue interference" in the electoral
process. It said voters would have to decide the issue on the proposition's merits, and the UFW set out on a massive campaign, helped immeasurably by the fraud charges. Growers attributed the charges
mainly to Brown's gubernatorial ambitions and had the state Agricultural Department issue, in the department's name, a misleading description of the proposition written by one of the growers' public relations men. But the charges put growers on the defensive.

Grower forces spent almost $500,000 on their campaign, complete
with TV commercials recreating scenes of violence that supposedly
had taken place in the fields at the instigation of UFW organizers.
The UFW spent about $150,000, part of it from provisions in some
of the union's contracts requiring members to contribute one day's
pay to a political action fund set up in response to the Farm Bureau's
legal campaign. The money was spent mainly on food, transportation
and lodging for hundreds of farm workers who traveled around the
state, sleeping in tent cities, gymnasiums and anywhere else they could
find cheap shelter, and pooling their meager funds for food. They
talked directly with as many voters as possible, registered some 50,000
others and stood at freeway off-ramps, along busy streets, in front of
supermarkets and at other gathering spots as "human billboards,"
holding huge signs that urged "No on 22." Chavez, barely recovered
from the fast in Arizona, campaigned exhaustively against "this fraud
which would destroy the farm workers union in California."

Proposition 22 was defeated by 4.6 million votes to 3.3 million.
That margin of defeat—58 percent to 42 percent—was larger than
the margin of victory for President Nixon in California in the same
election. The AFL-CIO, the Democratic Party, California's Catholic
bishops and others helped in the UFW campaign, but most of the
credit for the resounding defeat of Proposition 22 belonged to the
UFW. Now no one could doubt the union's ability to wage an extremely effective political campaign, and no other state would make a
serious attempt to enact such legislation.

Growers were struck another heavy blow a month later when the
state Supreme Court upheld the UFW's appeal against the lower court
orders that had prohibited the union from striking and boycotting

Salinas Valley lettuce growers who signed Teamster contracts in 1970. The Supreme Court ruled that growers had not complied with the Jurisdictional Strike Act, which had been applied in exempting them from UFW action. For to be protected by the act, employers "must maintain a strict neutrality between competing unions."

The court said growers had favored the Teamsters, "completely substituting" their choice for that of their workers, by signing Teamster agreements while "at least a substantial number and probably a majority" of the workers preferred UFW representation. The growers could not even pretend to neutrality, for there was "no suggestion on the record that the growers . . . attempted to ascertain whether their respective field workers desired to be represented by the Teamsters, or, indeed, that the question of their field workers' preference was even raised as a relevant consideration."

But though the California Supreme Court denied growers protection of the Jurisdictional Strike Act and allowed the UFW's lettuce strike and boycott to continue, it did not void the Teamster contracts. They were valid legal documents whatever the motivation behind their signing.

The growers and the Teamsters weren't taking any chances, however. The contracts had three years to run, but they quickly renegotiated them to increase pay and add new fringe benefits, in response to what was described as a grower desire for greater "stability" among workers. The Teamsters' Bill Grami assured reporters that this time the workers' desires also were considered; for even though they had not been allowed to vote on the new contract terms or on whether they wanted continued Teamster representation, they had been "consulted" prior to the renegotiation and promised that henceforth there would be "rank-and-file participation." The Teamsters would even begin servicing the two-year-old contracts by sending business agents into the fields to enforce all the terms except one. They would delay enforcing the provision that required workers to join the Teamsters Union; otherwise, the UFW, relying on no less an authority than the state Supreme Court, might very well sue growers and Teamsters for forcing workers to join a union they didn't support.

The renegotiation of the lettuce agreements signaled more than just an attempt to keep the UFW from signing contracts with vegetable growers. It was the start of a drive to keep the union from holding contracts with *any* growers. The Teamsters formed their own agricultural workers organizing committee, with a $3 million budget and the goal of signing workers throughout the West and Southwest. The first target would be the grape growers; their UFW contracts were nearing expiration, and they were eager to emulate the lettuce growers in the hope that signing Teamster contracts would accomplish what the growers' legal campaign had failed to do.

Any doubt that the drive against the UFW was a joint Teamster-grower effort was dispelled by Teamster President Frank Fitzsimmons in a speech to the American Farm Bureau Federation's annual convention in Los Angeles just a day before renegotiation of the lettuce contracts was announced. Fitzsimmons joined growers in attacking the UFW as "a revolutionary movement that is perpetrating a fraud on the American public" and asked the Farm Bureau for "an alliance . . . an accommodation which will work for the benefit of your organization and for mine."

Part of the "accommodation" was Farm Bureau support for extension of the National Labor Relations Act to agriculture. Most grower leaders had become convinced they could not get special legislation to destroy the UFW; but the NLRA's boycott limitations might now be enough, since the Teamsters were willing to challenge the UFW for the recognition rights guaranteed by the act. Besides, the chances for passage of an extension bill were slight, and growers could recognize a friendly Teamsters Union while pointing to their support of the NLRA as evidence that recognition was just another sign of their fairness in labor relations. Growers and Teamsters alike would insist that the workers preferred Teamster representation, and that the only fair way to prove otherwise would be through the elections provided for in the act. Until the act was extended to agriculture, they argued, growers had no choice but to recognize the Teamsters.

The Nixon Administration also was part of the effort, as a close ally of both the Farm Bureau and the Teamsters, the only major union to support President Nixon for reelection. It was no coincidence that Fitzsimmons' appearance at the Farm Bureau convention was arranged by Nixon's special counsel, Charles Colson, or that Colson was put on a $100,000-a-year retainer as a Teamster attorney when he left the White House following disclosure of his role in the Watergate scandals.

Nixon won Teamster support largely through his personal attentions to Fitzsimmons, a remarkably shallow man who was very impressed by dinner invitations to the White House. Fitzsimmons also was grateful to Nixon for meeting the demands of his union members by paroling former Teamster President James Hoffa from prison—but on condition that Hoffa not challenge Fitzsimmons for the Teamster presidency. There also was a moratorium declared by the Internal Revenue Service on $1.3 million owed in back taxes by another former Teamster president, Dave Beck, who switched allegiance from

Hoffa to Fitzsimmons; a Justice Department decision to drop prosecution of a fraud case against Fitzsimmons' son, Richard; and denial of an FBI request to seek further court-approved wiretaps in an investigation of an alleged underworld plan to use Teamster pension funds to set up crooked health and dental care plans.

The Teamsters went after the UFW's grape contracts in January of 1973. Representatives of the union's Western Conference met secretly with growers in the Coachella Valley, three months before their UFW contracts were to expire, and promised they would seek increased pay and benefits, but not the union voice in hiring and work operations required in the UFW agreements. Growers demanded the same weaker provisions in negotiating with the UFW on new contracts; while they negotiated, Teamster organizers went through the fields to get signatures on petitions asking the growers to sign with their union. The UFW contract negotiations eventually broke off, and nine hours after the old UFW contracts expired, Teamster and grower representatives announced they had negotiated contracts covering virtually all of the Coachella Valley's vineyards. The Teamsters not only would do away with the union hiring hall through the contracts, but also would sign agreements with labor contractors to help supply workers.

Teamster organizers claimed they had secured 4103 signatures on their petitions, despite reports from state employment offices that there were no more than 1500 workers in the fields at the time, a poll by the Catholic bishops' committee showing "the vast majority" of them wanted UFW contracts, and declarations from workers that their signatures were forged or that they had signed under the threat of losing their jobs.

The Teamster action touched off the most violent farm labor strife since the 1930s, a five-month battle in which two UFW members were killed, hundreds injured and more than 3500 arrested for violating nearly eighty injunctions against mass picketing, unlawful assembly and other demonstrations.

It started with a UFW strike that drew a vicious Teamster response and, as one consequence, unprecedented backing from the AFL-CIO. It was the best-financed and best-run strike in farm labor history. The UFW committed $1 million; AFL-CIO President George Meany raised $1.6 million from other affiliates and sent Organizing Director Bill Kircher and twenty aides to the valley to fight what Meany saw as an intolerable attempt by "the nation's largest union . . . to destroy this smaller union representing some of the most exploited workers in the nation." For the first time, agricultural strikers were able to leave their jobs without risking financial ruin; they received strike benefits of $35 to $90 a week, and could defy the inevitable injunctions against strikers with the assurance they would have bail money and the help of a large legal staff. But the Teamsters confronted them with another risk, that of serious physical injury.

Gangs of "guards" prowled the vineyard area, big, brutish men hired by the Teamsters from the union's hiring halls in Los Angeles or off the city's streets. They got $67 a day to "protect" nonstrikers from UFW pickets who massed outside vineyards and labor camps in defiance of court orders, noisily and angrily demanding that the workers inside also join the strike. Even Teamster officials called these so-called guards "the animals." They stood menacingly before the picket lines, glaring contemptuously through dark glasses, tattooed arms extending from the cut-off sleeves of ragged denim jackets emblazoned with motorcycle club symbols or bulging under bright blue jackets with the word "Teamsters" on the back and American flag patches below the shoulders. They taunted pickets with obscenities, provoked fights and frequently waded into them with flailing fists, chains, tire irons and a dangerous assortment of other weapons. After breaking up one picket line battle, a sheriff's captain reported coming up with "a small pile of rubber hoses, grape stakes, hatchets and small roofing hammers that had been taken from Teamsters."

Sheriff's deputies made dozens of arrests, but no one could thoroughly police the huge vineyard area where the "guards" patrolled in search of isolated picket lines. They even invaded labor camps to terrorize strikers' wives and children.

The strike area resembled a battle zone, with daily bulletins on violent skirmishes: 56 injured, 5 arrested in a melee between 400 pickets and 180 "guards" and Teamster supporters . . . 2 "guards" arrested for the kidnap and attempted murder of 2 workers they beat and stabbed with an ice pick . . . a sixty-year-old striker's collarbone broken . . . shots fired into a UFW organizer's house while he was talking with Chavez . . . gunfire at a picket line that included two of Chavez' sons . . . Chavez' car chased down a back road and stoned . . . a striker's house trailer set afire while he and his family were inside . . . the UFW office firebombed. . . .

One of the most highly publicized incidents involved a Catholic priest, John Bank, who was acting as the UFW's press liaison officer. Bank was set upon by a 300-pound "guard," Mike Falco, as the priest was having breakfast in a restaurant with a reporter. Falco sat down across from Bank, announced, "I may go to jail for this, but it's worth it," laughed, and then smashed his fist into the priest's nose. He broke three bones with the single blow.

Despite the furor, the Coachella Valley growers were able to harvest most of their crop, although they were forced to recruit a steady flow of inexperienced workers from Mexican border towns to replace strikers. This slowed the harvest, resulted in the shipment of poorly packed grapes to some markets and drove up costs in a year when unusual weather limited the crop and helped lower wholesale prices; but it was not enough to convince growers to meet the UFW strike demand for representation elections, much less to repudiate their Teamster contracts. Lionel Steinberg and K. K. Larson, the first Coachella Valley growers to sign with the UFW in 1970, had renegotiated their UFW contracts before the strike and held to them. But those two contracts were all that the UFW had left in the Coachella Valley; the union would even lose the Larson contract when it expired the next spring.

The battle moved north with the grape harvest to the San Joaquin Valley, where growers also discarded expired UFW contracts in favor of Teamster agreements. Hundreds of clerics, AFL-CIO members, legislators and other UFW supporters flocked to the vineyards, and by early summer the struggle was raging across six counties. The violence continued, but finally the publicity became too much even for the Teamsters' thick-skinned officials. They agreed to pull off their "guards" after 30 of them were arrested for charging into 200 pickets, sending three men and one woman to the hospital with injuries caused by blows from lead pipes, clubs and tire chains. Teamsters continued to blame the violence on UFW provocations and attempts to invade vineyards to get at nonstriking workers, but Bill Grami said the union was "assured that there are now enough law enforcement agents to protect our members."

Grami was correct, at any rate, in feeling that the Teamsters would get more "protection" from law officers. While certainly not sympathetic to the UFW, deputies in the Coachella Valley had rarely done any violence themselves. But San Joaquin Valley deputies, particularly in Kern and Tulare counties, chased, clubbed and maced pickets who openly defied orders against mass demonstrations and trespass or who allegedly tried to free fellow pickets who were being held by deputies. "They don't arrest us for trespassing," said Chavez. "They beat the hell out of us, both men and women."

In Kern County, the sheriff put half of his 200-man force on vineyard duty twelve hours a day, six days a week. In Tulare County, pickets faced squads of specially trained deputies in green flight suits, heavy boots and visored riot helmets, armed with pistols, yard-long clubs and tear gas canisters that hung forebodingly from wide webbed belts. In both counties, private patrolmen armed with shotguns stood behind the lines of deputies, and sheriff's helicopters circled low overhead.

Teamster intimidation continued as well. The "guards" were replaced by burly Teamster "organizers" and local high school athletes, some armed with baseball bats, whom the union hired. They stood at the edge of vineyards exchanging insults with pickets and trying to drown out their chants by playing music over the sound truck systems that were used on both sides of the picket lines.

More than 2000 UFW members and supporters were arrested during the summer. They jammed county jails to overflowing after the UFW ran short of bail money and decided that filling the jails was the best way to overturn the restrictive injunctions. In some cases, the orders limited the union to no more than one picket every 100 yards and said bullhorns and other sound equipment could not be used for more than one hour per day.

Priests, nuns, ministers, and women strikers with children in arms marched off to jail chanting UFW slogans with the others, and stayed for as long as two weeks despite court offers to release pickets on their own recognizance if they would promise not to resume their defiance of the injunctions. Among those jailed was a nun who looked on it as "spiritual renewal," and another nun who "wanted to show that the Church is with the farm workers not just in word, but in body." Dorothy Day, the celebrated seventy-six-year-old leader of the Catholic Worker organization, came from New York City to be jailed in support of "the most important thing that has ever happened to the U.S. labor movement."

The UFW strategy worked. Court calendars became so clogged with strikers' demands for jury trials and jails so full that deputies stopped arresting those who violated the injunctions. No union in U.S. history had ever drawn such support; yet the Teamster steamroller would not be halted. By the time the harvest reached the Delano area, virtually all the grape growers along the way had signed Teamster contracts.

The Delano growers hesitated, however. They were willing to renegotiate their UFW contracts—if the union would give them what the Teamsters had given the other growers by abandoning the hiring hall and the contract provisions giving workers a voice in how their jobs should be done. The UFW was making a last stand; but even so, the most it offered was a hiring hall jointly administered by growers and the union. To grant growers any more of what they demanded would destroy the very essence of the union.

The Delano growers allowed their UFW contracts to expire, but did not immediately sign with the Teamsters. The union was now hesitating, under the pressure of unfavorable public opinion which was undermining an expensive national campaign Fitzsimmons had launched to clean up the Teamster image. It was part of Fitzsimmons' own campaign to retain the union presidency against a challenge by Hoffa to win it back despite the conditions of his presidential parole. Fitzsimmons even had hopes of bringing the Teamsters back into the AFL-CIO, which had expelled the union for alleged corruption under Hoffa.

Fitzsimmons and other Teamster officials were already holding informal talks with AFL-CIO representatives at the request of AFL-CIO President George Meany on the possibility of another peace treaty with the UFW.

While those talks were going on in Washington, the UFW was putting most of its efforts into a strike against the Delano growers. The strike was ten days old when Meany sent the AFL-CIO's chief counsel and three vice presidents to continue the talks with Chavez and officials of the Western Conference of Teamsters at the conference headquarters south of San Francisco. Meany had promised Fitzsimmons to personally guarantee any UFW-Teamster agreement and to persuade Chavez to back extension of the NLRA to farm workers, so the UFW could no longer wage the boycotts that were hurting Teamsters and AFL-CIO members.

Progress was being made toward an agreement until word came in the midst of a negotiating session that the Delano growers had signed Teamster contracts, even as the Teamster and UFW representatives were trying to decide which of the unions should sign with the growers. Chavez and his aides stormed out of the session flamboyantly, past reporters who were outside awaiting word of a new peace treaty.

"Stabbed in the back!" shouted Chavez as he slid quickly into the front seat of a station wagon that would carry him back to the vineyard area. "Just like Pearl Harbor!" added the UFW's lawyer.

What the UFW representatives didn't say was that Teamster leaders had immediately repudiated the contracts. They were signed by the Teamsters' chief organizer in Delano, Jim Smith; but Fitzsimmons and Einar Mohn, the Western Conference director, maintained that Smith had acted in direct violation of their orders. Mohn declared the contracts "null and void," suspended Smith for two weeks and closed the Teamsters' Delano office. The AFL-CIO representatives backed Mohn's contention that there had been no duplicity by Teamster negotiators and agreed the peace talks should continue. But Chavez, reluctant to make concessions to the Teamsters anyway, decided to use the incident to generate more unfavorable publicity against the rival union. He announced he would not return to the talks until the Teamsters showed better evidence of "good faith."

Smith probably wasn't acting under the direction of Mohn and Fitzsimmons. He may have been acting merely under the pressure of his own ambition or with at least the tacit support of Hoffa and Grami, who saw victory in the vineyards as a way to further their ambitions for high union office. Peace could help only Fitzsimmons.

The result, in any case, was "victory" for the Teamsters. The twenty-nine growers who signed the contracts were "delighted," as John Giùmarra Jr. said, and would not give them up. The growers scoffed at the official Teamster repudiation as meaningless, put the contract terms into effect unilaterally and warned Teamster officials the union was legally bound to honor them. Growers refused to even respond to letters Fitzsimmons sent each of them declining representation of their workers, although "my response," said Giumarra's uncle, "would be, ha, ha!" Young Giumarra also was in a happy mood. "The UFW?" he asked. "I think they're out of business now."

The growers had reason to crow. Just one year earlier, the UFW held more than 150 contracts covering 50,000 workers and had about 30,000 year-round members. But now the union was down to a mere dozen contracts covering about 6500 workers, and had no more than 12,000 members.

A mood of angry frustration permeated both sides of the picket line in the vineyards where the UFW was struggling to win back lost contracts, putting a severe test on its commitment to nonviolence as well. Strikers did not plead with nonstrikers to join the picket lines; they demanded it, sometimes invading vineyards for face-to-face confrontation with workers who were universally abused as "scabs." Nonstrikers no longer turned aside sheepishly. Emboldened by sheriff's deputies and Teamster "organizers," they returned the bitter taunts of pickets and engaged in rock throwing contests with them.

Serious violence erupted when the UFW's peace talks with the Teamsters broke off. On that very day, two young pickets were wounded by gunshots fired from inside a struck vineyard. Three days later, one of the UFW's several hundred Arab members, twenty-four-year-old Nagi Daifullah, was killed in a scuffle with a deputy sheriff outside a bar frequented by strikers; three days after that, a sixty-year-old striker, Juan de la Cruz, was shot to death as he walked a picket line beside his wife.

A coroner's jury ruled Daifullah had died accidentally from a skull fracture, after the deputy had chased him for drunkenly interfering with the attempted arrest of another man inside the bar. The deputy struck Daifullah with a flashlight, but the jury ruled the fatal injury came when Daifullah fell while running from the deputy and struck his head on the pavement, even though UFW witnesses contended that the flashlight blow had killed Daifullah.

More than 5000 mourners marched in Daifullah's funeral procession, a line fully one and a half miles long, making their way slowly through Delano and down dusty, narrow roads in scorching 100-degree heat to UFW headquarters four miles away, carrying black flags and led by six of Daifullah's countrymen chanting an Arabic dirge.

Daifullah and more than 1200 others had been brought to the San Joaquin Valley from Yemen during the earlier vineyard strike, the latest group of poor immigrants to be used by growers against unionization, forced to live in isolated camps, unable to communicate with outsiders except through Arabic-speaking labor contractors. They were, as Chavez said of Daifullah in his eulogy, immigrants "who came here seeking opportunity and fell into the trap of poverty which has enslaved so many farm workers in the United States."

Even as Daifullah's mourners marched, funeral arrangements were being made for de la Cruz, who had been with the union from the beginning, as a striker at the DiGiorgio vineyards. A .22-caliber bullet had struck him just below the heart, one of five rifle shots fired from the cab of a pickup truck as it sped past a line of 100 pickets about sixty miles south of Delano. De la Cruz collapsed in the arms of his wife Maxima, as she held a canister of water for him. The driver of the truck and a twenty-year-old farm worker whom witnesses identified as the assailant were arrested forty-five minutes later. Three hours later, de la Cruz was dead.*

The UFW immediately called off all picketing and demanded an investigation by the Justice Department. Chavez said there would be "no more picketing until the federal law enforcement agencies guarantee our right to picket and see that our lives are safe and our civil rights not trampled on." Chavez also called for a general three-day fast "to rededicate ourselves to the principles of nonviolence." He said, "Farm workers everywhere are angry, but we will not fall into the trap of violence. We do not need to kill or destroy to win." The

---

* The truck driver was quickly released, and the young assailant was cleared by a jury three years later after claiming he had fired in response to a hail of rocks from pickets which had caused him and the driver to fear for their lives.

fast ended with the funeral services for de la Cruz, which brought
another 5000 mourners to join a Mass celebrated by three Roman
Catholic bishops and entertainers Joan Baez and Taj Mahal. Juan de
la Cruz, said Chavez, was "a martyr to a just cause."

With the vineyard picketing off, strikers were put to work on an
intensified boycott against grapes as well as lettuce. More than 500
UFW members set out after the de la Cruz funeral in a car caravan
headed for sixty-four cities. Growers and retailers would still protest
that shoppers were being asked to boycott produce picked by union
members, but they were *Teamster Union* members, and there was an
important new difference. It wasn't a Teamster Union member who
had died on the picket line; it wasn't Teamster Union members who
had been beaten and arrested.

As before, boycotters made a special target of Safeway Stores,
which already had bent far enough to wage an advertising campaign
for "free elections in farm labor negotiations" without the boycott
restrictions of the Labor Relations Act. In addition to applying boycott pressures that turned away an estimated 30,000 Safeway customers per week, UFW supporters had filed a series of suits charging
Safeway with a variety of illegal marketing practices, to the point
that Safeway filed a $150 million harassment suit.

Meany continued, meanwhile, to try to arrange resumption of the
UFW-Teamster peace talks, in hopes of lessening pressures on retail
clerks and other AFL-CIO members who were being hurt by the
boycott as well as protecting the AFL-CIO's most popular affiliate
from destruction by an outside union. Meany got Chavez to ease up
on the boycott, then he wooed the Teamsters, although perhaps not
intentionally, by echoing some of their complaints about the UFW
and implying he would correct the alleged problems. Meany agreed
that the hiring hall was run inefficiently and complained that UFW
members were required to pay dues year-round, whether working or
not, and had to pay dues owed for periods of unemployment before
being dispatched. Chavez, Meany added, was "a very unwise man"
to oppose extension of the NLRA to agriculture.

While Meany was talking with Fitzsimmons in Washington, the
UFW held its first constitutional convention, an event designed to
demonstrate that the union was firmly established despite the disastrous Teamster raids and had the broad public support necessary to
combat the raids.

It was the most unusual convention in contemporary labor history.
Just being there was rough for most of the 400 delegates. They were
not the usual collection of union officials with expensive clothes and

fat expense accounts who come to conventions to listen inattentively to a few speeches, adopt a few pro forma resolutions and quickly retire to hospitality suites in well-appointed convention hotels. They were poor rank-and-filers in work clothes. They stayed at the homes of local farm workers, and ate simple, sparse meals supplied by local churches and served in the convention hall, sometimes while they continued debate.

And the debate: There was forty-eight hours of it, in just three days, including a final session that ran twenty-two hours straight, presided over mainly by Chavez, who subsisted on gallons of carrot juice, and by Dolores Huerta, who had had her tenth child just two weeks previously. Yet most delegates stayed alert, to debate endlessly, to chant rhythmically, to sing, to dance and to pray.

The delegates put together a union structure that was as unusual as the convention. Like the UFW itself, the nine-member executive board was dominated by Mexican-Americans; but it also included a black worker, a woman, two Filipinos and a Jew. The union's new constitution required the officers to work full time for $5 a week and room and board; forbade the UFW from using violence "in any form, for any purpose whatsoever"; set up a Public Review Board of three outsiders to decide complaints from members disciplined by the union; and served notice on the Teamsters that the UFW's jurisdiction included "all farm workers in the United States." Dues requirements were changed so members would pay only when working, but the constitution also declared UFW support for "the unrestricted right to boycott" and gave union membership to those who worked on boycott committees in the United States and Canada.

Delegates were very careful in adopting the unusual 111-page constitution. They took nothing for granted, and they insisted on having the final say in everything. "Who is this Roberts?" a delegate demanded after Chavez explained that the proceedings were to be governed by Robert's Rules of Order. "Where's he from, and why should we follow his rules?"

Yet for all their fervor, delegates refused to put the UFW behind the one reform farm workers needed more than any other; they rejected a resolution proposed by a young boycott committee member who urged them to "join with the rest of organized labor in total opposition to the infamous nineteenth-century employers' system of piece rates." It is this system, as Chavez noted, that drives farm workers to "constant stooping and running" in competition with each other, and encourages employment of children to help increase their family's output. Chavez fought for the resolution behind the scenes, but young delegates would not be turned from the lure of a system that promised greater rewards to the strong and the swift. "Wait till they get older," Chavez said wistfully. "They'll be old and tired, and maybe. . . ."

Senator Edward Kennedy and other prominent political figures, Catholic bishops, leading rabbis and Protestant churchmen and top representatives of the AFL-CIO, the Auto Workers and the International Longshoremen's and Warehousemen's Union delivered pledges of major support to the convention.

Even some UFW sympathizers were beginning to predict the union's death. Had they looked closer at the convention, however, they would have seen a path to survival. Growers and Teamsters would face a potent combination of very powerful outside forces and highly dedicated members of a union that had now sunk its roots deeply.

12

Boycott!

Almost immediately after adjournment of the UFW convention, Chavez flew off to Washington for resumption of peace talks with the Teamsters. Chavez was skeptical, but in less than a week, negotiators announced "an agreement in principle." It needed only a few finishing touches from their attorneys and would go into effect as soon as those routine formalities were concluded.

Chavez was "elated." The organizing of *all* field workers would be left to the UFW. The Teamsters would "renounce and unilaterally rescind" all contracts the union had signed with grape growers, give up two major lettuce contracts immediately and give up the others when they expired in 1975. In return, the UFW would not boycott the lettuce growers who retained Teamster contracts and would not challenge Teamster jurisdiction over all workers involved in the processing, warehousing and trucking of produce. Any unresolved differences between the unions would be settled by Meany and Fitzsimmons.

Growers responded by asserting they would not give up their Teamster contracts; but there was no assurance they could make that stick, especially since some growers had secret understandings with the Teamsters to switch to the UFW in the event of a peace treaty.

Meany and Chavez were convinced the growers could not upset the agreement; they signed it quickly, after their lawyers looked it over. But Fitzsimmons claimed Teamster lawyers had found "some very serious legal problems," arising from grower threats to sue the union "to death" if it rescinded any contracts. Fitzsimmons stalled for nearly six weeks, then announced that the Teamsters would not sign the peace treaty after all. He said the union had decided to honor its "moral and legal obligations" to growers by keeping and "strictly enforcing" all 305 of its field worker contracts. Fitzsimmons asserted that what Meany described as "a full and complete agree-

ment" for the Teamsters to do otherwise had been merely an understanding that an agreement might be reached "contingent upon a
satisfactory settlement of the contract obligation question." He
added:

We have no alternative but to abide by those agreements which are legal
documents enforceable in the courts of the land . . . in every instance
the farm workers involved have freely chosen to be represented by the
Teamsters. . . . I cannot understand how the man who poses as head of
the American labor movement takes such a casual view of labor contracts,
when the welfare of millions of American working men and women depend
upon the sanctity of such contracts.

If Fitzsimmons really believed there had been no firm agreement
in the peace talks, he probably was the only party to the negotiations
who had that view. The Teamsters may never have intended to rescind the contracts anyway; but the delay in announcing their refusal
kept public heat off the union and diminished the flow of aid to the
UFW until after the harvest season was over and public attention was
diverted from agriculture.

It was clear, in any case, that Fitzsimmons was under heavy pressure to avoid an accommodation with the UFW. Hoffa was campaigning aggressively for Fitzsimmons' job, assuring Teamster members
that *he* wouldn't allow their union to give up *anything* to another
union, that he would "fight Chavez, just like we fight employers."
Those were welcome words to Grami and other influential leaders in
the Teamsters' Western Conference, and "rather than lose their support in the next Teamster election," AFL-CIO Vice President Paul
Jennings wrote Fitzsimmons, "you scuttled the pact." Other AFL-
CIO officials also cited pressure from Charles Colson, the Teamster
attorney and former Nixon aide, who did not want the union, a strong
supporter of the President, to cooperate in any way with Meany, who
was leading a campaign to impeach Nixon.

Fitzsimmons offered to resume peace talks with the AFL-CIO, but
while doing so he bitterly denounced Meany and Chavez. Meany was
outraged. He sent each of the AFL-CIO's 114 affiliates a 2000-word
"white paper" describing what occurred in the peace talks and con-
cluding with a pledge to support the UFW "for as long as is necessary
to win."

Chavez declared war on the Teamsters, who "have deceived us
every time." He put the UFW's full efforts into the lettuce and grape
boycott, in hopes of inflicting such economic damage on growers that

they would renounce their Teamster agreements. Chavez also reasoned that:

The Teamsters are in a bind because they can't keep both sides happy—only one side or the other—and in order to keep the growers happy and maintain their sweetheart arrangement they just can't afford to give the workers any representation. The moment they try to give the workers any representation and take care of grievances and get an adequate contract, at that moment they'll be thrown out in the street because the only reason the growers brought them in was to interfere with us and keep us from getting a legitimate contract, and so we're all the way out in the street, but we're in better shape than the Teamsters are.

"We'll break them," Chavez promised. "Don't ask me how long it will take, but we'll break them! Five years? Ten years? We're very patient. The other side has money; we have time . . . the great friend of the poor. And we have something else they don't have. We have people and a lot of love and understanding."

The UFW was spending about $200,000 a month, or more than it was taking in; but despite his pledge of support, Meany rejected Chavez' request for special funding. Meany complained that the AFL-CIO had not gotten a sufficient return for its $1.6 million contribution to the Coachella Valley strike. Yes, Meany said, he understood the problems of organizing farm workers; nevertheless, the strike had not won a single contract, and that made it a "disaster."

Meany finally did officially sanction the UFW's stepped-up boycott, but only after four months of argument within the AFL-CIO's executive council, and only on condition that the UFW not engage in secondary boycotts at markets where AFL-CIO members worked. Thus the UFW no longer said, "Boycott Safeway," but did continue to say, "Don't buy the lettuce and grapes sold at Safeway." Meany, who had been very hesitant in his previous boycott support, urged "the entire AFL-CIO membership to . . . support the boycott. . . . The success or failure of the UFW to win economic and social justice for farm workers will be heavily influenced by the energy and dedication with which the trade union movement pursues the boycott campaign." It would continue, Meany promised, "until the growers recognize the United Farm Workers as the legitimate collective bargaining representative of farm workers."

Other previously hesitant supporters came out in full support, including the National Conference of Catholic Bishops. The bishops had never put their collective strength behind a boycott, but announced that the UFW had "no other recourse." They urged Catholics to support the boycott until growers and Teamsters agreed to unrestricted union representation elections. Although he was a practicing Catholic, Fitzsimmons was not moved. "Why should we have an election," he asked, "if we already have the contracts?"

Fitzsimmons denounced the boycott as an unfair tactic, although his own union had used it in the past. In one notable instance, Bill Grami had directed an extremely effective apple boycott during a cannery workers strike in California. Teamster leaders also threatened to send their members through the picket lines of striking AFL-CIO unions, and cannery workers demanded the right to honor picket lines that Teamster farm workers threatened to put up to block the processing of produce picked by UFW members.

Fitzsimmons attempted to ease boycott pressures by shifting the blame for the previous summer's violence to the UFW in an open letter declaring that Meany and Chavez "must bear the blame" for any outbreaks during the forthcoming harvest. Meany, detecting sure signs of Charles Colson's style in the letter, called it "unmitigated gall." The previous year's violence, said Meany,

> resulted solely and simply because the Teamsters imported goons. Everyone—including Fitzsimmons—knows this. . . . For anyone to blame the Farm Workers for being the victims of violence is like blaming the victims of a mugging for walking on a public street. . . . It was Teamster goons who were indicted for beating up aged strikers, including women. . . . It was Farm Workers who were killed, beaten and hospitalized. . . . It was Teamster violence that forced the Farm Workers to halt picketing. . . . The time-tested and time-honored code of morality in the trade union movement has been that the strong help the weak; not that the strong destroy the weak.

Few AFL-CIO unions backed off from supporting the boycott, but some of the UFW's political allies did, now that two influential unions were competing for their support. The politicians said they must be "neutral."

Growers encouraged the public and politicians alike to remain neutral by picturing the dispute as a jurisdictional fight between unions that should be waged without outside interference. Alan Grant, the California Farm Bureau president who had been the most vociferously antiunion of the growers' spokesmen, suddenly was protesting that "the public is still led to believe that the struggle is between workers and growers, when in fact the growers are committed to union contracts." Hence it would be downright unfair to boycott the growers' produce.

Growers and market owners also tried to get around the boycott by securing dozens of injunctions against mass picketing by boycott committees and by putting UFW labels on boxes of Teamster-picked lettuce and grapes. The UFW added to the confusion and weakened what little grower support the union retained by advising supporters who were in doubt to simply boycott *all* lettuce and grapes, including shipments from growers who still held UFW contracts.

The UFW's nationwide network of boycott committees was extremely well organized, however, and continuously attracted energetic and dedicated newcomers to work with those who had learned valuable tactical lessons over the past five years. Their rallies and demonstrations, now held outside Teamster headquarters as well as in shopping areas, were coordinated with advertising, mail and telephone campaigns and an extremely wide array of other activities designed to keep UFW supporters active and interested and the image of a Teamster-grower conspiracy constantly before the public.

Sympathizers who couldn't actively participate in picketing and leafletting and a steady round of meetings and fund-raising affairs could buy UFW buttons, jewelry, posters, phonograph records, decals, commemorative stamps, flags, belt buckles, bumper strips, calendars. Boycott committee newsletters kept supporters well informed and in close contact, just as UFW members were drawn together through the bilingual union newspaper, *El Malcriado*. It told them of UFW and UFW support activities in the fields and in cities all over the world, provided them with practical advice on legal and health matters as well as on their own labor activities, and gave them a feeling of unity, importance and militancy. *El Malcriado* even had a gossip column, an employers' letter column ("Cowpies from the Growers") and an inspirational comic strip on the life of Emiliano Zapata.

Chavez embarked on a grueling round of speaking engagements that took him all over the country. He had become a major figure, and at every stop there inevitably was a news conference that gave him an opportunity to deliver the UFW's boycott plea to yet another group of consumers. Chavez' appearances served as well to help recruit the thousands of volunteers used in waging the boycott. One of Chavez' favorites was a sixty-year-old woman who came up to him at a meeting in Saginaw, Michigan, after he had called for volunteers. She said:

She couldn't get out there on the picket line, although she wanted to with all her life. But she just couldn't because her legs were bad. But she said she did go to the stores often to look for grapes and when she found them she always took a greeting from me to them. She said, "I go and I get their hand and I really squeeze their hand." She said, "I give you regards from Cesar Chavez." She looked like an angel. . . .

As intensive as it was, the UFW campaign swayed only a minority of shoppers. But, as a newspaper editorial noted, it "polarized the public to the point where friends have become estranged, refusing to eat salad or fruit at each other's tables," and it did have a noticeable impact, especially on grape sales and prices. One of the leading Delano growers, Louis Caratan, estimated his sales were down "10 percent or maybe 20 percent." Overall, grape growers lost at least $2 million in 1973; twice that, according to UFW reports.

Neither growers nor Teamsters would be moved, however, and the UFW campaign began lagging for lack of victories. Even George Meany declared he was "very pessimistic" about the future of the UFW. The union renewed its strikes against the grape and lettuce growers when the 1974 harvest began, and engaged in a flurry of brief, well-publicized strikes in a half-dozen other crops throughout California and Arizona, but also without winning contracts. Then, as the UFW had done so many times before, it found an issue to capture new public attention and support. The Gallo winery, which had abruptly switched to the Teamsters after holding UFW contracts for six years, was singled out as the major target; the cry of "Boycott Gallo!" would markedly transform the UFW campaign.

Gallo was a more formidable opponent than the grape and lettuce growers. It would take tremendous economic pressure to move the firm; Gallo alone produced 37 percent of the country's wine, 45 percent of that produced in California. This amounted to 150,000 cases per day and $250 million in sales per year, more than twice Gallo's nearest competitor. But Gallo's dominant position also would make it a highly visible target. Gallo wines were sold everywhere, year-round, and the boycott would draw thousands of new UFW supporters into action and give the union an extremely important new organizing tool.

The boycott also was designed to put pressure on the small grape growers who had resisted UFW demands, since Gallo relied on 2000 of those growers for most of its supplies. Gallo grew only about 10 percent of its own grapes, at vineyards that spread out around the firm's luxurious headquarters in Modesto, 110 miles southeast of San Francisco.

Huge stainless steel vats stood as towering, shining sentinels beside the headquarters building. It stood atop Modesto's only hill, its neo-colonial facade unblemished by the Gallo insignia or any other sign indicating that business was being transacted inside. Gallo had climbed to its preeminent position on the production and sale of low-grade fortified wine—"rot gut," as some inelegantly described it—but there was no clue of that beyond the tall hand-carved doors. The entire floor was a mammoth reception area. Along the edges of the marble floor fat carp swam lazily in clear, sparkling pools; above the pools, exotic multicolored parrots flitted among lush ferns and decorous overhanging trees. The entryway was covered with a carefully crafted rug, the initials "E & J" woven discreetly in the center. That would be Ernest and Julio Gallo, the founders and masters of the Gallo wine empire; proud, aloof men who didn't easily share authority with others.

The Gallos and their families lived nearby in sequestered luxury, with tennis courts and swimming pools shielded from the public eye by stands of tall shade trees.

The men and women who harvested the Gallos' grapes lived in camps down the road, also in houses owned by the Gallo family. Many of them were Portuguese, brought from the Azores Islands after termination of the bracero program curtailed the supply of Mexican workers. One of their camps consisted of twenty one-room apartments, fourteen of them housing families of five and six, the single small rooms divided by faded drapery slung over ropes strung between the walls. Camp residents shared a communal bathroom facility, a dimly lit cement-floored building containing a few leaky toilets. Flies, rats and cockroaches were not uncommon.

The UFW's dispute with the Gallos had begun in the summer of 1973, after negotiators failed to reach agreement on renewing the union's expired contract. Gallo had operated without serious complaint under two UFW contracts; but like the grape growers in Delano who were negotiating with the UFW on new contracts during the same period, Gallo suddenly objected to those provisions that gave the UFW and its members a voice in hiring and operations. For the Teamsters had also offered Gallo the irresistible opportunity to sign contracts that would not infringe greatly on employer authority.

Gallo negotiators demanded that the UFW give up the hiring hall and its right to determine the seniority of workers and discipline them for violating union rules. Gallo claimed to be acting for employees who complained of "favoritism and cronyism" in the dispatching of workers and of facing loss of "good standing" in the UFW and thus loss of their jobs for not making back dues payments and not taking part in lettuce boycott demonstrations and other activities as required by their union constitution.

Such attempted employer interference in internal union affairs was unusual, to say the least; but Gallo's concerns were not those of its employees, in any case. The main concern was what Ernest Gallo called the UFW's "inefficiency" and lack of a "businesslike" approach. Gallo did not relish dealing with the elected committee of workers that negotiated the UFW's contracts and carried out their day-to-day enforcement. He wanted to deal directly with Chavez, one to one, as the employers of Teamsters often deal solely with Teamster officials, unhindered by the direct demands of their employees. Said Gallo:

> Leaving it up to the ranch committee was entirely impractical. . . . When you leave it up to the workers, how energetic are they going to be? There was no control of the worker by the field boss and owner. This has resulted in complete loss of discipline, excessive labor costs and poor quality of work. . . . Teamsters are more professional and experienced in administering contracts.

Some of Gallo's workers saw the situation a bit differently, however. One, Manuel Hernandez, recalled:

> Before the UFW contract, everybody had to run working, had to take three steps each vine and they had to be sort of running steps. You always had the foreman right behind your back. They would yell at you quite a bit. . . . If it wasn't the foreman yelling at you, it was the supervisor, the superintendent.

Ernest Gallo made his comments after signing the Teamster contract that replaced the expired UFW agreement. While Gallo representatives were negotiating with the UFW on a new contract and telling reporters the UFW doubtlessly represented Gallo's workers, Teamster organizers were allowed into the winery's vineyards. Then, after the UFW negotiations broke off over Gallo's demand for a "businesslike" contract, the winery announced it would begin negotiations with Teamster representatives. Such a procedure is illegal under the NLRA, which Gallo claimed to support; but the act, of course, did not cover agriculture.

Gallo and the Teamsters claimed a heavy majority of field workers had signed petitions urging Gallo to switch unions; at least half of the workers nevertheless struck to protest Teamster recognition. Undeterred, Gallo hired replacements and quickly concluded negotiations with the Teamsters.

The new contract would, of course, require Gallo employees to join the Teamsters. But there would be no need for them to take part in union activities. All they needed to do to remain in "good standing" was to pay their dues. There would be no bothersome election of worker committees to press grievances and discuss work procedures, the use of pesticides and other safety matters with supervisors, no troublesome hiring hall to allot work according to seniority. There wouldn't even be any union meetings.

This was true for all farm workers under Teamster contracts, as Einar Mohn, the Teamsters' Western Conference director, explained in an unusually candid interview with a graduate student, Jane Yett Kiely, who was assigned by Safeway Stores to make an independent study of the Teamster-UFW dispute. Mohn told Kiely:

> It will be a couple of years before they can start having membership meetings, before we can use the farm workers' ideas in the union. . . . I'm not sure how effective a union can be when it is composed of Mexican-Americans and Mexican nationals with temporary visas. Maybe as agriculture becomes more sophisticated, more mechanized, with fewer transients, fewer green carders, and as jobs become more attractive to whites, then we can build a union that can have structure and that can negotiate from strength and have membership participation.

Kiely wondered what would happen to workers displaced by mechanization; was "there any protection in the contracts for them?" No, said Mohn:

> That isn't a problem to solve in this way. Shortage of jobs is the problem. If there weren't such a shortage of jobs, Mexican-Americans could get jobs. I don't know what will happen to the Mexican-Americans. After all, you can't expect whites to step aside and let Mexican-Americans and Negroes have the [machine] jobs they have had for years.

Publication of Mohn's remarks touched off a controversy; but though Mohn claimed Kiely's report was "misleading," he reiterated that "it will be a couple of years before farm workers will be able to take any real part in membership meetings."

In practice, the Teamster approach meant that at Gallo's vineyards appointed Teamster business agents came by occasionally to see how things were going, but that hiring and firing, determination of seniority and how work should be performed was handled by Gallo alone. It was more efficient that way.

Gallo claimed its workers ratified the contract 158–1; but there were another 173 Gallo employees on the picket line by then, and they all had signed authorization cards indicating they wanted a UFW contract. They demanded an election to prove it. The Teamsters, however, were "not going to go for any Mickey Mouse election of any nature," according to the chief Teamster organizer, Jim Smith—the same Jim Smith who had signed with the Delano growers during the UFW-Teamster peace talks.

Gallo offered strikers a chance to return to work under the Teamster contract; those who didn't were fired and ordered out of the company camps. Many had no place else to stay, however, and there were twenty-four families who wouldn't budge from one camp. Gallo tried eviction notices and orders against trespassing, then cut off garbage collection and maintenance service. Toilets clogged, the septic tank sprang a leak and drinking water became contaminated, but still they wouldn't leave. Finally, the UFW filed a $3.5 million suit demanding repairs and Gallo agreed to clean up the camp. Gallo insisted it had tried to repair the deteriorating facilities, but that strikers kept maintenance men at bay with showers of rocks—until after the UFW filed its damage suit. Gallo suspected the UFW was just seeking publicity for its boycott. And that's just what the union got—lots of it.

The boycott cause wasn't hurt, either, by the arrest of sixty strikers for entering a Gallo vineyard and doing battle with nonstrikers. Twenty-five of the strikers were held for nine days in a stifling, windowless warehouse that served as a temporary jail, until a judge dropped a bail requirement of $300 per striker and released them on their own recognizance.

The UFW could not get official AFL-CIO support for the Gallo boycott because of objections from the distillery workers and bottle makers unions, whose members worked inside Gallo's winery. But the union recruited at least as potent a force among college students and other young UFW supporters who made up a significant segment of Gallo's market. They formed a virtual boycott army, constantly popping up in front of liquor stores in thousands of neighborhoods across the country. It was a never-ending task, however. A store might agree to take Gallo off its shelves, but there always was another store down the street or around the corner that still stocked the wine, and even those who went along with the boycott had a habit of putting Gallo bottles back on the shelves after the pickets left.

Gallo and liquor store associations also waged a strong counter-campaign. Gallo advertised extensively, pleading that the firm was caught in a jurisdictional dispute, citing its alleged support for extending the NLRA to agriculture and claiming Gallo field workers were now the highest paid in the continental United States.* "Don't boycott

---

* Gallo employees were paid $3.10 to $4.05 an hour plus piece rates under the Teamster contract, which did put them among the highest paid workers on an hourly basis (although not necessarily on an annual basis). But the rate was no higher than that in most UFW contracts and probably no higher than the UFW would have won from Gallo had the union abandoned its opposition to the terms that Gallo later demanded of the Teamsters in exchange for the pay rate, and thus been able to renegotiate its contract with the winery.

Gallo wines," the ads argued. "They are 100 percent union made." Gallo also sent letters to thousands of churches and synagogues, asserting that the winery's purpose was to maintain "a warm family-like relationship" with its workers and "protect" them from the UFW.

In California, liquor stores secured injunctions severely limiting the number of boycott pickets, on grounds that mass picketing was creating "the fear of immediate violence" in customers and potential customers. Boycott supporters defied the court orders, got free time on radio and television stations to respond to Gallo's ads and took legal action of their own. They charged Gallo with illegally hiding its identity by not putting the firm name on the labels of some of the wines it marketed under more than a dozen different brand names and with using its dominant position to "artificially inflate prices" and engage in other illegal marketing practices.

The UFW also sought support through a campaign against a heavy influx of illegal aliens from Mexico who were being hired by struck growers and otherwise being used to undercut the pay and conditions of domestic workers and to hinder unionization. The situation was much like that under the defunct bracero program, except that the Mexican workers now being brought in were denied even the minimal protections that had been available under that program.

The illegal aliens paid contractors—*coyotes,* as they were called—from $100 to $500 to smuggle them across the border in rickety trucks and buses, sometimes in the trunks of autos or in closed containers. They were cramped together in shacks that often were no more than crudely converted chicken coops, hidden from agents of the Immigration and Naturalization Service, paying whatever the grower demanded for food and their primitive lodgings and working at whatever pace he set. They were desperately poor and there were no effective legal sanctions against their employers, so few dared complain; if they did, they could be deported immediately and possibly fined.

The conditions endured by the illegal aliens were described graphically by author Christopher Biffle, who visited one of the crumbling houses where they lived in hiding:

The room . . . was long and narrow, had probably once been the living room, but now was crammed with rotting cots and mattresses. The walls had large holes where the plaster was smashed in, some of these had been patched with bits of cardboard boxes. Fifteen or twenty men were sitting in this one small room, most were stripped to the waist and sweating. . . . All the beds were sheetless and coverless; most of them were very thin mattresses on cotlike frames. The mattresses were old, filthy from having been slept on without a covering, and many were split apart, spilling their filling. I could see small black bugs everywhere on them and inside them. . . . They had one very small stove in the kitchen. . . . The cupboards had no doors and contained a surprisingly small amount of food for the number of men. There was one bathroom. The toilet worked but the bathtub didn't. . . . The walls in the house seemed to have been painted white at one time, but they had all turned a muddy color from years of dust and sweat. There were no closets; the men had strung clotheslines across the corners of the rooms and had hung their work clothes neatly over these. . . . Everything in this house seemed drowned in smell; it made the strongest single impression. The walls seemed to have gone dark with it and at first it was choking. It was the rank, powerful odor of men who had worked in dirt and this was laid, season after season, on top of the smell of the food they cooked—a smell of sweat and lard and then the reek of the mattresses and dank plaster that had absorbed these smells.*

Federal officials estimated that perhaps one-third of California's farm workers were illegal aliens, and farm workers commonly believed that by 1974 at least half the workers on San Joaquin Valley farms were "illegals." They put the number as high as 50,000. Many growers privately agreed with the farm workers' estimate, but claimed, as they had under the bracero program, that they needed Mexican workers to get their crops harvested.

UFW investigators found 2200 illegal aliens in one six-county area alone, as evidence of what Chavez called "the worst invasion of illegal aliens in our history." Chavez got ready agreement from the woefully understaffed Immigration and Naturalization Service; its agents were still fortunate if they apprehended one illegal alien in five, yet the number of arrests had doubled since 1970. Arrests were being made in the valley at a rate of more than 1000 a month and the total was rising steadily. At the same time, however, the number of agents was being held down; there were only ten agents to cover the valley's major farm area, but local officials pleaded in vain for more help from Washington.

Chavez blamed it on a "conspiracy" among growers and the Nixon Administration; for "if we could get the illegals out of the grape fields and if we could get the illegals out of the lettuce fields, the growers would have to come and meet with us in 24 hours. . . . We do not blame the illegals—who are our brothers and sisters—because they are only the tools used by others to try and destroy our movement. But their pressure hurts the aspirations of all farm workers for a decent life, a decent job and a decent wage."

* Christopher Biffle, "Illegal Aliens, 'Late on a Moonless Night.' " *The Nation,* January 25, 1975, p. 80.

The UFW set up a "border patrol" of its own to try to stop aliens as they crossed the border in southwest Arizona to take jobs with struck lemon growers. Tents were set up along a line fifty yards from the border to shelter UFW patrolmen who drove up and down border roads while a spotter plane circled above them. Aliens caught coming over the low border fence were taken to a central gathering point and urged to return home, or were turned over to border patrolmen from the Immigration and Naturalization Service.

The UFW's opposition to illegal aliens brought the union into serious conflict with Mexican-American organizations; they felt the growing attacks on illegal aliens were discriminatory to the aliens and to Mexicans and Mexican-Americans generally. The UFW agreed, and soon took another position. It would not flatly oppose entry of illegal aliens, who apparently couldn't be stopped anyway. The union would merely oppose their employment as replacements for strikers; and it would try to organize the aliens, as it had organized Mexicans who had come into the country legally for temporary work over UFW objections. The decision was formalized in a UFW convention resolution declaring that "if growers can bring illegal workers to this country for the purpose of exploiting them, then we can organize illegal workers to liberate them." All workers here illegally, the resolution added, should be declared "legal" and granted amnesty from deportation and other penalty.

Widespread public concern prompted introduction of legislation by Chairman Peter Rodino of the House Judiciary Committee that would supposedly curb the flow of illegal aliens by imposing penalties on employers who "knowingly" hired them. The UFW had called for such legislation in the past, and many of its liberal backers endorsed the bill; but the union now joined the forces that blocked its passage on the grounds that it did not carry a specific prohibition against using illegal aliens as strikebreakers, did not impose strict enough penalties to deter employers, did not ease restrictions on the legal immigration of Latin Americans and would discriminate against all Mexican and Mexican-American workers by requiring them to prove they were legal residents.

The UFW's unceasing campaign against the labor contractor system permitted by Teamster contracts also was brought to broad public attention after the crash of a contractor's bus near Blythe in the Imperial Valley. Nineteen workers were killed when the bus careened around a curve just before dawn and skidded into a water-filled ditch, trapping workers inside in a mass of seats so flimsily moored that all of them tore loose on impact. The driver had worked a full day in the fields before picking up the bus at 2 o'clock that morning, and had already driven more than 250 miles when he turned into that curve; it was posted for 20 miles an hour, but highway patrolmen said the bus was going at least 45 miles an hour.

Although the workers were under a Teamster contract, it was the UFW that provided aid and comfort. Chavez and others from the union and the Migrant Ministry rushed to the scene, helped make funeral arrangements and collected $2000 from farm workers to aid the families of the dead.

"We are united in our sorrow, but also in our anger," Chavez told some 2000 mourners at a memorial Mass two days after the crash. "This tragedy happened because of the greed of the big growers who do not care about the safety of workers and expose them to great dangers when they transport them in wheeled coffins to the fields. . . . These accidents happen because employers allow labor contractors to treat us as if we were not important human beings."

Chavez estimated that "90 percent of the labor buses in California could not pass inspection and are not fit to be on the roads." Inspections carried out later under new state regulations prompted by the UFW's outcry indicated Chavez may not have been exaggerating in the slightest. Highway patrolmen who inspected about one-fourth of the 2100 vehicles used to transport farm workers found that 95 percent failed their tests, about half because they were unsafe mechanically. Inspectors discovered leaky mufflers, dangerously loose nuts, bolts, screws, and wheels, dim taillights, missing clutch and brake springs, and that many of the vehicles did not even carry spare tires.

Attempts to require drivers to undergo special training and to otherwise tighten the law further were rejected, however, and serious accidents continued. Less than two months after the accident near Blythe, twelve workers were killed in a crash near the Mexican border.

Despite the UFW's stress on Gallo as the major boycott target, the union did not entirely neglect the grape and lettuce campaigns. Attempts by growers to increase sales in Europe, which already accounted for almost 15 percent of their market, sent Chavez on a three-week tour in the fall of 1974. He met with Pope Paul VI, Dr. Phillip Potter, executive secretary of the World Council of Churches, and with other religious, labor and political leaders in Britain and on the continent, drawing extensive media coverage and pledges of support.

The UFW's ever-busy legal staff also continued pressing suits against growers and Teamster officials—more than two dozen of them detailing a variety of actions that allegedly violated the right of farm workers to choose their own representatives. It resulted, finally, in a most unusual court order that prohibited the UFW from filing any further suits against the Teamsters, or even against growers charged with firing UFW supporters. A superior court judge issued the order after Teamster lawyers complained the UFW was "abusing the lawful process of the courts" by filing "piecemeal, repetitious and baseless litigation . . . for the purpose of harassing the Teamsters and their officers." The American Civil Liberties Union, the deans of major California law schools and others rose quickly to defend the UFW from what the union condemned as "a fundamental attack on the Bill of Rights," and the order was rescinded after two and a half months on grounds that it did indeed violate basic constitutional rights.

13

A Union of Their Own

The UFW's steady pressures did not noticeably slow the Teamsters. The union, which already held more than 300 farm labor contracts covering 50,000 workers in California and Arizona, moved ahead with plans to organize thousands more throughout all thirteen western states. That would add at least $100,000 a month to the $2.4 million the Teamsters had spent on agricultural organizing so far.

The vehicle for the drive would be a brand-new Teamster local, No. 1973, which was chartered in the summer of 1974 at ceremonies in a richly appointed lodge south of the new local's headquarters in Salinas. Teamster President Frank Fitzsimmons himself was there, in a thickly carpeted reception room close by a golf course, flanked by the West's top Teamster leaders. Three dozen farm workers, brought from around the state by the Teamsters and paid $60 for the day, were deployed about the room, awkwardly balancing cocktails and hors d'oeuvres and telling reporters how much they appreciated working under Teamster contracts. The glass doors leading to the reception area were locked; outside, below low wooden barriers, Teamster organizers and private guards scrutinized arriving cars for uninvited guests. Salinas growers had been invited, but they were otherwise occupied; more than 1000 of their workers had struck that day to protest the chartering of Local 1973—even though most of the workers were under Teamster contracts.

Despite the precautions, about 100 of the strikers managed to get onto the lodge grounds. They gathered angrily below the low balcony outside the reception room, waving the red and black flags of the UFW and spoiling the Teamsters' attempt to tell their story without contradiction.

As the demonstrators outside booed and jeered, Fitzsimmons took the podium to declare that "we are bringing a strong trade union movement into the fields and vineyards and we are proud of this role

in the better working conditions, pay and benefits that this development represents for the minority Americans who make up such a large
part of the farm worker force . . . for the first time there is a strong
union of farm workers of their own choosing."

Fitzsimmons denounced Chavez as "no more a labor leader than
the man on the moon. . . . We're not interested in causes; we're interested in having a union that will properly represent all the farm
workers."

As head of Local 1973, Fitzsimmons appointed a Mexican-American, David Castro, who appeared to have nothing in common with
Chavez beyond his ancestry. Castro had worked for a Teamster cannery workers local for the past twenty-one years, but an official biog-
raphy assured reporters he had been a migrant for many years before
that and "engaged in his first walkout from the fields in 1934, at the
tender age of nine." Lest reporters get another impression from his
styled hair, fashionable eyeglasses, expensive doubleknit suit and
$550-a-week salary, Castro hastened to explain that "ever since I
could afford it, I like to wear a suit and tie, and in all my working
days in the fields I was never hungry or dirty."

It wasn't just appearance that set Castro off from Chavez. Chavez
might believe in building a union from the bottom up, but Castro had
other ideas. There would be no elections in Local 1973 for at least
two years, until he was "better known among the workers." Nor would
members decide for themselves how the local should be run or what
went into its contracts with growers. The members' "primary responsibility," said Castro, was to learn and follow the procedures laid
down by their appointed officials and to learn and abide by the terms
of the contracts the officials had negotiated.

But Local 1973 would try to do well for its members. For starters,
the workers who had been brought to the charter ceremony were
whisked off to a Salinas motel to be wined and dined from midafter-
noon until well past midnight (the bar bill alone ran to more than
$500). The local hired sixty organizers at $200 to $325 a week each
plus expenses and set up a complete social service department.

Five months later, Local 1973 was all but abolished. Its jurisdiction was cut back from the thirteen western states to the area just
around Salinas, the social services department closed and members
outside Salinas assigned to Teamster locals in their areas that were
controlled by Anglo truck drivers. Castro and most of the organizers
were fired or shifted elsewhere.

The official explanation, as voiced by a Teamster public relations
man, was that "we want to streamline our operations and make them

more efficient. . . . Rather than carry on any massive organizing campaign . . . we want to sell the services of the Teamsters to those we already have under contract, and then we can expect growth because our reputation will be spread by word of mouth."

Local 1973 actually fell victim to a power struggle within the Teamsters. As director of field organizing for the union's Western Conference, Bill Grami had taken control of the local, and that gave him a huge power base. For one thing, it would give Grami a lot of votes at the next Teamster convention in support of Hoffa's attempt to oust Fitzsimmons as union president. Fitzsimmons had replaced Einar Mohn as Western Conference director with a younger, more aggressive man, Andy Anderson, and when Anderson saw Grami's growing power, he quickly cut back Local 1973 and eliminated Castro and the organizers who were loyal to Grami. Grami was assigned to another job in the conference hierarchy and Castro shifted to a small Arizona town at a pay cut of $200 a week. Grami took it quietly, but Castro made the mistake of writing Fitzsimmons a letter in which he complained that "I was used by you, Frank . . . subjected to crap, ignored and humiliated like a man with leprosy." Fitzsimmons forwarded the letter to Anderson, and Castro was fired. Castro filed complaints with government agencies, seeking $4600 in back wages and charging the Teamsters with "a systematic policy and practice of removing Mexican-Americans from positions of authority," but he never did get his job back.

The UFW greeted the cutback of Local 1973 as a sign that the Teamsters would leave agriculture entirely. But though the Teamsters did not do any further organizing of consequence, the union held tenaciously to the contracts that had to be overturned if the UFW was to grow. Chavez counseled patience, insisting that the UFW's boycotts and other activities eventually would force out the Teamsters. He urged workers at farms under Teamster contract to "build and organize! Do it quietly, but do it! Do it clandestinely, but do it! Do it silently, but do it!" Chavez also suggested they withhold dues from the Teamsters and told those in Salinas that "when you work in the lettuce, don't do such a careful job—slow down."

But the media, which had done so much to build the broad public support that sustained the UFW, would not be patient. It became the journalistic fashion to proclaim that the UFW was in its death throes. *Time* magazine spoke of "a public that seems to have grown tired of causes great and small" and a writer for *The New York Times Magazine* discovered that "the charisma and the cause" were giving way to the "shrewd skill and raw power of the Teamsters Union." The journalists did not understand the power of the forces they had helped bring into play or the built-in staying power of the UFW and the nature of its opponents. "The Teamsters and the growers have money, education, political influence and public relations firms," said Chavez. "They have the kind of power that is easily recognized in America in 1974; but they do not reach the hearts and consciences of people. They have to pay for everything they do."

The predictions of the UFW's coming death suddenly disappeared after one sunny day in the spring of 1975 when nearly 15,000 people marched past the Gallo Winery in Modesto and into that city's Graceda Park. Never had there been such a massive demonstration for the UFW, not even at the end of the dramatic march to Sacramento that had started the union toward its first major success nine years earlier.

More than 250 of the demonstrators had walked the entire 110 miles from San Francisco to Modesto in a week-long march intended to show Gallo, the general public and especially California's newly-elected governor, Edmund G. Brown Jr., that the UFW was indeed very much alive. The marchers led a procession fully a mile long into the park; they filed in four to eight abreast, waving red banners and chanting, "Cesar *si,* Teamsters no, Gallo Wine has got to go!" There were farm workers, young people, priests, nuns, ministers, people from seemingly every walk of life, thunderously applauding Chavez' promise that "we will win our contracts back!" It was the same coalition of supporters that had helped win the contracts originally—with the notable exception of the AFL-CIO, which would have no part in a boycott against a winery that employed its members. As a matter of fact, the AFL-CIO's local Labor Council sent a message of protest to be read at the demonstration, declaring Gallo to be "a fair employer." But the demonstrators barely noticed it among the dozens of messages of support from liberal Democratic politicians, prominent church leaders, entertainers and officers of independent unions such as the Auto Workers.

Gallo fought back with a series of full-page newspaper ads reiterating the winery's assertion that it treated field workers well, was caught between two unions and would support an election between the two under the NLRA or equivalent procedures.* Gallo's eager public

* The UFW took up Gallo's proposal by offering to submit to an election under NLRA rules, which prohibit losers from boycotting, striking or making any other attempts to continue pressing their recognition demands for a year after the vote. The union said it would put up a $1 million performance bond as a guarantee; but Gallo balked, on grounds that the Teamsters would not

relations men emphasized the message by hanging a huge banner beneath the windows of an upper floor of San Francisco's stately St. Francis Hotel, overlooking the outdoor rally which inaugurated the march; it read: "Gallo's Farm Workers Best Paid in U.S. Marching Wrong Way, Cesar?" Another banner was draped across Gallo's headquarters' building as marchers filed past a week later. It told them there were "73 More Miles to Go. Gallo Asks UFW to Support NLRA-type Laws in Sacramento to Guarantee Farm Worker Rights."

Ernest Gallo almost never met directly with reporters, but the march moved him to call one of his first news conferences. Gallo sat stiffly behind a long table, his public relations director standing between him and reporters seated at rows of tables, the rear of the room filled with Gallo office workers and representatives of the distillery workers and bottle makers unions, who joined Gallo in denouncing the UFW's boycott and march.

Reporters asked Gallo about reports in *The Wall Street Journal* and trade publications indicating Gallo sales had dropped 9 percent over the year nationally, much more in some college towns and other particular markets, while sales of other wines increased. Could that be attributed to the boycott, or perhaps, as some analysts said, to overproduction of so-called pop wines? It couldn't be attributed to anything, said Gallo, because *sales had not dropped.* He would not elaborate, however: "The Gallo Winery, as you know, is a family organization. Our figures are not made public. You must take my word for it. . . ."

Gallo charged that farm workers had been forced to take part in the march because of the UFW contract provisions requiring participation in union activities. He said it was "that very type of tactic which caused our workers to join the Teamsters; they were forced to go out of town during weekends." It was "a really sad sight . . . children who had been dragged through the parade, parents who had been taken from their jobs. . . ."

Gallo held the news conference immediately after conclusion of the rally that ended the march, but he hardly could be expected to overcome the impact of such a demonstration. It was more than enough to convince Governor Brown and a majority of state legislators that the

---

take part in any election until after their contract expired in 1977. An informal poll was taken by a task force from the National Council of Churches just before the march, and it showed an "overwhelming preference" for the UFW among Gallo workers. The Task Force reported that the Teamsters had not represented the workers "in an effective, vigorous, democratic fashion" and had engaged in "systematic discrimination" against Mexican-Americans and other minority workers.

UFW retained a sizable and influential constituency and great organizational ability. They would listen very seriously to the UFW's demand for a state farm labor law significantly different from the "NLRA-type law" sought by Gallo, the Teamsters and other growers. The law proposed by the UFW would grant the government protection and union representation elections of the NLRA, but it also would allow farm workers to retain the economic weapons necessary to realize their contract demands.

The UFW had proposed such legislation before, but grower and Teamster lobbyists blocked it by backing union representation bills of their own that *would prohibit* secondary boycotts. It wouldn't have done the UFW much good to get the bills through the legislature anyway, since former Governor Reagan would certainly have vetoed them. But Governor Brown was not a grower ally: as California's Secretary of State, he had helped the UFW fight off the crippling law proposed by growers in their initiative campaign of 1972; he had marched with the UFW, had appointed one of Chavez' long-time assistants as one of his own key aides and had replaced Alan Grant, the antiunion president of the state Board of Agriculture, with Lionel Steinberg, the only Coachella Valley grower to retain a UFW contract.

Brown cited passage of a farm labor bill as a first priority and felt certain legislators would cooperate because of growing public concern that serious violence would break out in the fields if they didn't act soon. It was a gamble, but success was one sure way to firmly establish the new administration in a position of leadership and dispel doubts being raised over the inexperience of the thirty-seven-year-old governor. Brown was careful not to say he would seek a UFW-approved bill; he told the legislature, in fact, that the "appropriate bill . . . will not fully satisfy any of the parties to the dispute." With that, Brown set out on a course that would indeed mark him as a master of political strategy.

He had his staff prepare an administration bill proposing gubernatorial appointment of an Agricultural Labor Relations Board to hear unfair labor practice charges from unions and growers and to conduct elections at the call of a majority of those working for any grower during his peak harvest period. Strikers and anyone else who had worked for the grower during the past three years would be eligible to vote, and the winning union would be able to strike and boycott and require future employees to become members.

Brown had his bill introduced into both the state Assembly, where UFW allies predominated, and the Senate, where Teamster and grower forces prevailed, and then began an intensive campaign to win widespread public support. For two weeks the governor traveled the state, meeting daily with influential people on all sides of the issue. Brown also sent letters to 18,000 key people—"bankers and labor leaders, clergy and growers, those who are directly and even emotionally involved who might have heard a description of the proposal from others," according to the governor's executive secretary.

The descriptions they were hearing from others were not complimentary. Each of the factions involved had its own bill that differed significantly from Brown's measure, and was angered that he had not endorsed its proposal instead of offering his own. The UFW raised the loudest objections, attacking the bill as "basically deceptive." Andy Anderson of the Teamsters called the bill "immoral" because it did not ban the secondary boycott or protect the Teamsters' currently held farm contracts from challenge by election. Growers were less vehement; they were even silent on the fact that the governor's bill would permit strikes at harvest time. But a key grower said they were "dead set" against the provision allowing secondary boycotts.

The UFW felt the rights to strike and boycott were too limited. The UFW's bill put no limit on their use, whereas Brown's measure said they could be used only to press contract demands against growers who had already recognized the union. They could not be used to win recognition; that could come only through government-supervised elections. But the UFW's main objection was that the bill would not automatically void contracts previously signed by the Teamsters. Brown's bill would invalidate Teamster contracts held by growers whose employees voted for UFW representation; but the UFW protested that allowing the contracts to remain in force in the meantime would give them unmerited legal standing and give the Teamsters an advantage in elections at farms where they were in effect.

Brown overcame the grower and UFW objections with compromises worked out during two all-night sessions in his office. Growers accepted the secondary boycott, and the UFW agreed to the restrictions on its use. The UFW nevertheless got most of the important concessions carried in the twenty-six amendments that were put into Brown's bill, including one that would allow the union to challenge Teamster contracts in court prior to elections.

Teamster representatives maintained their opposition; they backed off from insisting that their contracts be immune from challenge, but now claimed Brown's bill threatened to automatically void the contracts, despite the certainty of Brown and the UFW that it did no such thing. Worse, new opposition rose from the state AFL-CIO, its Building and Construction Trades Council and the Packinghouse Workers

Union. They protested an amendment, demanded by the UFW, that would put all of a grower's employees into a single voting unit, whatever their job. This was seen as a clear threat to the building trades' jurisdiction over carpenters, heavy equipment operators and other farm craftsmen, and the Packinghouse Workers' jurisdiction over packing shed workers.

Brown was fearful of upsetting the delicate compromise worked out between the UFW and growers, but had to meet the heavy pressures of AFL-CIO and Teamster forces by proposing three further amendments. They set up separate voting units for packing shed workers, excluded craftsmen from the bill, and specifically guaranteed that Teamster contracts would remain in effect until successfully challenged by an election or in court.

The amendments were accepted by all parties during another long session in Brown's office, and the governor quickly called a special session to hear the bill. The legislature's Republican minority continued to oppose the measure on behalf of a few grower groups, but this had no decisive effect; for the legislature had been presented with a farm labor bill that would satisfy all the fiercely competing interests whose intense distrust of each other had made compromise impossible until Brown, by doggedly refusing to side with any one interest, became a powerful neutral figure through whom they could compromise.

Brown was helped considerably by significant changes in the political climate. The UFW was eager to reach an agreement on just about any measure that would guarantee legitimate elections, since the union was now confident it could win such votes, and the Teamsters could no longer politically oppose free elections. Growers realized the Teamsters could not save them after all; they were still being battered by boycotts, precisely because they had turned to the Teamsters, and UFW pressures were forcing the Teamsters to make stronger contract demands. Growers and Teamsters also were aware that the chance to be involved in a compromise settlement was the best they could expect from a liberal governor and legislature. They could have stalled for a year, but a bill eventually would have passed, and it undoubtedly would have been a lot less to their liking than the compromise bill.

Despite the compromises, the result was as clear a victory for the UFW as for Governor Brown: the first collective bargaining law for farm workers outside Hawaii, and one recognizing that the special problems of farm workers could not be met by the National Labor Relations Act. Most important, as the Catholic Bishops Council of California noted, was the law's "focus on protecting the rights of individual farm workers." It gave them the means to form a strong union of their own choosing to take lasting and effective economic action, with the assurance that nothing would be done until they voted to do it.

Brown wisely cautioned those at the bill signing ceremony not to "overstate what's going on here today; this is the beginning, not the end." There were still tens of thousands of farm workers to organize, hundreds of elections to be conducted, hundreds of contracts to be negotiated, and it would be extremely rough going. But if the law could be made to work it would set an extremely important precedent in U.S. labor-management relations.

Four months later, Brown signed another important bill, granting unemployment insurance to farm workers. The legislature had passed the bill four times previously; but though farm workers suffered more from unemployment than most workers who were covered, Reagan had vetoed the bill each time. He argued it would have put California growers at a disadvantage with growers in other states, since employers finance unemployment benefits. What Reagan hadn't said, however, was that without unemployment insurance, farm workers had to draw welfare benefits, which were financed by property taxes. State reports showed that farm workers were drawing more than $7.5 million a year in welfare payments; and Brown and the legislature saw that as an unwarranted subsidy to growers whose low pay scales and system of using workers on a seasonal basis had caused much of the farm workers' need.

Growers also lost out to the Brown Administration in an attempt to retain use of the short-handled hoe, which kept thousands of field workers bent almost double for most of their working day. Most growers had abandoned it for tools that allowed workers to stand upright, but California's lettuce growers insisted the short-handled hoe was needed for speed and efficiency. Their argument had prevailed during the Reagan Administration, despite physicians' reports of workers who had suffered ruptured spinal disks, arthritis of the spine and other serious back injuries because they were forced to use what the UFW called "this despised tool." But Brown's Division of Industrial Safety ruled, over strong grower objections, that the short-handled hoe was an unsafe tool and could no longer be used. From now on, hoes used by California farm workers would have to be at least four feet long.*

The boycott campaign that had strengthened the UFW for its legal victories was now shown to be the most effective in U.S. history.

---

* Some growers defied the ban on the short-handled hoe by requiring workers to use their bare hands to perform work previously done with the aid of the hoe.

A Louis Harris Poll released in the fall of 1975 showed that 12 percent of the country's adult population—17 million people—had stopped buying grapes because of the boycott; 11 percent, or 14 million, had stopped buying lettuce; 8 percent, or 11 million, had stopped buying Gallo wines. Of those surveyed, 45 percent supported the UFW, only 7 percent backed the Teamsters; 14 percent supported both unions or neither, and 35 percent were uncertain. The UFW got support from 34 percent of those asked to choose between that union and growers, but growers got 29 percent. Harris concluded that "backing for Chavez' union runs strongest among professional people and the college-educated, who support the UFW against growers by roughly a 2–1 margin and who sympathize with the UFW more than the Teamsters by almost 10 to one."

Growers had demanded that the boycott be called off immediately after passage of the new farm labor law. But the UFW intensified it, largely in hopes of forcing growers to hold elections before the law actually went into effect or to at least allow UFW organizers onto their farms to campaign and gather the signatures necessary to call for elections under the law. Teamster organizers were already campaigning on some 400 farms where their union held contracts, but it was a rare grower who allowed access to the UFW.

The UFW began its campaigning with another march—a 59-day, 1000-mile march from the Mexican border through the state's major farm areas, led by Chavez and 60 UFW members and supporters. They might not be able to get onto farms to talk with workers, but their rallies brought workers off the farms to sign election petitions and to hear of the rights which the new law conferred on them—most especially the right not to be intimidated by growers and Teamsters who were telling them how they should vote.

The Teamsters were moved to hold their first meeting of farm workers since the union began signing field contracts on a major scale 5 years earlier. But 1000 chanting UFW supporters showed up at the gathering in Salinas, and the Teamsters quickly decided to hold no further meetings. The union did gets its campaign started off strongly, however, by signing new contracts with 165 lettuce growers which raised base pay by a whopping 42½ cents an hour, or 16 percent, and increased fringe benefits by another 9 percent. That raised minimum pay to $2.96 an hour, compared with the $2.45 in the UFW's few lettuce contracts.

Grower negotiators agreed to the big increase without any fuss but claimed, in their public explanations, that they had no choice because the Teamsters threatened a strike. But as one negotiator said privately, growers also "were willing to give them a damned good contract" in hopes it would help defeat the UFW in the coming elections and free growers from the boycott at last, since the law prohibited such activity by election losers. This gambit would help the Teamsters considerably among the lettuce workers, since voting against the Teamsters would mean nullifying that fat contract and gambling that the UFW could get as much in the contract it would have to negotiate after the election. Teamster organizers also used the lettuce contract in campaigning in other crops, pointing to it as a concrete example of what could be expected from Teamster representation.

Passage of the farm labor law did not shift the conflict entirely to the fields. Brown's nominees to the five-member board which would administer the law came under attack from grower and Teamster lobbyists who almost blocked their confirmation by the state senate. The heaviest attack was directed against Brown's appointment of LeRoy Chatfield, a former Christian Brother who was his director of administration. Chatfield, commended in a UFW convention resolution as "one of the most valuable people the union has ever had in its ranks," had run the UFW's campaigns against Safeway and the growers' antiunion initiative, had set up and administered its medical program and otherwise served as one of Chavez' closest aides for eight years before joining Brown's staff. There was also strong opposition to Board Chairman Roger Mahony, the auxiliary bishop of Fresno, who had long been active in the Catholic bishops' committee which helped the UFW get its first contracts, backed its boycotts and provided other help. The other appointees included a Mexican-American attorney who was active in civil rights affairs and a lawyer who, while handling Teamster matters, also was very active in liberal Democratic Party circles. There was only one grower partisan on the board, a former assistant to the president of the California Farm Bureau, and grower spokesmen protested, as one said, that "the board is oriented toward unionization."

The growers were correct; but what they couldn't—or wouldn't—understand was that it was supposed to be that way. The purpose of the new law, as of the original National Labor Relations Act, was precisely to bring about unionization as a way to end conflict which had been occurring because of widespread efforts to secure it in the absence of orderly legal procedures. The law was not designed to help anyone block unionization but to try to make unionization come about smoothly, and not solely on the terms of the Teamsters which growers had chosen as the lesser of the two union evils they saw facing them.

Grower refusal to accept that essential premise would cause serious problems in administering California's farm labor law.

Argument over the rules which were to govern elections kept the law from going into effect on schedule. The UFW won a fight to have its well-known black eagle and other symbols printed on ballots for the benefit of the thousands of illiterate farm workers but lost in opposing a rule which allowed the Teamsters to call for elections on the mere showing of a majority of the dues authorization cards which were signed as a condition of employment by workers on farms with Teamster contracts. The greatest controversy was over the question of allowing organizers access to farms. The Farm Labor Board took a middle ground by allowing access for limited periods before and after working hours and during lunch and other work breaks. The UFW, which wanted unlimited access, accepted the rule; but growers continued to insist that they alone should decide when—and if—organizers should enter their property. Growers openly defied the access rule with the encouragement of Farm Bureau officials and the help of sheriffs and rural judges who agreed it violated the growers' "constitutional right" against trespassing. Growers freely acknowledged that Teamster organizers were given access to those farms with Teamster contracts; how else, they asked, was the union to administer the contracts? If growers chose to allow only Teamster organizers onto other farms as well, or to allow no organizers at all, they felt that was their legal prerogative.

The Farm Labor Board got a ruling from the state supreme court which stayed the lower court orders against the access rule pending a hearing, but many growers and sheriff's deputies ignored it by claiming the court eventually would uphold their position.* Growers had deputies arrest several hundred UFW members and supporters for trespassing; in some cases, growers hired armed guards or stood guard themselves. In one incident, eight UFW organizers were confronted outside a tomato field near Stockton by forty armed members of the "Posse Commitatus," one of several vigilante groups which had sprung up around the country to "defend" the Constitution against judges and others who interpreted the laws in ways not to their liking. The orga-

---

* The state court eventually upheld the access rule, in a 4-3 decision which cited federal court decisions granting union organizers access to lumber and mining camps and oil tankers when there was no other reasonable way for them to reach workers. Grower attorneys appealed the California decision to the U.S. Supreme Court, but the court ruled it lacked jurisdiction, despite grower claims that constitutional property rights were involved.

nizers backed off; but when deputy sheriffs moved in, the posse leveled
its weapons and one member fired a shotgun blast within an inch of a
deputy's ear, touching off a melee which resulted in the arrest of three
people, including a fourteen-year-old packing an Army rifle.

Both the state and federal attorneys general nevertheless refused
requests from the AFL-CIO to order growers to disarm their guards
and to investigate the conduct of local law enforcement agencies;
threats, intimidation and violence continued. The Farm Labor Board
got a taste of it when seventy-five Teamster adherents led by the
union's chief organizers in Delano and Salinas attacked Bishop Mahony and Chatfield at the board's offices in Sacramento. They kicked
a hole in a wall, pushed Chatfield against it, pinned Teamster buttons
all over his clothing, threw dirt in his face, struck him with picket
signs and made "all kinds of threats . . . like I should resign if I
knew what's good for me." When Bishop Mahony tried to leave, he
was shoved against his car while Teamster buttons were pinned to his
coat and the car's tires slashed.

Even where access was granted to organizers there was likely to be
intimidation. The Farm Labor Board cited Gallo, for example, with
sixty preelection violations that included "taking thousands of pictures
of UFW organizers talking to Gallo workers." Gallo also was charged
with firing pro-UFW employees, purposely hiring Teamster supporters,
displaying pro-Teamster literature and otherwise telling employees
how they should vote.

The UFW filed more than 1000 complaints with the board charging dozens of other growers with similar violations. Some were charged
with padding voting lists with ineligible employees who would vote
against even holding an election and with threatening workers with
bodily harm, loss of jobs or lesser pay, benefits or living quarters if
they even talked with a UFW organizer. The UFW contended that
more than 1800 workers were fired and an undetermined number laid
off because of their UFW sympathies and that illegal aliens who supported the union were reported to the government before they could
vote.

The Labor Board went ahead with the elections nevertheless because of the basic rule that complaints should be investigated *after*
elections in order not to delay voting past the harvest season. The
elections were conducted in an extremely tense atmosphere. Union ob-
servers and agents from the Farm Labor Board were on hand, but
voting took place on grower property, in the presence of armed guards
and grower supervisors, and in most cases workers were brought to
the polls by growers and supervisors. The first results amounted to a

stalemate between the two unions. It was clear most workers wanted union representation, since only seventeen of the first month's elections resulted in victory for the "no union" position. But the other results showed the UFW winning seventy-four elections, the Teamsters winning seventy-three, and each getting roughly the same number of votes.

Chavez blamed intimidation for the UFW's failure to overwhelm the Teamsters. But though that may have been the crucial factor, the UFW had other serious problems. Circumstances had forced the union to abandon its strategy of slowly building an organization of members educated in the principles of self-determination; it had to seek out thousands of new members in a hurriedly conducted election campaign in which the more easily grasped issue of better pay was stressed. Many workers were impressed by the size and power of the Teamsters and the relatively high pay the union had won from growers, and were indifferent at best to the UFW's deeper concerns. Unlike the UFW's dedicated core of members, they did not necessarily want a union of their own; they wanted a union that would *serve them,* without requiring them to do much in return.

"They were always making us go to meetings and rallies," ran a typical complaint from a former UFW member who voted for the Teamsters. There were also complaints against the UFW hiring hall; it was described in Teamster leaflets not as a place where workers decided among themselves on allocating jobs but as a place that "takes away the workers' pride" by forcing them to "beg" for jobs. "With the Teamsters," declared a fifty-five-year-old grape picker who voted against the UFW, "it's like not having a union at all—you are free to work where you want."

Official certification of most elections was held up, pending investigation of complaints. Growers challenged virtually every election in which strikers voted, in defiance of the board rule allowing them to participate; and Teamsters filed complaints against UFW electioneering at the polls; but more than 90 percent of the complaints were from the UFW, which continued filing them in a steady, angry stream that led even sympathetic state officials to grumble privately that the union was bent on clogging the election machinery. Chavez charged that "every election is tainted" and blamed it on the Farm Labor Board's agents and its chief counsel, Walter Kintz, a 16-year veteran of the NLRB staff. Chavez attempted to draw maximum public attention by demanding that Kintz resign; Kintz was "evil," said Chavez, and purposely allowed growers and Teamsters to violate board rules.

The real blame lay with the legislature, for demanding that elections be held so quickly after passage of the law, and with Governor

Brown, for appointing Kintz rather than one of the many talented and imaginative young men on the governor's staff. Kintz was not "evil," but he was no more than an honest and competent bureaucrat, unfitted for the enormous and unprecedented task of administering the new law. Kintz was given just a little more than a month to recruit and train a staff, write regulations and then, in the first month of operation after that, conduct five times more elections than the NLRB had conducted in its entire first year of existence. Kintz' staff, a mixture of NLRB veterans and young people, had neither the time nor experience to deal with the work that swamped the new state agency. During the first five months of operations, through the beginning of 1976, the staff conducted more than 400 elections, was asked to investigate nearly three times that many unfair labor practice charges and had to defend itself against at least 200 lawsuits. The staff had not even anticipated such a work load, because of what Kintz acknowledged as his failure to gauge the extreme depth of farm workers' frustrations and suspicions and the extreme height of their expectations. Kintz defended his staff members for accomplishing "more than anyone could reasonably expect" and praised their "superhuman efforts," but he conceded nonetheless that his agency was doing "less than a satisfactory job."

The chief problem was that failure to resolve most of the unfair labor practice charges resulted in the certification of only 75 elections by the end of 1975. Among those certified was the election at Inter Harvest, the largest of the state's lettuce growers, where the UFW won overwhelmingly and was able to negotiate a precedent-setting contract raising pay 26 percent. But ballot challenges delayed election decisions and contract negotiations at most other major union targets, including Gallo and the Giumarra Corporation, the largest of the grape growers.

Overall unofficial results showed the UFW running far ahead, despite its earlier difficulties in the elections at farms with Teamster contracts, largely because the Teamsters concentrated on defending those contracts and others the union already held rather than seeking recognition from uncommitted growers who might be less helpful to the union's campaign. So, although the Teamsters won about half of the elections on farms with Teamster contracts, the union did not even challenge the UFW on many farms where neither union held a contract. The UFW also won at all 11 farms where it still held contracts, and emerged from the first round of elections with 205 apparently firm victories covering more than 30,000 workers, while the Teamsters ended up with 102 victories covering about 11,000 workers.

It was only a small, shaky start, however; there were more than 200,000 other farm workers in California who had not even had the chance to vote, and challenges continued to block contract negotiations between election winners and growers, seriously undermine the Farm Labor Board's effectiveness and cloud the board's future.

Because of the unanticipated workload, the board quickly used up the $2.5 million the state provided for its first year. At the beginning of 1976, only halfway through the year, the board was forced to lay off its 175 employees and suspend operations for 5 months pending its regular budget appropriation in midyear. This held up certification of more than 200 election results, decisions on more than 1000 unfair labor practice complaints and the processing of hundreds of election petitions. On many of the farms where election results had been certified, growers refused to negotiate contracts with the winners, since there were no board agents to act against those refusing to bargain. In some cases, growers refused to recognize votes by their employees to switch from Teamster to UFW representation. The UFW charged that some other growers took advantage of the situation by firing more than 500 employees for engaging in the union activity protected by the dormant law.

The state legislature was asked for an emergency appropriation to keep the Farm Labor Board operating after its funds were depleted. But that would have taken a two-thirds majority, and Republican and rural Democratic opponents had enough votes to block it, on behalf of grower and Teamster representatives who asserted that the UFW's success in the elections was the result of bias by the board and demanded changes in the board's makeup and operations.*

Kintz resigned during the interim period, as did three board members, including Chatfield, the opponents' main target. Governor Brown indicated he would appoint "neutrals" to the vacant posts, and he and legislative supporters of the farm labor act offered to work with grower and union officials on modifying board operations. But that was not enough for the opponents; they demanded immediate changes which, as one of the UFW's legislative supporters noted, "would amount to a repeal of the act." The changes would have limited sanctions on growers charged with unfair labor practices, curtailed the voting rights of seasonal workers, virtually denied organizers access to farms, trans-

---

* Actually, the Farm Labor Board showed little—if any—bias. All but 5 of the 72 decisions which the board rendered before it suspended operations were unanimous, meaning that in 93 percent of the cases decided, the Teamster and grower representatives on the board sided with the three allegedly pro-UFW members.

ferred many board functions to other agencies and otherwise have
made it easier for growers to escape unionization. The opponents were
adamant: Unless those changes were made, they would not vote to
re-fund the Farm Labor Board. But Governor Brown also was adamant. "I am not going to sell out the farm workers," he promised.
"Compromise is one thing, but betrayal is another."

Opponents also temporarily blocked the board's regular budget appropriation when it came before the legislature in June. They backed
off after the UFW waged a successful campaign for an initiative to
require the legislature to fund the board on a continuous basis, as
well as guarantee organizers the absolute right of access, subject growers to treble damages for unfair labor practices and make it impossible
to further amend the farm labor act except by popular vote. The ease
with which the UFW secured signatures to place the initiative on the
state's November ballot—the union got nearly 720,000, or twice as
many as needed, in just 29 days—convinced opponents to change position, in hopes that if the original law was functioning properly, Californians might be less likely to vote for the initiative, which would
make the law even less palatable to grower and Teamster forces. As
one of the growers' chief legislative allies remarked, "We've got to
have the board in business as a way of defeating the initiative."

All that was needed to secure full legislative support for re-funding
the Farm Labor Board was a face-saving device. Governor Brown all
but abandoned executive functions during the spring and early summer to campaign unsuccessfully for the Democratic presidential nomi-
nation with the major support of Chavez and hundreds of UFW volunteers, pointedly using his uncompromising position on re-funding the
board as an issue; but he finally gave the opponents a way out by
appointing three "neutral" lawyers to the board vacancies. The governor's appointees included Gerald Brown (no relation), a former
member of the NLRB; he was named chairman in place of Bishop
Mahony, who announced he would resign from the board later in the
year.

Once the board was re-funded and the farm labor law became
operative again, growers and their allies launched a successful fight
against the UFW's ballot initiative. The grower forces were careful
not to directly attack their real targets—the UFW and the law itself.
Instead, they spent $1.8 million on a highly deceptive but highly effec-
tive media campaign that characterized the initiative, not as a measure
to keep the law from being further eroded, but as an assault on *everyone's* property rights, because one of its provisions would have written
the Farm Labor Board's access rule into law. The provision said union

organizers could have access to farm property only during three speci-
fied hours per day, strictly limited their number and restricted them to
designated areas. It was aimed, furthermore, at the corporate growers
—7 percent of California's growers overall—who employ three-
fourths of the state's farm workers and thus are the chief targets of
UFW organizers. Yet campaign ads, paid for largely by oil firms and
other corporate interests such as the Southern Pacific Land Company,
featured "grassroots farmers" urging voters to "help me protect my
personal property rights and yours" and implying that organizers
would be allowed to invade their homes and that urban as well as
rural residents—especially wives and daughters—would be threatened
if the initiative passed. "I've raised my family and *daughters* on this
farm and *we* feel threatened," declared one "grassroots farmer." Another small grower—a woman—warned that "I will have no protection or privacy."

The UFW raised almost as much money as the grower forces through
contributions from more than 400,000 individual supporters and put
2,500 volunteers and organizers into its campaign with the backing
of Governor Brown and other leading Democrats, including the party's
successful presidential candidate, Jimmy Carter. But the initiative was
defeated by a margin of more than three to two. This was partly because many of the UFW's supporters apparently felt the union's major
need was met when the legislature re-funded the law, and they believed, as the Los Angeles *Times* said, that "public issues should not
be removed from the give-and-take of the legislative process and
frozen into law by initiative."

The union also was hurt by the reluctance of some supporters to
act with the same enthusiasm as they had before the UFW gained the
power to exert the political influence responsible for passage of the
farm labor act. Their ardor cooled once the UFW moved into a position that required compromise and political partisanship and subjected Chavez to charges, invariably made against successful labor
leaders, that he is a "union boss" seeking personal power.

Failure of the initiative and the weakening of UFW support have
led to serious challenges that continue to hamper the farm labor
law. Growers maintain their strong opposition and are pushing the
legislature to weaken the law and limit its financing.

The law, in short, is far from realizing its potential of bringing
economic justice and peace to California agriculture and pointing
the way to enactment of similar laws elsewhere—especially in Congress, where a substantial body of Democrats is anxiously awaiting a
sign of success.

Even a well-functioning law would present the UFW with almost as formidable a task as it faced during the decade in which the union had no legal protection. The California law only requires growers to *bargain* with election winners and, as Chavez observed, "90 percent of the growers won't sign contracts until after we hurt them with strikes and boycotts." Winning contracts will not end the job, either; administering and policing them will take tremendous effort. For while the UFW has shown unique skill in running strikes and boycotts, it has yet to demonstrate the administrative ability required to successfully run an established union.

The crucial goals lie far beyond winning and adequately enforcing contracts, however. Contracts are merely tools which can force agricultural interests to reform their archaic system of planting crops for the convenience of employers, economic speculators and consumers with little regard for the instability that is imposed on those who harvest them at the times when others decide they should be harvested and who drift from area to area, finding work only irregularly. The laws of nature do not mandate this; thanks to modern irrigation methods, planting can be done in a way to provide year-round jobs and do away with the seasonal and migratory nature of agricultural work, which is at the heart of the farm workers' severe problems. Longshoremen, construction workers and others forced their industries to regularize employment many years ago through strong unions and strongly enforced contracts built around union-controlled hiring halls, and farm workers can reform their industry, too.

Agriculture is perhaps the most irrational industry in the United States; overproduction, cutthroat competition and sloppy and outmoded production, management and marketing practices are the general rule. Those traits once characterized other industries as well, but they disappeared under the pressures of a stabilized work force whose very nature demands rational planning. As Henry Anderson noted in those days when he and others in the Agricultural Workers Organizing Committee were painfully laying the groundwork for what the UFW finally brought about, growers "have been able to survive in their disorganized state by requiring their employees to exist in a disorganized state."

The changes will include heavy use of mechanized production methods; the process already has started under the impetus of union organizing. That will surely destroy jobs, but it will make those that remain less onerous, and no one who represents workers opposes such a development in an industry that still relies on the back-breaking methods of the nineteenth century. What is needed is a guarantee that

the profits of mechanization will be shared with workers, in the form
of higher pay and other benefits, as well as assurances that no one will
be summarily displaced by machines. That is what the UFW seeks in
its contracts and, as has been demonstrated on Hawaii's plantations,
that is what a strong union can get.

Growers will continue to argue nonetheless that the costs of effective unionization will be too great to bear, by claiming that pressures
from the UFW and the Teamsters already have forced deep cuts in
farm profits. Growers will find it very difficult to prove their argument, however. State and federal reports show that farm pay in California has increased 120 percent in the decade since the rise of the
UFW; but at the same time, worker productivity has increased more
than 70 percent, crop output 25 percent, and the net income of California growers overall has more than doubled, that of the average individual grower almost tripled.*

Struggle though they will, growers will not escape the unionization
which has come to other employers. The UFW has proved its staying
power in one of the most rigorous tests any union has ever faced; it
has built a basic structure and organization too firmly established and
too broadly based to be overturned; it has rooted the farm workers'
cause solidly in the mainstream of the country's labor, political and
social movements, and neither the UFW nor its influential and dedicated supporters give the least indication of abandoning the goal of a
strong, effective union for California's farm workers and, eventually,
for farm workers everywhere.

That such a union is needed cannot be disputed. Despite the de-
velopments in California, the status of U.S. farm workers generally
remains almost as low as it has been for a century. The federal minimum wage has been extended to about one-third of the workers, and
pay has risen steadily—but very slowly. Most farm workers still exist
on earnings well below the poverty level and must endure long periods
of unemployment. In 1975, for instance, the average income for the
2.7 million men, women and children who worked on U.S. farms was
less than $2000, the average number of working days only 114—and
1.6 million of the workers could find no employment outside agriculture through which to supplement their meager farm earnings.

Farm workers, in short, remain the country's most oppressed workers, subject to the systematic exploitation of growers and labor con-

---

* Pay, averaging $1.10 to $1.35 an hour in 1964, has risen to about $3 an
hour. Growers' gross income overall went from $3.7 billion in 1964 to $8.5
billion in 1974, net income from $1 billion to $2.1 billion. The average grower's net income increased from $11,378 to $33,070.

tractors, with woefully inadequate diets, housing, health care and schooling their common lot.

Social insurance and welfare programs have been extended to farm workers, but in practice the programs have provided very little aid. Nor has there been much improvement in the lax enforcement of the laws enacted to regulate the marginal working conditions which accompany the low pay in agriculture.

But change finally is coming. For the only real questions now are *when* unionization will come on a broad scale, and on what terms. Will it be on the terms of orthodox unions such as the Teamsters, which operate like service clubs, performing important services in exchange for dues? Or will it be in the manner of the UFW, which has fought to involve its members in a broad movement for social, economic and political reform? The final outcome is a long way off, but pressures from the Teamsters and the AFL-CIO and pressures for moderation which come with organizational success could force the farm workers' union to narrow its vision to the limited goals which were set by most other unions after they won their struggles to become established.

Should the pressures prevail, something vitally important will be denied farm workers. Yet even so, farm workers will still have what they have sought since the Industrial Workers of the World raised their banners over the fields of California so long ago. They will have their own strong union. They will exert their collective strength against those whose power has overwhelmed them for almost a century.

Cesar Chavez was correct. *Si se puede.* It can be done.

ACKNOWLEDGMENTS

Thanking all of the hundreds of people who helped me during the eighteen years of reporting on farm labor that went into my work on this book would be impossible. But I would never have been able to do that work at all without the incredible patience, understanding, love, inspiration, skills and knowledge of my wife Gerry.

I also especially want to thank some of my friends and colleagues whose support, aid, and comfort was absolutely essential. Above all, there is Harry Bernstein of the Los Angeles *Times,* whose reporting has made his newspaper by far the country's most important source of information on farm labor and, indeed, on every aspect of labor; Sidney Roger, former editor of the ILWU *Dispatcher;* Ron Taylor of the Fresno *Bee;* Sam Kushner of the *People's World;* Scott Blakey, formerly of KQED-TV in San Francisco, an assignment editor who *understood;* and four filmmakers of extreme sensitivity, Charles Rudnick, Blair Stapp, Lorne Morrison and Peter Hobe. Special thanks and appreciation are due as well to Carey McWilliams of *The Nation,* who first encouraged me to explore the subject, and to Ralph Helstein of the Packinghouse Workers Union, whose early advice proved to be an invaluable guide.

Cesar Chavez' aid also was considerable, from that very first night so long ago when he sat for hours assuring a skeptical reporter from San Francisco that, yes, *it could be done.* Hundreds of others associated with his union, rank and filers, officers and staff members, have been equally helpful, particularly Fred Ross Jr., Jerry Cohen, Jim Drake, Wendy Goepel, Cathy Murphy and Marc Grossman. Special thanks also to Paul Schrade of the United Auto Workers; Glenn Martin and Mike Peevey of the California Labor Federation; Einar Mohn and Bill Kelly of the Western Conference of Teamsters; Tor Torland of the U.S. Labor Department; Al Tieburg, former director of California's Department of Employment; Congressman Phillip Burton of San Francisco; Les Hubbard and Tom Ellick, formerly of the Council of California Growers; and John Giumarra Jr. All were invariably accessible, candid and helpful, often under extremely trying circumstances.

DICK MEISTER

Many people helped me in gathering information for this book, but I would like to thank especially H. L. Mitchell, Paul S. Taylor, and Father James Vizzard for promptly responding to my frequent questions. Also, I want to express my gratitude to Rachelle Marshall and Jean Simpson for dedicated assistance in research. Karl Yoneda gave me background material, including his own writings, on Asian farm workers and early farm labor organizing in California, and I also received useful documents from Pat Chambers, Rosemary Cooperrider and Henry Clay East.

Professor Lawrence DeLucia of the State University of New York, Patricia Palmer, the head of the manuscript collections at the Stanford University Library, and Willa Baum and Malca Chall of the Regional Oral History Office at the University of California in Berkeley advised me on sources of information on farm labor. I would also like to thank Fay Bennett, formerly on the staff of the Rural Advancement Fund, Dorothy Day and her partners in the Catholic Worker movement, and Maena Hendricks, Barbara Baer, Jackson Benson, Devon McFarland, Blanche Nosworthy, Dr. Hubert Phillips, Susan Riggs, and Susan Drake, who all have a connection, either active or literary, with farm labor and shared their insights with me. As always, Bruce Bliven and Mort Lewis helped me as mentors. Elizabeth B. Mason and Louis M. Starr of the Oral History Office of Columbia University gave valuable assistance.

Above all, I have relied on the involvement of my family and the inspiration that came from Chris Hartmire and my committed friends from the summer of 1973.

ANNE LOFTIS

NOTE ON SOURCES

Written material used in the preparation of this book has come from hundreds of sources. The most important dealing with the period since 1940 were the Los Angeles *Times;* Fresno *Bee; People's World; El Malcriado; The Nation; California Farmer; California Farm Bureau Federation Monthly; The Farm Quarterly;* the writings of Chris Hartmire for the National Farm Worker Ministry and of Howard Matson for the Unitarian Universalist Migrant Ministry; of Sidney Roger, Barry Silverman, Dave Thompson and Morris Watson in the *Dispatcher* and other ILWU publications, and the papers of Ronald Haughton and Irwin DeShetler in the Walter Reuther Library at Wayne State University.

Especially valuable material on the IWW and the 1930s period came from the papers of Simon J. Lubin and Paul S. Taylor in the Bancroft Library at the University of California in Berkeley, from the papers of Carey McWilliams at the University of California at Los Angeles, and from two theses, Herman Weintraub, *The IWW in California, 1905–1931* (UCLA, 1947), and Samuel Edgeton Wood, *The California State Commission on Immigration and Housing: A Study of Administrative Organization and the Growth of Function* (UC Berkeley, 1942). Also invaluable were the papers of the Southern Tenant Farmers' Union at the University of North Carolina (quoted on pages 51–52 and 53) and material on the bracero program in the papers of Ernesto Galarza at Stanford University and of Father James Vizzard, S.J., at the University of Santa Clara.

Dozens of reports from government agencies and congressional and legislative committees have been consulted, including especially the La Follette Committee report on the 1933 cotton strike (part 54 of the U.S. Senate Committee on Education and Labor hearings pursuant to S. Res. 266, 74th Congress), *Migratory Labor in California* (State Relief Administration, 1936), Stuart Jamieson's *Labor Unionism in American Agriculture* (U.S. Labor Department Bulletin No. 836, 1945) and proceedings of the Special House Subcommittee on Labor in 1967 (pursuant to HR 4769, 90th Congress). Useful as well were two reports from the National

Advisory Committee on Farm Labor, *Farm Labor Organizing, 1905–1967* (1967), and *The Grape Strike* (1966).

The most important books included *The Casual Laborer and Other Essays* by Carleton H. Parker (Harcourt, Brace and Howe, 1920); *Revolt Among the Sharecroppers,* Howard Kester (Covici-Friede, 1936); *Rebel Voices: An I.W.W. Anthology,* Joyce Kornbluh (University of Michigan Press, 1964); *Merchants of Labor: The Mexican Bracero Story,* Ernesto Galarza (Rosicrucian Press, 1964); *History of the Labor Movement in the United States, Vol. 4, the I.W.W., 1903–1917,* Philip S. Foner (International Publishers, 1965); *The Slaves We Rent,* Truman E. Moore (Random House, 1965); *Huelga: The First Hundred Days of the Great Delano Grape Strike,* Eugene Nelson (Farm Worker Press, 1966); *We Shall Be All: A History of the Industrial Workers of the World,* Melvyn Dubofsky (Quadrangle Books, 1969); *Sal Si Puedes: Cesar Chavez and the New American Revolution,* Peter Matthiessen (Random House, 1969); *So Shall Ye Reap: The Story of Cesar Chavez and the Farm Workers' Movement,* Joan London and Henry Anderson (Crowell, 1970); *Factories in the Field,* Carey McWilliams (Peregrine Press, 1971; original edition, Little, Brown, 1939); *Cry from the Cotton: The Southern Tenant Farmers' Union and the New Deal,* Donald Grubbs (University of North Carolina Press, 1971); *Delano: The Story of the California Grape Strike,* John Gregory Dunne (Farrar, Strauss & Giroux, 1971); *Harry Bridges: The Rise and Fall of Radical Labor in the United States,* Charles Larrowe (Lawrence Hill and Co., 1972); *Sky Full of Storm: A Brief History of California Labor,* David F. Selvin (California Historical Society, 1975); *Chavez and the Farm Workers,* Ronald B. Taylor (Beacon Press, 1975).

INDEX

235

DATE DUE

APR 1 0 2007			
GAYLORD			PRINTED IN U.S.A.